Content Warnings

I'm a fan of content warnings, both as a reader and an author, which is why I include them at the start of all my books. If content warnings aren't your thing, feel free to skip this page. However, something you should probably know in advance (not a spoiler, don't worry) is that this book is recommended for mature readers only. Happy reading!

Before starting Allie and Travis's story, please note the following content warnings: on-page child kidnapping, mentions of human trafficking, PTSD, brief mention of suicidal thoughts, profanity, and explicit sexual content (chapter 43 in its entirety).

THE
LAIR

LISINA CONEY

ISBN: 978-84-09-69075-6

Cover design by Melissa Doughty – Mel D. Designs

Editing by Hot Tree Editing

Proofreading by My Brother's Editor

Formatting by Zarin Madiyha

For everyone who feels like they have to hide who they truly are.
The real you is always worth it.
-

And for myself, who stayed quiet one too many times for fear of ruffling people's feathers.
Never again.

Prologue

Age 9

"ARE YOU BROKEN OR SOMETHING, ALLISON? *SMILE.*"

My mother huffed and put down her phone with an annoyed sigh.

The disdain in that gesture made my eyes get glassy. I knew I had to smile. I did it all the time when I played with my friends at school, so why did it feel so impossible?

"Hold the doll up higher," she instructed in a not-so-nice voice, kneeling in front of the couch where I was sitting so she could get the best shot. Our dog, Milo, wagged his tail, looking for attention, but she brushed him off with a small push. "And, for the hundredth time, *smile.* I need this picture today, and you're already late for school. You know what will happen if you don't smile, don't you?"

My stomach dropped at the threat woven into her words. I didn't want to be there, but my mother had always been very clear about what would happen if I didn't smile for pictures and videos—no new toys for Christmas, no going out to eat on the weekends, and no new house.

"Yeah," I uttered.

It was a weak, anxious sound.

1

"Then do it."

It's just a smile.

I adjusted the doll on my lap and pushed down the tears collecting in my eyes, giving her the smile she wanted.

"You can't even smile right," she said with a roll of her eyes. I hated it when she did that. It made me feel like I'd ruined everything. "This doll is a gift they sent you for free. Do you have any idea how hard I have to work to get this for you? The only thing you have to do is look like you're happy, so stop this attention-seeking charade."

I didn't ask for this doll is what I wanted to scream at her, but I stayed quiet. She always called me ungrateful when I did that, and I didn't want to fight.

The pressure weighed me down as I sneaked furtive glances at the clock. There was no way we would get to school on time. There were too many cars on the road at this hour.

If I was late to school, I would get in trouble with the principal again. And as much as I didn't want that, I also didn't want to disappoint my mother no matter how much I hated posing for pictures.

So I propped the doll higher and smiled until my face hurt.

"That'll do," she dismissed a few clicks later, still unconvinced. Her attention shifted to the phone always glued to her hand. "Get in the car. You've made us late again."

Chapter One

Once upon a time, there was a ferocious bear and a tiny rabbit who found themselves trapped in the same lair because the universe had a shitty sense of humor.

And then the bear ate the rabbit. The end.

"Allie. A word."

I forgot to mention that, in this tale, the bear could talk.

And it's called Travis Ward.

I shut my eyes, taking advantage of the fact that my back is turned to him, and press my lips into a thin line. Who am I kidding? There's no getting out of this.

"What's up, boss man?"

I also forgot to say the rabbit had had an exhausting week and just wanted to go home, open a bottle of cheap wine, and watch reality TV on her phone because she doesn't have cable.

When I saw Travis earlier today, taking inventory with that familiar scowl on his face, I already knew he wasn't in a great mood. Which, for him, doesn't mean much—the storm in him never clears.

Whatever advantage I think I have is short-lived. His heavy

footsteps on the floor I mopped just minutes ago approach me with a daunting rhythm.

Too slowly, the tank-sized man who has been my boss for a little over a year steps into my line of vision—well, his chest does. At five foot two, I consider myself to be on the shorter side, but my boss makes me feel all the more minuscule. He's what, six four? Six five, maybe, if I'm generous. With that dark brown hair and thick, short beard, he's not beating the bear allegations anytime soon, that's for sure.

"You know what you did." That rough, deep voice doesn't need to ask any questions. He knows I messed up, and I don't have it in me to play coy.

Yet I don't answer right away. My shift finishes in five minutes, so maybe if I stay really quiet and stand really still, he'll forget I'm here. And when I make my escape in five—now four—minutes, it'll be too late for a scolding.

People can say what they want about Travis, but he never makes us stay a minute past our shifts at the bar and is equally as strict with our arrival times. It's in his ex-Navy SEAL blood, I bet.

But luck hasn't been on my side for the past twenty-five years, and it's not going to start now.

"Allie."

He says my name in a way that sounds more like a grunt.

When he crosses those bulky arms over his chest, I know he's pissed. Travis isn't a huge talker, which means I've memorized his body language to a T. But even if I hadn't, the tightness of his jaw and the permanent notch between his brows paint a very clear picture.

"I messed up the stock order, didn't I?"

He says nothing, as if he were waiting for me to answer my own stupid question.

I've endured much worse than this grumpy mountain of a

man—ex-military or not—so instead of begging for his oh-so-great forgiveness, I ask, "How can I fix it?"

His answer is, of course, "You can't."

Okay, now he's being pessimistic for no reason.

I square my shoulders and keep my gaze on his unwavering mossy green eyes, barely paying any attention to his massive upper body that belongs in wrestling matches where sweaty, half-naked men beat each other up for fun.

"What are we short on? Rum? Rye whiskey? I can stop by the liquor store and come back in"—I glance at the clock on the wall—"twenty minutes. I'll pay for them out of my own pocket."

When he says nothing, I know my attempt at a reconciliation isn't working. But I don't give up.

"How many bottles do we need? Just say."

Travis doesn't waver. Good thing I'm a master at reading his poker faces, or else we would have much more frustrating one-sided conversations.

"Look," I start as the clock strikes the end of my shift, "I'm sorry I messed up the stock order. I wish I could say it won't happen again, but we both know it might because that computer hates me. I can promise I will pay more attention, though."

Honesty is all I can give him.

And not even that if I'm being technical.

My brain betrays me as our stare off contest continues. Because now is *not* the time to think that his perpetually pissed-off look suits him. In a weird way, it does. That grouchy face makes him look handsome but not approachable, like an awe-inducing wild animal.

I really need to stop thinking about his rugged-in-an-attractive-way face, or his thick, short beard that would cover his lips if it weren't so carefully trimmed, or how black his hair looks under the lights of the bar even though I know it's dark brown. I really should.

Travis shifts his stance, only to cross his arms tighter. The deep, frustrated sigh he lets out parts the hairs on my bangs.

"You ordered six bottles of scotch, three bottles of brandy, and four bottles of apple vodka." A pause. I don't like this pause. It makes my skin crawl and my stomach drop. "You had to order boxes, not bottles."

I wince. "I can't get all of that at the store, right?"

"Right."

This...is bad. Really bad. Making an honest mistake or two is okay, part of human nature and all that, but this is different. Because I didn't just mess up one stock order last week—three months ago, I messed up another one, and just yesterday, I tripped over Charlie's stupid backpack in the changing room, and in a desperate attempt to save my nose from being broken, I broke the door handle instead.

I hate disappointing people who are counting on me. It doesn't matter that Travis fixed the door handle in two minutes or that a few messed-up stock orders here and there won't put The Lair out of business. I didn't get yelled at—not that boss man ever raises his voice to start with—but what difference does it make? I still feel like crap.

I really like this job, damn it. I'm happy here.

I'm happy for the first time in a very, very long time.

"How can I fix it?" I insist, a sudden lump of guilt and embarrassment clogging my throat.

His face remains stoic. If I didn't know him, I'd fear he'd turned into stone right in front of my eyes. But because I do, I only wait in agony for the two-word answer I already suspect he's going to give me.

"You can't."

I hate how I want to fix it, but he won't let me. How I'm the only employee who's messed up two stock orders in less than three months.

And I hate that it makes me think that my mother was right. That I'm not good at anything but being a bother.

"Go home, Allie," Travis orders in that authoritative voice that usually makes my skin tingle.

"But—"

"Be here at four tomorrow."

I blink. "I'm not fired?"

I expected this to be the last straw. It's not like I'm the most qualified waitress in the history of customer service even though I take my job very seriously. He could get a replacement within twenty-four hours if he tried.

But he won't because I'll still have a job tomorrow. Figure that one out.

"Go home," he repeats.

"All right. See you tomorrow," I mutter.

My shoulder brushes his arm as I walk past him, heading to the changing room. He doesn't add anything else. And when I reach the threshold and glance over my shoulder, he is nowhere to be seen.

I wish I'd imagined that whole exchange, but I'm not that lucky. I've never been.

* * *

It all started thirteen months ago.

Well, technically, it started sixteen years ago, but I like to pretend it didn't.

Either way, thirteen months ago, I found myself in the small town of Bannport, Maine. It wasn't my original destination, given how I didn't know this place existed until a sign on the road told me so. But something happened that day—something that made me stop.

My car broke down.

Also, my hair needed a desperate round of dye.

By some miracle, I managed to pull into a car repair shop and was told it wouldn't take them long to take a look. Since I had errands to run, I ventured into town with nothing but my purse and a hungry stomach.

Two bottles of brown hair dye later, I saw it.

The Lair.

A typical small-town sports bar, by the looks of it. The sign above the door was well-kept. Clean too. I could read the white, Western-style letters just fine, which meant dust hadn't collected. The red bricks of the building gave it a cozy feeling, so at odds with the sports bars I'd been to so far.

As a young woman traveling alone, maybe I should've thought twice about stepping into a possibly all-male place called The Lair. But then someone exited the bar, and the mouthwatering smell of grilled meat drifted to my about-to-pass-out-from-hunger self, and I was sold.

Pushing past the Staff Needed sign on the door, I kept one eye on the four occupied tables while I took a seat in a secluded corner, near the pool table at the back and as far away from the TV as I could, since that's where everyone's attention was. Nobody glanced my way, which allowed me to relax just enough to scan the menu for that grilled burger I'd smelled earlier.

The smell of food in the air mixed with the pine-clean scent coming from my table, which meant someone had wiped it just moments before. If that hadn't given it away, the lack of grease on the surface would have.

I glanced around me—dozens of bottles of liquor behind the bar, neon signs on the brick wall, not many tables.

And then him.

"What can I get you?"

I had never heard such a gruff yet soothing voice in my life.

It made a strange jolt run down my rigid spine. When I looked up, I understood why this place was called The Lair—a bear-man was hiding in here.

And that in itself might have been the understatement of the century. Tall, much taller than me, stood a huge man with a scowl so deep, it rivaled my mother's. Only his didn't have that layer of cruelty I'd learned to spot so easily.

A flannel shirt covered everything from his collarbone down to his hairy forearms, which I could see because his sleeves were rolled up, as if he'd been doing some kind of handiwork. With those ginormous hands and long, thick fingers, it wouldn't faze me if he could build a house from the ground up.

For someone working in customer service, I thought he had the grouchiest face. And that was saying something, considering I'd seen many faces in the past six years. Too many.

Yet I didn't feel an immediate urge to run away. The thinnest layer of kindness shone in his green eyes—or maybe it was wishful thinking. Because no kindness meant I could very easily end up in a ditch by the end of my meal.

Don't think about that. Not anymore.

I could tell his lips were plump and kind of rosy, even though they were pressed into a thin, hard line. Straight nose, bushy eyebrows. Mid- to late thirties, if I had to guess, which would make him a decade older than me. Not that this stranger's age was any of my business.

My perusal couldn't have lasted longer than two seconds, but it was enough to make things awkward. I remember he repeated, voice slightly more irritated, "Can I get you anything?"

He knew I'd been staring, and it was nothing short of mortifying.

"A cheeseburger and a Budweiser, please."

Bear-man only narrowed his eyes at me, silent for a moment that stretched and stretched.

"How old are you?"

Ah, of course. A classic.

Society needed to get rid of the notion that chubby cheeks were baby-like features because some grown people couldn't do anything about them—nor did we want to. Plus, it's not like I looked like a teenager.

But I knew there was nothing I could do or say to convince this massive stranger I wasn't underage except for handing him my ID, as mortifying as it was. The piece of plastic trembled between my fingers—only slightly—as I held it out for him to inspect.

Those narrowed eyes narrowed a little more, and I found myself gulping even though I had nothing to hide—not regarding my age.

"California." It wasn't a question or an accusation, but it felt like both to me. "Long way from Maine."

I said nothing, and he didn't ask me anymore not-questions. Without another word, he disappeared behind the bar.

Like a coward, I rolled my eyes when I knew he wasn't looking. If he wasn't back in five minutes with my beer, I would find another place in this godforsaken town to drown my hangry demons in.

My phone vibrated in my pocket, and I slipped my hand inside as I kept my eyes on the four occupied tables. Every man in this place had decided to ignore the female newcomer, and I was all about that.

I held my phone under the table, as I had done countless times in high school, and was relieved to find a notification from Jada. She'd caught me sneaking furtive glances at my phone more than once during her lessons, but never told my parents. She knew I had enough on my plate as it was.

JADA

Where are you now?

I typed out my reply before a gigantic shadow was cast over me.

ME

Bannport, Maine

A cold Budweiser was placed in front of me, and I almost cried from joy.

"Thank you." I smiled up at the grouchy stranger, and I got exactly what I suspected he'd give me in return—a scowl.

Whatever.

He left as quickly as he came, and I went back to my conversation with Jada.

JADA

How long are you staying there?

I didn't consider Bannport an option, more like a quick stop. What did this town in the middle of nowhere have to offer?

A home, maybe.

Ha. The voice inside my head decided to crack some jokes today.

Home. I didn't know the meaning of that word. Never had and suspected I never would.

ME

I wasn't planning on staying here.

JADA

Where are you running away to, honey?

A lump formed in my throat as two conflicting emotions crashed into me.

I hadn't talked to Jada in four days, and I missed her voice terribly. I missed seeing her in person, too, but that wasn't an option, and it wouldn't be for a while.

I missed her *pollo guisado*, her warm hugs, the rich scent of the jasmine candles she burned at home, and the term of affection she'd been calling me since I was twelve. Since that day she stopped being just my schoolteacher and became the adult I needed to survive.

I gulped down half of my beer in a failed attempt to banish the painful memories, but when I set it back down with a thump, the questions were still there.

Am I still running away? Do I even know how to stop?

ME

I'm not running away.

JADA

Can I call you?

One quick look at my battery percentage told me the answer, and it wasn't the one I would've liked.

ME

My phone is about to die, but maybe tonight?

JADA

Whenever you can, Allie. You know we're here for you.

Tears pricked my eyes, but I was *not* going to start crying in the middle of a random sports bar while I was all alone. I was *not* going to show anyone around me weakness, let alone grown men ten times bigger and stronger than I was.

But Jada was right. I was running away—hadn't stopped for the past few years—and maybe I needed to think about my next move for longer than two seconds.

ME

Thank you. I love you both.

JADA

We love you too. Take care of yourself.

Putting my phone back inside my pocket, I started to peel off the wet label on the bottle, thinking about my options. As I saw it, I had three.

One was to keep moving. After years on the road, I was finally where I wanted to be. I was here, in Maine, at last. I'd made it. Nobody was forcing me to leave or stay or do anything at all.

Option two was to go back the way I came. Once they gave my car the green light, I could drive anywhere in the country, and that notion made me breathe a little easier. I didn't miss the scorching sun of Texas or the incessant traffic of North Carolina, but maybe I felt like that because deep down, I knew I was simply passing by every place I'd been to.

And option three...

Was I really considering option three?

Two hours ago, I didn't know Bannport existed, and now I was thinking about staying here for good? Or at least until I had a more solid plan.

I pulled out my phone again. A quick search online told me Bannport was far more popular than I initially gave it credit for. Bannport Lake was a big tourist attraction during the summer, and so were the hiking trails not far from here. The town celebrated some kind of music festival in the spring, and there was even a museum only ten minutes away.

A school, several bars and supermarkets, a gym, hair and nail salons, a bank, a farmers' market, a library...

Fine, so maybe Bannport wasn't some random godforsaken town after all. Who would've known.

I was still undecided when bear-man came back with the most delicious-smelling burger I'd ever seen. But I didn't let the goodness in front of me distract me for too long. I was a woman on a mission. One I wasn't too sure about in the first place, but life was about living and taking risks.

Now that I finally had the privilege of freedom, I wasn't going to let self-doubts take it from me. I owed it to myself after what I'd survived.

"Hey," I called out to the man as he retreated without a word.

He didn't turn around, not fully. Those attentive eyes surveilled me from over his shoulder, and the words almost got stuck in my tongue.

"Could you point me to a nearby inn or a hotel, please?"

I was doing it. I was staying in Bannport, at least for a night. I had enough money to last me about six weeks if I couldn't find a job, and that was if I cut my expenses by half again.

But it was fine. I'd done it before, and I could do it again as many times as I needed to. Anything was better than my old life.

"There's a hotel down the street."

Was that a grumble?

"Could you write down the address for me, please?"

He disappeared behind the bar without giving me a proper answer. Maybe I was testing his patience, or maybe I was over-thinking my interactions with him way too much. Both seemed plausible.

If he didn't want to help me, I could find a hotel on my own. I was by no means a stranger to being independent, to doing things myself because nobody was going to step in and help. I didn't need anyone to.

Three bites into my burger, though, a piece of paper landed next to my empty beer. I arched an eyebrow, mouth full of beef. Slowly, I swallowed.

His only answer was "The hotel."

I examined his neat handwriting for all of two seconds before I saw him move out of the corner of my eye.

And then I did something that altered the course of my life forever.

"I saw you're hiring."

Chapter Two

I keep my gaze trained on the shot glasses I'm filling with tequila, the loud tables of hockey fans shouting over the sound of the TV. Drunk laughter engulfs me, along with the unmistakable click of glasses meeting one another.

Bannport really fooled me. There's nothing small about this small town's Saturday nights, especially not when hockey is on.

Someone slams their fists into the bar, turning the tequila shots I was pouring into a small waterfall. I lose count of the number of times patrons have called my name or at least have called for me—*beautiful* seems to be a favorite tonight.

But I'd be lying if I said I didn't thrive during The Lair's busy nights.

"Show me that smile, Allie Cat."

Charlie winks as he approaches, spinning his empty tray on his fingers like a basketball. I give him an eye roll for that, painfully aware that I'm starting to embody Travis.

"Get me some peanuts for tables twelve and seven, pretty please," he says as he reaches for a wet cloth behind the bar. "Someone spilled his drink. *A-fucking-gain.*"

"Sucks to suck." I grab the peanuts and stick my tongue out

at him as I place them on his tray. "At least the tips will be good."

"They'd better be," Charlie agrees, running a hand through his dirty-blond hair. The strong smell of his cologne hits my nostrils as he leans in conspiratorially and whispers, "Fuck hockey night," right before he leaves with his peanuts.

I only snort and shake my head.

Charlie is...Charlie. There's no other way to describe him.

Travis hired him three months ago when our previous waitress left for the big city. As far as replacements go, I can't complain about Charlie. He's a year younger than me and a recent college graduate. For whatever reason, he decided to move back to his hometown instead of trying to make it as a marketing mogul in the city. He must have hit his head or something.

Says the girl who decided to stay in Bannport, too, instead of going literally anywhere else.

And I might, one day. Maybe.

Regardless of his sometimes obnoxious and very often over-the-top attitude, I'm happy to have Charlie around. He's either a breath of fresh air or a pain in the ass, and there's no way to tell until it's too late.

All thoughts about my co-worker get interrupted when a loud thump comes from my left side, making me jump.

"What does one have to do to get a fucking old-fashioned around here?"

I crack my neck, readying myself for battle, and manage a tight smile.

David, Danny, or whatever his name is, is no stranger to late-night drinks at The Lair, and I always avoid serving him when I can. He's loud, rude, and he threw up once. As in, on his lap. While sitting at the bar.

I don't like him one bit. And if the mean scowl he throws me every week is any indication, I'd say he isn't my biggest fan either.

Avoiding him tonight isn't an option, though, so I ignore the other four people yelling for drinks and get on with the old-fashioned. "Coming right up."

Charlie is busy with the tables, and Travis....

Where the hell is Travis?

I steal a look around as I finish off the drink, but I don't see him anywhere.

"I'm falling asleep here, girl," David/Danny/asshole grunts, and it takes all my willpower and then some not to smash the drink into his wrinkly, sweaty forehead.

In reality, I would never hurt anyone. I don't believe in violence as an answer. And even if I did, I'm too chicken to face the consequences. All it takes is the thought of my face in the newspapers to banish the idea very, *very* quickly.

I summon a fake smile because giving him attitude and risking making a scene won't be worth it, even if that's exactly what I want to do. "There you go."

I set the old-fashioned in front of him—I should cut him off after this one—and don't wait for a thank you that'll never come. Someone else is already demanding my attention, and for the next minute, I drown myself in the sounds of shouts, laughter, and the celebration of a hat trick.

Until he yells again.

"You call this a fucking old-fashioned?" A glass—*his* glass—slams on the bar, liquid spilling everywhere, and I shut my eyes to brace myself for what's to come.

People around him shift their gazes, alarmed, but ultimately ignore him. Nobody in their right mind would want to mess with a pissed off drunk, and I'm no exception.

But I get paid for this.

I like my job. I like the people I work with. I like this town.

I'm lucky to have a roof over my head and food on the table. I can't compromise that.

"What's wrong?" I smile tightly once more, trying to summon Charlie with my mind to no avail. He's only a few feet away, and I'm definitely in his line of vision, but chances are he can't hear anything over the loud throng, including this old man's yells.

He smacks the glass on the bar again, making my pulse go all the way up to my throat, and I catch it just in time before it topples to the ground. "Are you even old enough to serve me a fucking drink? This is bullshit."

"Excuse me—" I start, bits of subdued rage swirling in my stomach, but he doesn't give me a chance to finish.

"Where's my fucking orange peel?" he sneers.

I blink.

"You forgot the orange peel," he points out, looking at the now-half-empty glass as if I'd filled it with poison.

He's being rude, dramatic, and scary because of an *orange peel*? Is this a joke?

"I can get you another—"

I don't miss his cheek twitching as he leans in and points a crooked finger at me. "You shouldn't be here. Get me a man to make me a fucking drink or get out of my face."

Wow. Okay.

Taking a deep breath, I tell myself he's drunk and won't really hurt me. We're in the middle of a crowded bar, and there's a huge wooden barrier between us I'm not planning to jump over.

My mother's voice echoes in my head before I can stop it, making everything else turn dark.

Damn it, Allison. You can never do anything right. Do you even care about your family?

I shut my eyes, but the memory assaults me just the same.

Go away, go away, go away.

It takes me an embarrassingly long number of seconds to realize I've zoned out, and David/Danny is staring at me like I've grown a second head.

"I can get you another one," I say, fighting the strong grip the not-too-old memories have on my heart.

"I want nothing from you." The sneer is back in full force. "And I'm not paying for shit tonight. I'm not taking drinks from you."

I ignore the jab because I've got bigger fish to fry, as I'm pretty sure boss man will have my head if I let a customer leave the bar without paying their tab.

"We don't offer free drinks."

My tight smile is gone, replaced by what I can only hope is a serious expression.

"Bulls—"

David/Danny doesn't finish his sentence.

A huge hand that is at least twice the size of mine maneuvers around me and gently grabs the old-fashioned from my trembling fingers, placing it somewhere behind me.

I would recognize those calloused fingers anywhere—not like they are easily mistakable. His presence at my back is warm, yet I know the look on his face I would find if I turned around won't be.

Travis doesn't shout, doesn't raise his voice at all. He never needs to.

"Out."

That deep, authoritative one-word rumble travels all the way down my spine and settles at its base, where a tingling sensation remains.

"Give this old man a break, Ward." He tries to play it cool, but he fails.

A single sentence from my boss and David/Danny doesn't appear to be so drunk anymore. *Huh.*

His glassy eyes land on me, hard and unforgiving, as if I were to blame for the situation he got himself into all on his own. I didn't call Travis, don't even know where he's been for the past hour, but he doesn't seem to care.

Feeling braver now that I've got my boss at my back, my only answer is to arch an eyebrow in a "now what?" expression.

The old man throws his hands up in mock surrender. "Got it. No need to throw me out like some drunk."

I'm not too sure about that. If Travis hadn't shown up, I'd still be having a one-sided argument with him. I'm not going to cry because some random man was mean to me while under the influence. I have thick skin, if nothing else.

I'd like to think I'm as independent as they come, but I'm also not stupid enough to turn down the help of an ex-Navy SEAL to get out of a sticky situation if he offers. I know how to pick my battles.

I can't bask in the sweet, sweet sight of David/Danny leaving The Lair with fifty less dollars in his pocket because hockey fans have mercy on no one. For the next hour, I lose myself in the chaos until the bar starts to clear out.

As I lock the front door when the last patron walks out, Charlie appears out of nowhere. "I saw you and Travis having a stare off contest with Dean earlier."

So that's his name. No David or Danny after all.

I grab the mop and suppress a yawn. I haven't felt this tired in a while, but at least I'll fall asleep faster tonight. That's always a plus.

"Yeah. He refused to pay for his drinks because I forgot the orange peel in his old-fashioned," I tell him.

Charlie roars out a laugh. "Oh, Drunk Dean. So that's why

Travis was sending him death glares from across the bar? Checks out."

Travis and throwing death glares go hand in hand, so Charlie's words don't surprise me.

"Let's finish up," I say a little under my breath, desperate to rest for a minute but knowing I'll fall asleep on the spot if I do.

I mop the floors in record time and check if Jude, one of our cooks, needs any help in the kitchen. In his sixties, he and his wife, Sandra, are responsible for the burger-induced comas I fall into every week. Not that I have any complaints.

His tired smile mirrors mine. "Thanks, Smith, but all's under control."

I ignore the way *Smith* catches all the air in my lungs, even though it's been his nickname for me since my first day on the job.

The lights in the bar turn off one by one then—Travis's silent way of telling us we're done for the day. Sometimes I believe he takes the "no wasting saliva" policy a bit too far. A simple "Let's go" would suffice, but what do I know?

After a quick stop by the changing room to grab my bag with the spare clothes I'm too exhausted to change into, I say goodbye to Jude and Charlie before they disappear into the changing room.

As much as my legs ache and my arms hurt from the long hours of lifting heavy bottles and pouring drinks, I still manage to beam at Travis as I pass by him at the front door. "See you tomorrow, boss man."

A grunt is the only answer I get, but I don't take it personally.

Sometimes I have a hard time understanding how on earth I managed to land this job. I'm a quick learner and give my two hundred percent on everything I do, but I don't think Travis likes me very much. He doesn't seem to like *anyone* very much. I'm not the most social of butterflies out there, either, so I get it.

Outside, the cold November air seeps under my puffer jacket, making me shiver until I get inside my car. After I turn on the engine and get the heater running, I glance down the street at The Lair out of habit.

Travis is standing at the door, his eyes on me. He doesn't go back inside until I drive away.

Chapter Three

HERE'S THE THING—SOMETIMES, YOU HAVE TO MAKE uncomfortable choices knowing they will set you free later.

When I decided to leave behind my old life in California six years ago with nothing but a suitcase, a car that had seen better days, and an envelope full of cash I technically stole but also technically owned, I had nobody on my mind but me. I'm not ashamed to admit I was being selfish, greedy, and all those other things my mother always accused me of. But I did what I had to do to save myself.

Yet it took me nearly two years to recognize the face I saw in the mirror every day. The brown hair that wasn't mine, the long hair turned short, the bangs I'd never considered cutting.

I mix the hair dye in the stained plastic bowl and avoid my gaze in the mirror. The deep breath I take isn't enough to stop the anxiety from sinking its claws into my chest, making it difficult to get air in and out of my lungs.

After using some Vaseline to prevent the dye from staining my scalp, I get on with lie number one.

I know what most people would say—"But Allie, dyeing your hair doesn't make you a liar!"—and they'd be right. It doesn't. People change their appearance all the time, and that doesn't make them a better or worse person. But the *why* I'm doing it is what makes me hate myself a little more every day.

My dark eyes stare back at me as I thoroughly apply the dye, and I make a mental note to add a few more boxes to my grocery list later. I don't want to run out just in case there's an emergency.

Right, because my social and/or romantic life is so intense.

I snort at my own thoughts as I cover the last few strands with the foul-smelling chemical. My hair brushes my shoulders, which is the shortest I've ever worn it. Paired with the wispy bangs I never thought would suit me, but I've grown to love, I don't look like the Allie from six years ago. At all.

That was the goal all along.

My phone pings with a notification, and I frown. Jada is working right now, and I rarely get texts from anyone else. Other than the group chat we have for The Lair—which Charlie spams, and Travis never participates in—my phone has been quiet all day.

Speak of the devil.

CHARLIE

Allie Cat!!!!!!

I try not to smile and fail. It's not the first time he's texted me privately, and it's always for the same reason.

CHARLIE

My friends and I are going to a bonfire party after work on Friday. Wanna tag along?

You only have one option btw.

And it is to say yes.

Once my hair is done, I take off my disposable gloves, rinse my hands in the sink for good measure, and grab my phone from where I set it earlier on the toilet. And then I stare at Charlie's texts and wait for the guilt to make itself at home like it always does.

I tried to fight it since that first day he introduced himself at The Lair with his contagious smile and kind eyes, but I can't deny it anymore—Charlie is my friend.

A friendship that shouldn't have happened, but then he went and made a point to include me in every single one of his plans with his friend group, claiming that, "You spend too much time on your own, Allie Cat. That can't be good for the soul. You're more than welcome to hang out with us."

At some point, he got so insistent, I asked him if he was flirting or if he liked me or *something*. I have zero experience with men, but that's what they do when they're interested in someone, right? They pester them to death.

But he only laughed and said, "You're beautiful, but I only like you as a friend. Please tell me I didn't just break your heart."

Charlie is like an annoying younger brother to me, which makes it worse when I always text him the same thing.

ME

I'm not sure.

I know I'm not going, and he knows I'm not going, but we both want to pretend otherwise.

CHARLIE

Only for an hour? Pretty please?

I'm typing that no, I don't think I'll make it, when he texts again.

CHARLIE

I'll bring carrot cake.

26

That makes me reconsider. Narrowing my eyes at the screen as if he could see the suspicion in them, I text back.

> ME
>
> To a bonfire party?

CHARLIE

What can I say, I'm full of surprises.

> ME
>
> Full of shit too.

CHARLIE

Hahaha

Don't Travis me.

And why my heart leaps at the mention of our boss will forever remain a mystery.

Charlie found out carrot cake is my all-time favorite food two months ago when Sandra brought a huge one to the bar on her birthday. I had one slice and took two home, and he has been teasing me about my obsession with it ever since. I'm not bothered by it.

For a moment, I allow myself to imagine what it would be like to accept Charlie's invitation and have fun at the bonfire with his friends. Being with them, even if only for an hour, would help me feel that sense of normalcy I've been craving for years.

"Friends make the world a little brighter," Jada would always tell me.

But then I remember all the reasons I shouldn't get close to them. Why it would be better for everyone that I stay away.

> ME
>
> I don't think I can make it.
>
> I'll let you know if I change my mind.

We both know I won't. I never do.

He texts something back, but I don't read it. Looking at my phone is making me light-headed, so I focus on wiping the excess dye off my neck and forehead before I get in the shower to rinse it all off.

Charlie might think he wants to hang out with me, but I'm saving him from heartbreak. Because no matter how many times I tell myself that I'm doing this because I need to, because it sets me free, I can't ignore the truth.

I'm lying to everyone in this town.

Chapter Four

Age 11

Mocking laughter invaded my eardrums as I rushed down the packed hall, keeping my head down.

Maybe if I didn't look at them, everyone would forget I was there. Maybe they would forget what they saw.

I spotted my friend Marie in the classroom, whispering something into Eve's ear. As soon as she saw me, she pulled away and gave me a wavering smile.

"Hey," I greeted them, pretending I didn't know all eyes were on me. Pretending I couldn't hear the hushed whispers.

"Um, hi," Marie said nervously, looking around awkwardly.

A quick glance at the clock told me Mrs. Jada wouldn't be here for another few minutes, so I busied myself taking out my notebook and colored pencils. I wrote down the date in fancy lettering—an attempt at making myself look busy and unbothered. But pretending I couldn't hear them didn't make the whispers stop.

"It was like she wet the bed but more gross."

"She's so embarrassing."

"I watched that video, like, ten times, and somehow it kept getting worse."

"I can't believe it's all over the internet. It's crazy."

An uncomfortable, heavy weight settled in the middle of my chest and didn't let me breathe. As I doodled, pretending nothing was wrong, I angrily wondered why me.

Why did I have to be the butt of the joke?

Why did I have to be strong, pretend I was fine, while everyone laughed at me?

What did I ever do wrong to deserve this?

Mrs. Jada entered the classroom as my eyes started watering. She shushed everyone, stealing a quick glance at me that told me she knew what was going on. But I didn't feel judged by her or laughed at. Never by Mrs. Jada.

"I hope you're done wasting precious geometry time, or I'll have to send home some extra homework today," she started, her voice leaving no room for arguments.

My classmates groaned, and the whispers died down. A couple of boys and a girl stole quick glances back at me, as if they couldn't get the images of my period stains all over my bed off their brains. Because my mother thought it was necessary to tell—and show—the world about my first period. And even though the video eventually got taken down, it didn't make much of a difference.

In a way, I couldn't blame them.

For the next twenty minutes, I drowned myself in the logical and mechanical ways of geometry. Math was my favorite subject, always had been. No emotions were needed, and if I disconnected my brain for a mere second, I would fail. Math kept my mind busy and quiet in a way nothing else did. It challenged me, gave me a sense of purpose—even if that purpose was only to get good grades.

"Can anyone tell me what the area of the triangle on the screen is?" Mrs. Jada asked.

I lowered my head to my notebook, doing a quick calculation. When I was done, I raised my hand. "It should be twenty."

Mrs. Jada gave me an approving smile. "That's correct."

I beamed, finding my first spark of happiness today. Until Keith two rows in front of me extinguished it again.

"Well done, Bloody Allie."

The weight in my chest dragged me down, down, *down*.

Everyone snickered around me, glancing my way with mirth in their eyes that felt like a personal attack. It *was*.

Mrs. Jada wasn't amused. "See yourself out to the principal's office, Keith."

"But—"

"Do as you're told and stop wasting any more of our time."

A few of his friends laughed at his demise, but it didn't make me feel better.

Bloody Allie.

I knew the nickname would follow me forever, no matter how much I tried to hide from the consequences of my mother's choices.

Chapter Five

THE THING ABOUT HIDING IS THAT, SOONER OR LATER, someone always finds you.

"What the hell are you doing here?"

Travis's deep grumble makes me jump, and I curse under my breath. As much as I appreciate his stern-looking face on a normal day, he's the last person I want to see right now.

I don't think my nonchalant smile is too convincing. "Nothing, boss man."

I've had a few moments in the past six years where I've wanted the ground to swallow me and never spit me back out. One of those happened two years ago. I was in Greensboro and accidentally spilled my soda on a child behind me in the line at a fast-food restaurant. *A child.* The poor boy must have been seven or eight. I still remember those eyes, glancing at me with confusion and fear.

If his mother didn't beat me up on the spot—even though I'd apologized profusely and offered to pay for a new T-shirt—it was only because I'm a fast runner.

That was pretty bad, and this might be right up there with it.

As expected, Travis doesn't buy my smile or my words. If his massive arms crossed in front of his equally enormous chest are any indication, not only does he not buy it, but he's angry with me. Again.

I press my thighs together and hide my lower area with my intertwined hands, hoping and praying and then hoping some more that he doesn't think I'm being a weirdo.

"All's fine and dandy." *Not.*

My boss watches me with quiet fury, standing very still right outside the door. The supply closet isn't big, so if he took a single step, he'd be in my face in seconds. But he doesn't move or say anything at all.

That familiar weight reappears in the middle of my chest. Flashbacks from that day in Jada's class assault my head while my brain chants *Bloody Allie* with a vengeance.

Why did this have to happen now?

With the light coming from the bar at his back, Travis's face is clouded in darkness. Even so, I don't need to see it to know his left cheek is probably ticking with annoyance, or his eyes are narrowed at me.

I don't need to look at him because I sneak glances at his face more often than I should.

"Why are you in the supply closet instead of working?" he asks in a tone that isn't nice but also isn't rude.

I know lying is bad—most of the time. I have been and still am forced to do it from time to time, even if it makes me hate myself every single day. So maybe that's why, as Travis shifts on his feet and appears a whole foot taller, I tell him the truth.

"I just got my period."

The words feel sharp on my tongue.

Travis stares ahead, not saying anything, waiting for me to elaborate. So, I take a shaky breath and remind myself Travis is a grown man who won't make fun of me for this.

He doesn't know what happened. He doesn't know who I am. Who I really am.

"It stained my jeans. I was looking for something I could wear for the rest of my shift."

When a beat of silence goes by, followed by five more, I'm pretty sure I broke him.

Everything I know about Travis Ward I have learned against my will. It's not that I don't care about him. It's just that he doesn't speak much, let alone share the details of his personal life with his co-workers. But Jude and Sandra have told me some things about him, and so has his uncle Neil, who he inherited the bar from. The old man stops by sometimes and is known for joking around—the polar opposite of his nephew.

Over the past thirteen months, I have learned that Travis is an ex-Navy SEAL and is thirty-seven, has two dogs, lives on a farm somewhere not far from The Lair, and hasn't been in a relationship in years.

Thank you, Uncle Neil, for that last piece of information.

I also know he's an only child, has no kids, and grew up with his uncle (no aunt) before he enlisted, which must mean he doesn't have much experience with periods. I'm assuming.

That would explain the deafening silence and the way the air seems to shift around us, turning awkward for the first time since we met.

"But I'm fine," I'm quick to amend. "If I could run to my apartment—"

"What do you need?"

My only reply is to stand very still and wait for some huffing and puffing. But when none of that happens, I ask, "What do you mean?"

"From the store. What do you need?"

I'm pretty sure my eyes are bugging out of my skull as I stare at him, waiting for an "I'm just kidding. Go back to work" that never comes.

My boss, this stoic man who has never given me any reason to think he likes me in the first place, is now asking me what I need from the store?

"I don't have all day, Allie," he grumbles, snapping me back to the present.

"Sorry. Yeah, um, I need tampons. And a pair of leggings."

Mortification settles in when I realize my underwear is ruined too. But there's no way in hell I'm asking my boss to buy me panties of all things, so I guess I'm going commando for the rest of my shift. It wouldn't be the worst thing I've endured.

"What kind of tampons?" he asks, making me die a little bit inside.

I know periods are normal and not something to be ashamed of, and I agree. Truly. It took me many years to come to terms with this, and it was only thanks to Jada's multiple interventions. But the damage my mother did to my experience with periods isn't fully gone, which is why I wince at Travis's words and wish there was literally anyone else in this supply closet with me right now.

"Travis, you really don't need to—"

"Regular ones?"

I swallow back my embarrassment. Well, then. "Yes. Thank you."

"What size leggings do you wear?"

This definitely beats the spilling-soda-on-a-child moment.

My throat is so dry, my voice comes out a little raspy. "Medium."

He doesn't give me time to object, to insist that he doesn't have to do this. He simply says, "I'll be back in fifteen. Stay here if you want." And then leaves.

I don't have time to overthink what just happened because

Sandra, one of our cooks and Jude's wife, pops her head into the supply closet and gives me one of her motherly smiles.

"Oh, dear. Are you okay? Travis said you needed me."

Travis said what now?

I smile back at Sandra because I may be a mess right now, but I love this woman to death. "I had a little accident."

She stays with me for the time it takes Travis to come back, distracting me with stories about her one-year-old grandson.

I know where the conversation is heading before she asks. And when she does, I try my best to keep all the muscles on my face and body relaxed.

"Where were you from again, dear? I keep forgetting."

I love Sandra and Jude with all I've got. Not only because they make the best hamburgers in town, but also because they are always there for me when I need them. Ran out of gas? They will lend me their car for a whole week if I ask. Can't afford groceries? They will stock up my fridge until I get back on my feet.

They are some of the most generous people I have ever met, rivaling Jada and her husband, Paul, which is why lying to her makes me feel like the worst person alive.

"California."

That's not a lie.

"And how's your family doing? Are they coming to visit soon?"

"They're doing well." My smile doesn't waver as I picture Jada and Paul. They aren't the people she's asking about, but they are the only ones I consider my family. "Work keeps them busy, but we talk often."

"Being busy with work is always good." Her eyes wrinkle with her sincere smile, making the nausea in my stomach rise to my throat. "Our son is busy, too, but we're hoping to visit next month."

36

The change of direction in our conversation makes breathing easier.

"Going to the big city, huh? Are you sure Jude is ready for all those people speeding down the street, pretending to have somewhere important to be?" I tease her, knowing how her husband isn't a fan of crowds. He loves small-town life a bit too much, and I don't blame him because I do too.

She pushes back her glasses and sends me a playful look. "If he isn't, I'll make him."

I laugh at that, imagining poor Jude being dragged through the Boston streets by his wife.

Their love is what I've always imagined for myself before reality hit me square in the face. Someone I could joke with, someone to hold me when I needed to crumble, someone to create a loving home with. Someone with a kind heart and good intentions. But that future isn't for me, and I have to come to terms with that.

No one deserves to be with a liar.

"You could come with us," Sandra offers next. "To visit our son."

My heart pounds. "Oh, I wouldn't want to intrude."

"You really wouldn't, dear. The more, the merrier." Her smile hides a hint of worry. "You never go anywhere, never leave Bannport. A change of scenery could be good for you. I don't want to overstep, of course, but please know you're always welcome where Jude and I are."

My eyes start to sting, and I know it's not my hormones giving me a hard time. "Thank you."

Just then, Travis walks into the supply closet. He doesn't bother with pleasantries. "Your stuff."

My heart jumps when his fingers brush mine as he passes me a grocery bag.

When he turns to the older woman, his voice softens as

much as it's able to. "Thank you, Sandra. You can go back to work."

She gives me a reassuring smile as she leaves the supply closet, squeezing Travis's forearm as she goes.

I peek inside the bag. A box of tampons and a pair of black leggings, just like I asked. Before I can say anything, he starts turning around.

"Wait! Travis, wait." I walk up to him awkwardly, feeling dirty and sticky and everything that is wrong with this world, but not wanting to part ways without telling him, "Thank you for going to the store for me. You didn't have to, but I really appreciate it. How much was it? I'll pay you back."

I resist the urge to give him a quick hug because we aren't there yet. I don't think we'll ever be, and that's okay.

He doesn't reply immediately, those hard eyes scanning every inch of my face. And when he finally does, my shoulders sag. "Charlie has been covering for you. Hurry up."

"But I—"

"You don't have to pay me back, Allie." The firm way he says my name sends a chill down my spine. "Go back to work. We're crowded."

I try to keep a smile on my face but fail.

Out of all the men in the world my heart could beat for, it *had* to be my asshole of a boss. Of course.

I'm not in love with Travis. I know where we stand, and I'm not looking to get my heart broken anytime soon—or ever. I've had enough drama over the past few years to last me several lifetimes, and a silly workplace crush doesn't need to be added to the mix.

He might be a full-on grouch most of the time, but he isn't unnecessarily mean. He doesn't treat his staff or his customers with disrespect, and he doesn't think he's better than anyone else. He's open to feedback from his uncle—and even from us—

and he puts a lot of care into making sure The Lair runs smoothly. Our paychecks arrive on time, and he splits the tips equally—a luxury I haven't experienced many times before.

Travis might not be easy to be around sometimes, but he isn't a bad man. A bad man wouldn't have bought me tampons and new leggings while I was in distress. He would've told me periods aren't a big deal and to go back to work.

So what if I steal furtive glances at him more often than I should?

Maybe I'm just confused. That must be it. It's not like he would ever be interested in one of his employees—one who happens to be twelve years younger than him and a massive liar at that. Not that he's aware of the latter, but the point still stands.

Travis and I are what we are—boss and employee—and that's it. It's enough, and it will continue to be.

I can't afford to be anything else to anyone.

Chapter Six

Two weeks after messing up my second stock order, I almost kill somebody.

At The Lair, all our menus include allergy disclaimers for every dish. Since customers are able to check them, I have never bothered asking if anyone was allergic to something. People can always communicate their needs, right?

Wrong.

"She's trying to kill me!" our customer bellows.

Before today, I'd never seen this woman in my life, but even if I had, I can guarantee I wouldn't try to kill her. Not that she knows my intentions, but come on.

"Ma'am—" Charlie starts, having come to my rescue after hearing her loud screeches from across the bar.

"I don't want to hear it." The woman, who doesn't look much older than us, sends my co-worker a cutting glare before sliding it toward me. "I am allergic to onions, and look what this burger comes with—*onions*. See? It's here between the meat and the bun. This is *unacceptable*. I want to speak to the manager."

I breathe in and out, willing my inner peace to come back.

This is Travis's business, and I don't want to ruin its hard-earned good reputation.

"I am so sorry this happened," I start because, at the end of the day, I want to keep my job. I show her the menu. "As you can see, every dish includes allergy disclaimers, as well as every ingredient. In the description of the burger you ordered, onions are the third ingredient listed. If you had warned me about your food restrictions, we would have taken care of it appropriately. Still, I apologize for not checking beforehand."

I know I'm not imagining the way my fingers tremble as I hold the menu in her direction, but I keep my shoulders straight and my chin high.

This was an unfortunate mistake. Maybe I should have double-checked, but I have never had this problem before, and I sure as hell wasn't trying to kill anybody.

"Oh, so now it's *my* fault?" When she raises her voice, the man next to her grabs her arm, trying to calm her down, but it's like she can't even hear him. "I told you I was allergic to onions, and I asked for them to be removed."

I blink. "No, you didn't."

She *didn't*. I wouldn't forget something like that.

She looks at me as if I had just verbally slapped her. "Excuse me?"

"Mindy," the man next to her tries once again. "It's okay. It wasn't her fault." When he looks at me, his mortified expression makes me feel bad for him. "Could she get another burger without onions, please?"

I'm quick to nod. "Of course."

"I don't want another burger." Mindy grabs her purse and stands from their booth. Charlie shifts closer to me. "And I'm also not paying for that shit that almost killed me. Where's your manager?"

41

What's with people refusing to pay for their food and drinks lately?

"He isn't here right now," Charlie says, which isn't a lie. Travis was here this morning when my shift started, but I haven't seen him since. "If you would like to file a complaint form, I will get one for you, but we can't let you leave the restaurant without paying the tab, ma'am."

Her companion stands after her and gives Charlie a tight smile. "That won't be necessary. And of course we'll pay."

"Like hell we will." Mindy shakes off his grip and drills those hard, cruel eyes into me.

But then something shifts.

It happens in slow motion. First, the confused frown. Then the change in her gaze from furious to unsure. And finally, she asks the question.

A question I've only been asked once before in the past six years.

A question that made me flee Nashville months before planned.

"Do I know you from somewhere?" And then she makes it worse. "You look *so* familiar."

Sweat collects at the back of my neck.

My pulse throbs, turning my vision into a blur. My lungs cinch tighter, not letting air in, as adrenaline surges through me.

Three things happen all at once.

One—I panic.

Two—I get a strong urge to cry.

Three—I need to throw up.

Now.

But Mindy's eyes are on me, and I need to think of something before recognition dawns on her. *Anything.*

She looks the part. Maybe I'm being too judgmental, or maybe it's the way she's dressed in the latest trends or how tightly she grips her phone, not putting it down for one second. When I took their order, she was browsing through a popular app, so it wouldn't be far-fetched to think that she...

Leave. Leave. Leave.

I smile and hope she doesn't notice how the corners of my mouth are also trembling. "I'm here all the time, so you may have seen me around."

"It's not that." She peruses my face again. "I'm not from here, but I swear you remind me of—"

"Mindy," the man beside her interrupts. "Let's go, please. They have work to do."

"I'm sorry about our misunderstanding," I'm quick to say. "I need to see to other tables. Charlie?"

His eyes pinball between the couple and me. "Sure thing."

I don't stay long enough to check if Mindy says anything else or agrees to pay the tab without making a fuss.

I don't stay long enough to spot Travis walking back into the bar and pulling Charlie aside before taking care of Mindy and her poor companion himself.

I don't see any of that because, not even a minute later, I'm shutting the bathroom door behind me and throwing up in the toilet.

That woman recognized me.

She knows who I am.

She knows *where* I am.

All these years covering my tracks, for nothing.

All my attempts at leaving my past behind, ruined.

An image of Mindy scrolling through her phone flashes in my mind, and another wave of nausea hits me. I brace myself on the toilet and empty my stomach as the tears fall.

If she tells anybody...

They can't force me to go back or to do anything I don't want to do. I'm an adult now.

The thought doesn't make me feel better. Maybe because being yelled at and demanded I go back wouldn't be the worst thing that could happen.

I flush the toilet and lean my weight on the cold wall behind me, waiting until my legs stop shaking to exit the bathroom. Everything in me is willing my anxiety to go away, but it remains, fiercely gripping my chest.

Logically, I know what my next step should be. If someone has found out where I live, I have to leave. I need to make myself scarce once again, go somewhere else. Maine has enough small towns to start over a few times.

So what if the thought of leaving this life behind makes me nauseous again? A job I love, my co-workers, the nice people of Bannport, my freedom...

Am I ready to give it up because someone *might* have recognized me?

I don't get to answer my own question because the bathroom door opens, and my boss walks in. The space isn't too big —it's just one stall and a sink—so there's no place for me to hide, no way for him to miss me. To miss how much of a mess I am.

Travis doesn't say a word as he opens the tap, the sound of water filling the silence between us. I keep my face down, wiping away my tears with my sleeve and hoping there isn't vomit on the corners of my mouth. *Oh hell.*

Could this be worse than the period stain?

My brain doesn't register what he's doing until he nudges my hands with a wet towel. It looks comically small between his fingers, and it takes me a moment to peel my gaze off them. I only do so because he pushes the towel into my hands again, his silent way of telling me to grab it.

We don't speak.

I hate that he's seeing me like this, but at least it's only him watching me in my most vulnerable state. It wasn't always like that.

When the towel meets my skin, its warmth soothes me a little. Once I make sure my face is as clean as it's going to get, I give him a tiny smile.

"Thank you." My voice doesn't sound much louder than a whisper, but he's close enough to hear me, close enough for the woodsy scent of his cologne to wrap around my lungs.

The only response I get is a grunt.

Or, at least, that's what I think until he asks in that deep voice, "Are you sick?"

I think I might be, but not in the way he thinks.

"I'm fine. It's probably just a bug."

It's not. I threw up because I panicked, but I can't tell him that. I don't want to answer the million questions that will come after that. Although this is Travis I'm talking about, so more like two.

But after fourteen months of being around him, I should know better than to think I can fool an ex-military man who seems to read minds.

"I know what happened with those people," he says.

I'm sure you don't. "It's fine."

I fold the towel into a perfect square and give it back to him. He accepts it wordlessly, his gaze trained on my face as if he were looking for something I'm sure he won't find.

"It's really okay," I assure him. "It's not the first time a customer's been rude to me. I'll get over it. Thanks for checking on me, boss man."

I fight the urge to overthink why he followed me here in the first place. Travis isn't the caring type. At work, he keeps conversations strictly business—at least with me. Maybe he has in-depth talks with Jude and Sandra after hours, but I wouldn't know or care.

Liar.

But he's here now, and maybe it means something.

That he wants me to go back to work, possibly.

I'm about to leave when my eyes land on a box of tampons and pads on the bathroom counter.

"Did you get those?" I ask him, my throat dry.

The stiff nods he gives me makes my heart leap. "Just in case customers need them."

He bought tampons for the bathroom. For the remainder of my shift, I'm unable to think about anything else, forgetting about my breakdown.

I can't stop thinking about how his actions speak for him more than he knows, how he's the best boss I've ever had, how his grumpiness is endearing, how I always feel safe when he's around.

And then I force myself to draft my two-week notice when I get home.

* * *

One thing I'm not going to miss about Bannport is my apartment, that's for sure.

I was lucky to find something within my limited budget, but Apartment B isn't the best. It isn't even *great* or *good*. My landlord, the mechanic I took my car to when it broke down the day I arrived in Bannport, conveniently forgot to tell me about the humidity problem in the building—which makes black mold grow on my walls. I clean it up as soon as it appears, but...mold.

Finding an apartment in this small town is a pain, I've come to learn. It's full of vacation rentals, which I would have to move out of every few months. I'm not about that at all.

But hey, at least I have a place to stay, mold and all. My apartment has a small kitchen and living room area, and my bedroom and bathroom are decent sized. I've had it much, *much* worse while living in the lap of luxury.

If nothing else, I'm thankful for my independence. I have a roof over my head I can afford all on my own, food in my fridge, a car that still runs, and money in my bank account to buy as much hair dye as I need.

And up until today, I had a job I loved and co-workers I felt comfortable around. I haven't resigned yet, but my mind is set.

I think.

"Honey," Jada greets me from the other end of the line when I call her later that day. She sounds way more enthusiastic than I'm feeling. "Do you know what you'll be doing for Christmas?"

Jada and Paul invite me over to their home every year, but I haven't been back to Los Angeles in six years. Much to their disappointment, I won't start now.

I plop down on my thrifted couch I got the same day I signed my lease and stare up at the popcorn ceiling. "I'll be staying here, I think."

"You think?"

I let out a deep sigh and decide I don't have the mental strength to beat around the bush today. "I'm considering turning in my two-week notice."

"Okay," she concedes. But she says it in that voice she'd use when one of us gave her an incorrect answer in math class that she didn't want us to feel bad about. "Aren't you happy at work? Is it your boss?"

When I first started working at The Lair, I told Jada about Travis's grumpiness. I always made a point to remark how he was never rude to me, just a bit stoic in general. But I haven't complained about him in a while—haven't even mentioned his name—so her assumption is surprising.

"It's not Travis." In a way, I wish Travis were the reason I

47

was considering leaving this town. It would make things much easier. "Someone..." *God. I can't believe this is happening right now.* "At the bar, someone recognized me today. A customer. At least I think she did."

"That's impossible," my former teacher blurts out, as if the mere thought is insane. "It's been what? Five, six years? And you look so different now, Allie. Did she say something to you?"

"She said she knew me from somewhere. That I looked familiar."

I don't tell her about my date with the toilet. The less I upset her, the better.

"All right. Let's slow down," she instructs, using that teacher voice again. "I thought you were happy at The Lair. In Bannport. Did something else happen?"

"No." It's the truth.

"And you want to run away because someone *might* have recognized you?"

I don't miss the way she says "run away" and not "leave." Not "move."

"I saw it in her eyes, Jada. She knew who I was. She was young, too, so she might know who my family is. Might know... everything."

The thought of that stranger, of any stranger, having a front-row seat to my private life makes my stomach turn again. I haven't felt this in a while, haven't allowed myself to remember that my life will never belong to me again.

"Allie." She sighs, sounding a little tired. "Listen to me—it's *very* unlikely that anyone would recognize you after all these years. You've grown up, not to mention changed your appearance."

"My face was all over the news. Jada, it was bad. I don't need to remind you." The more logical part of me wants to believe her, but... "Someone already recognized me not that long ago. Remember Nashville?"

"All right. It happened once," she concedes.

"So, not that unlikely," I mutter.

"Do you really want to uproot your entire life because of a woman who probably won't do anything about it even if she actually recognized you?"

"I did it once. I could do it again."

I could do it a thousand times if I had to. If I could leave behind everything I knew for a chance at a life worth living, I know I have the strength to resign from The Lair and never set foot in Bannport again.

But do I want to?

"That isn't the point, honey." She sighs again after she says it, which lets me know I'm in trouble. Well, as much trouble as I can get in with the absolute angel that is Jada. "Tell me something—do you feel at peace in Bannport with the life you are creating for yourself?"

The answer comes easily. "Yes."

"Then here's what we're going to do," she starts, always the beacon during my storms. "I'll search in every corner of the internet, and if I find something about this, I'll tell you. Once we know how serious this is or isn't, you can decide what to do. But don't overreact for now."

What she's saying sounds reasonable, but...

"What if it's already out there?"

"I'll start searching right now. I'm putting Paul on the task too," she says. Her husband hates being online as much as I do, so the fact that he's doing this for me means more than he will ever know. "We'll keep looking every day this week in case she decides to post something later. Don't worry about it, okay? Stay offline."

She doesn't have to tell me twice.

I let out a shaky breath. "Thank you, Jada. I love you so much."

"We love you too, Allie. Don't make any impulsive decisions you might regret later. Think about how precious the life you're building for yourself is, and don't let anybody ruin it. Not even yourself."

Not even yourself.

That has always been the hardest part.

Chapter Seven

AFTER LOOKING FOR SEVEN DAYS AND SEVEN NIGHTS, JADA and Paul don't find anything. Not a single trace of me or my whereabouts on the internet.

"Maybe she didn't know who you were after all," Jada suggested. "Your hair probably threw her off."

"Or maybe she recognized you," Paul offered over our video call last night, which didn't really help, but I still love him, "but she chose not to say anything."

I stomped down the idea that she could have recognized me *and* gone directly to my mother because that would be insane. But now, twenty-four hours later, I'm not proud to admit it has resurfaced.

And now isn't the best time for distractions.

The Lair is packed to the brim with Travis's friends. A guy named Josh turns forty tonight, and he chose The Lair as the place to celebrate. Apparently, he offered Travis a ridiculous sum of money to rent the bar for a private party.

The first hour goes by as normal as any birthday party full of half-drunk people would—an indecent number of shots, loud conversations, and endless laughter. That's until I notice something unacceptable.

"What are you doing?" I arch a curious eyebrow at Travis, who doesn't so much as spare me a glance as he gets some drinks ready.

"Working," he says.

I roll my eyes. "Why are you working tonight? Isn't it your friend's birthday party?"

He sets two beers in front of a waiting customer before turning to me. Those green eyes scream boredom as he asks, "Your point?"

"Travis..."

"Allie."

So, this is how it's going to go.

I watch his profile as he cleans some spilled beer from the counter. "Shouldn't you be celebrating with them? I'm not asking you to get first in line for karaoke, but you could let loose for a bit."

I know what he's going to say before he says it, and I'm ready to fight him on this.

Travis is one of the most—if not *the* most—hardworking people I know. He's here every day before anyone else and is always the last one to leave. Whenever there's an issue with any of the patrons, he gets involved and doesn't relent until the customer leaves satisfied or at least less pissed off.

Granted, I have no clue what he does in his spare time. He could have the most active of social lives known to humankind, but I doubt it. I mean, he's pretty much here fifteen hours a day, and he doesn't seem to have a problem with that. But right now, I do.

"I have to work," he says in that deep voice, which is exactly what I expected of him.

"Charlie and I can take care of everything for a bit if you want to grab a drink with them," I offer.

But of course, the next thing he tells me is, "I don't drink on the clock."

"Then get off the clock."

"Allie."

A warning.

"Boss man."

He shoots me a bored stare that, for some reason, I find amusing.

"One drink, and I'll stop pestering you," I tell him. "Sounds like a great deal to me, considering I'm planning to keep pestering you if you don't agree."

He isn't amused, which only makes this even more fun for me. So what if I enjoy poking the bear? It's not like he'll fire me over this—he's had enough reasons to before today, yet here I am.

When he still doesn't answer, I circle the bar until I get to the other side, open the cooler, and take out a cold beer. Then I shove it into Travis's giant hand as his eyes scan every inch of my face, probably looking for the audacity.

"You touched it, so now it's yours."

A beat passes. Travis only blinks.

"Go, boss man. Charlie and I got this."

And then I make a mistake.

In an effort to convince Travis that the world won't end if he has a drink with his friends, I wrap my hand around his forearm to guide him to their table. But when I touch his bare, hairy, firm skin, something weird happens.

Something weird and *bad*.

A sudden jolt of electricity climbs up all the way from my hand and lands in the pit of my stomach—and that traitorous jolt of electricity flutters. Just once, but it's enough for me to recognize what is going on.

A butterfly.

A stupid butterfly has taken flight in my stomach, bumping into every corner of it.

I let go of his arm as if he were on fire. Travis hasn't moved an inch from his original spot.

Wearing what I'm pretty sure is a nervous smile, I say, "I need to go back to my tables, but think about it. Even if it's only for ten minutes, you deserve a break. We'll be fine, and it's not like you'll be leaving the bar anyway. If we mess up, feel free to yell at me."

His body still hasn't moved. Those eyes travel from the hand that just touched him to my face in one slow, agonizing swipe that makes the single butterfly in my stomach flap its wings a little faster.

And then he says, "I would never yell at you."

My heart jumps.

Yes, someone not yelling at me should be the bare minimum, but I'm not focusing on that. Travis never yells at anyone.

It's the way he says it that makes the butterfly in my stomach start getting ideas. It's the subtle change in his voice, from gruff and annoyed to gruff and almost soft. Softer, at least. As if the mere idea of yelling at me made him sick to his stomach.

Or maybe I'm just seeing things.

The small smile I give him is genuine and maybe a little freaked out because *what the hell is happening to me, and can it stop?* "I know. It's just a figure of speech."

"I don't like it."

I bite the inside of my cheek. "Okay."

We stare at each other, neither of us brave enough to end

the safety of this silence. It takes one of his friends calling his name for him to break our impromptu stare off contest.

"Go with them." I nudge him one last time. If he insists on being a workaholic grump, at least I tried.

But the planets or stars must be aligned because Travis lets out a deep breath—one that tells me he's already tired of dealing with me—and says the last thing I expected. "Fine. Ten minutes."

Because I'm a little shit, I say, "Make it twenty."

I don't imagine that growl. "You won't drop this, will you?"

"Nope."

And if my playful smirk bothers him, he doesn't say.

"Fine."

Feeling an immense sense of accomplishment, I give him a thumbs-up before going back to my tables and telling Charlie we'll be on our own for a bit.

Ten minutes deep into the chaos that is running The Lair without Travis's extra help, a guy flags me over to their table.

"What can I get you?" I ask with a smile.

After months of bartending, I have grown quite the thick skin when it comes to dealing with drunk people—mostly men—and their flirty natures. Flirty is better than aggressive, so I'll take it even if they still make my skin crawl.

Yet nothing could've prepared me for this guy to wrap an arm around my shoulders and press me against his sweaty side.

"I don't need anything else now that you're here," he drawls, the alcohol on his breath all the more evident now that he's so close.

"Mike," one of the women at the table warns.

I send her a grateful look and swiftly slither my way out from under his arm. I smile to be polite, but I'm struggling to find any of this funny at all.

"I'm working right now. What can I get you?" I ask again.

The drunk man, Mike, pouts at me. A grown man, pouting. "How about when your shift ends? We can go somewhere, you and I."

"I'm not interested," I tell him, my voice losing all traces of politeness.

"Oh, burn." One of his friends at the table laughs.

The woman is still glancing at me, an apologetic look in her eyes. She turns to Mike. "I think it's time to call it a night and stop bothering Travis's employees, don't you?"

Mike tsks before giving me a once-over, that sly smile back on his face. "Come with me to the karaoke machine. We'll have a good time."

I don't want to draw attention to myself, so I don't lash out as I maybe should. Instead, I ask the table in an even voice, "Did you want anything?"

"I think he wants his fucking teeth knocked out," a familiar voice says behind me. A deep, rough voice that makes my heart skip a beat. "Don't you, Mike?"

The next thing I feel is a gentle hand on my elbow, guiding me away from the man who looks like he's just peed his pants a little. I can't bring myself to feel bad about it.

A shiver travels down my spine, and my brain shifts all its attention to that warm hand on my skin. A hand that belongs to a man who has been coming to my rescue one too many times recently.

Towering over me in all his ex-Navy SEAL glory, Travis stares down at Mike as if he already knows how to get rid of his body.

"Sorry, man." Mike backs down, considerably paler, as his eyes pinball between me and my boss. "Didn't know she was yours."

His?

With Travis's body against mine, it's impossible to miss

the tension in his wide shoulders or his strong yet gentle grip on my arm, but not a single part of me feels threatened right now. Not by Asshole Mike and certainly not by Travis's closeness.

If anything, the latter makes me feel shielded.

He tips down that handsome face to look at me, his eyes asking me what his words won't. *Are you okay?*

Only when I give him a small nod does he turn to Mike.

"Get the fuck out of my bar."

The other people around the table say nothing. One of the guys sends Mike a death glare, which he misses since he's too busy gaping at my boss. "The fuck, man?"

"You mess with my staff, you get the fuck out."

His staff.

Right. I mean, yes, that's who I am to Travis. It makes sense that he would come to the rescue so fast. He probably fears I would sue the bar or something for not feeling safe at the workplace. I shouldn't overthink this.

Those long fingers curl a little tighter around my elbow as Mike leaves his chair and takes a step closer. Travis positions himself in front of me.

"Sorry, man," Mike says, a hint of remorse in his voice. "I apologize," he tells me while I'm still partially hidden behind Travis's tense back. "I didn't mean to make you uncomfortable. I'm not having the best day, and it's just... never mind. It's not an excuse. I'm sorry. I'm leaving now."

I say nothing. Travis doesn't move until Mike exits the bar, his huge military-style boots planted like tree roots. His jaw does that ticking thing again before he drops my elbow.

But before I can say anything, he surprises me by turning around and asking first, "Are you okay?"

Dragging my eyes up his waist to his shoulders and then his face, I nod. "Yeah." I swallow, giving him a smile. "I would've punched him in the balls if he had crossed any more lines, but thanks for coming to the rescue."

A strange sound escapes the back of his throat, and it takes me a second to realize what it is.

A chuckle.

Travis is *chuckling*. At something I said.

Is he sick?

"My break's over." He tilts his head toward the bar. But his voice sounds... lighter. He points to the bar with his bearded chin. "I'll be there."

I'll be there in case you need me is how my brain has decided to finish his perfectly complete sentence.

I'm so delusional.

Travis said it himself—I'm part of his staff, which is the only reason he worries about me. I shouldn't entertain any other crazy ideas or focus too much on how the warmth of his hand seems to have settled within my skin, leaving a tingly sensation behind.

I'm too young for him, and he'd never be interested. He doesn't *know* me either. Not really.

And despite all the reasons why crushing on my boss is a disaster waiting to happen, my heart refuses to get the memo.

Chapter Eight

As my tired feet drag me inside the grocery store on my morning off, I keep wondering if what happened last night was only a fever dream. A butterfly-inducing one, but febrile nonetheless.

I've never been an overly cuddly person, but there is a difference between being clingy and not having been hugged in months—the last hug I got was from Jada, nearly a year ago. If my body reacted that way to Travis's hand on my elbow, it must be because I'm touch starved.

I grab some orange juice on my way to the hair products aisle and decide the world won't end if I allow some honesty into my system just for one second.

Okay, maybe five.

Five seconds, and I'll stop thinking about my crush on Travis forever.

The feel of his big, warm body so close to mine.

The hard muscles on his arms that I may or may not have daydreamed about touching a couple of times since I've known him. (I only want to poke them a little to see if they're real because there's simply no way they can be so huge.)

Five seconds are up.

The grip of that massive but surprisingly gentle hand on my elbow.

How he positioned himself in front of me in a protective gesture, his body a shield.

Stop it.

The woodsy smell of his cologne.

How invincible it made me feel to have him by my side.

What am I doing?

I can't be attracted to Travis. Not to the point where I'm unable to stop my thoughts from spiraling.

Falling for my boss is inconvenient enough, but falling for my much-older boss who doesn't give two craps about me outside of the workplace? That's *bad*.

Which means this...attraction or whatever the hell I feel for Travis needs to stop *now*.

If I had the tiniest of chances with him, maybe I would throw caution to the wind—but I don't. I know where we stand, and it's okay. He will never set his sights on a woman more than a decade younger than him, and my past is too heavy of a secret burden to ignore.

This is the path I chose for myself, the sacrifices I decided to make, the lies I chose to tell. I made my own bed, and I will lie in it.

Shutting down my intrusive thoughts, I grab two packs of hair dye and head for the register. Only I don't make it that far.

Something—someone—catches my eye in one of the aisles. Like a puppet on a string, I turn in the direction of the last person I expected or needed to see on my morning off.

Travis hasn't spotted me yet, but I have no doubts I only have a seconds-long advantage before he does. He's scratching his beard as he ponders something in front of...

The toy aisle?

Why is Travis looking at children's toys?

He has a whole cart full of them behind him. A mix of pinks and blues, yellows and greens, and *holy crap*. There must be at least twenty different things inside that cart.

My mind scans for the piece of information I must be missing, but I come up empty-handed. Travis doesn't have children; it would have come up in the year I've been working for him.

And I distinctly remember—for reasons that are neither here nor there—Uncle Neil saying how he was still waiting for grandkids. Or grandnieces and grandnephews, technically. So no, Travis isn't a dad. I would know.

I also remember he's an only child, so maybe all those toys are for his friends' kids? But so many? Christmas is only three weeks away, yet...

As I remind myself that whatever he spends his money on is none of my business and that it's not socially acceptable to blatantly stare at people, his head turns in my direction.

Shit.

I try to hide the two boxes of hair dye behind my back, but I'm too slow. His gaze shifts from my hands to my face, and a muscle in his jaw ticks.

Before I know what I'm doing, and because it would look weird if I just ran away, I give him a tight-lipped smile and move closer to him. Enough for him to hear me when I say, "Morning, boss man. Doing some shopping?"

The tension in the corners of his mouth catches my eye, and so do those wide shoulders clad in the same flannel shirt he was wearing when we met.

His head tilts just barely, a small nod of acknowledgment that feels too much like a dismissal. "Allie."

And that's it. No "How are you doing?" No "How's your shopping trip going?" No nothing.

Fair enough. He doesn't owe me a thing outside of the bar.

61

That realization doesn't make the stinging sensation go away, though.

"I'll see you around," I say, hoping my voice doesn't come out too awkward. I think I fail.

He's seen my hair dye, and I've seen his toys, but neither of us brings it up. We don't acknowledge the reasons why my hair color might not be natural or why he needs to give gifts to so many children. To be fair, I don't think I have the right to ask.

I give him a smile I'm sure doesn't reach my eyes, and he only nods again.

When I said he isn't big on wasting saliva, I really meant it. There's no reason for me to be upset that he doesn't look too enthusiastic about bumping into me.

So why does Travis ignoring me outside of The Lair, like I don't even exist when I'm off the clock, hurt my heart so damn much?

* * *

The next day, my foot is barely out of the changing room after our shift ends when Charlie declares, "This might be my best idea yet."

To nobody's surprise, Travis doesn't entertain him. "Did you check if the back door was locked?"

"Yes, boss. It is locked."

"Good."

"About my idea," Charlie insists, unfazed by our boss's dismissal. He sets his gaze on me, then on Jude and Sandra, who have just left the kitchen for the night. "Two words: Secret Santa."

Someone groans. I think it's Jude.

"Come on, it'll be fun. We can set a budget of, like, fifteen dollars. We don't have to make super meaningful gifts or anything," he keeps going. "Honestly, I'd be happy with some cookies."

"Aw." That's Sandra. "What a sweet idea, Charlie. It sounds fun. Count me in."

He lets out a victorious cry. "Jude? Your wife is all for it, so that means you have to agree."

"Whatever," he mutters. Sandra hooks an arm around his and plants a loud kiss on his cheek, which makes me smile. When she notices me looking at them, she winks.

"You're weak, Jude," I tease him.

He shrugs. "Can't deny it."

When I look away from them, I find Charlie pretty much in my face. "Allie Cat? You have to say yes."

I arch an amused eyebrow. "*Have* to?"

"It's the law. You don't want the authorities to come knocking at your door, do you?"

I know he's only teasing. I *know* this, but his words make the air whoosh out of my lungs all the same. My throat works a heavy swallow, and I barely notice the tightness in Travis's voice as he says, "Back off, Charlie."

"Sorry." He gives me a pleading look. "Say yes?"

I can't even think straight right now. I think I mutter, "Okay."

I take a deep breath through my nose, telling my brain that we're safe. Nobody is coming after me—Jada and Paul checked. They would tell me if something was up.

Charlie moves on to his last victim. "Boss? Everyone said yes, so you can't be the only one not playing."

Travis isn't one to succumb to peer pressure. "I'm not playing."

"Please?"

"No."

"With a cherry on top?"

63

Charlie's playful smile is making Travis's cheek tick, so I jump in. "Come on, Travis. It could be fun."

His eyes narrow on me, but I don't back down. He might be the most intimidating man I've ever seen, but I'm so determined to get him to play Secret Santa, it's as if my life depends on it. He needs to let loose, and maybe...

Okay. Maybe I'd love to buy something for him.

I'm 99 percent sure he's going to shut me off and tell us to get the hell out of the bar since we're already closed, but then the unexpected happens.

"Fine."

Did I hear that right? He's *agreeing*?

Charlie beams. "This is going to be epic. Let me grab some scraps of paper, and I'll do the raffle really quick."

Jude's still smiling as he looks from me to Travis. "Never thought I'd see the day, Ward."

The only response poor Jude gets is a grunt.

Charlie reappears with a pen and five pieces of paper. "This is how we're gonna do it," he starts, leaning on the bar to write something down. "I'm writing one name on each piece of paper. Then we'll put them inside my hat, and finally we'll take turns picking one. But you can't share the name with anyone else, otherwise it's no fun."

"What happens if we get our own name?" Jude asks.

"You show everyone, so we make sure you're not cheating, and then you grab another one."

"I'm so excited," Sandra says, sending me a wide smile I can't help but mimic.

I've heard of Secret Santa before, but I've never played. Jada and Paul aren't big on gifts, and years ago, we decided not to send one another any Christmas or birthday presents. At this point in my life, a phone call or a hug means way more than any material good could. But I can't say I'm not excited to make and receive a gift soon, even if it sounds shallow.

Maybe I should start being unapologetic about the things that make me happy, no matter how silly they might sound to others.

Charlie grabs the wool hat he was wearing this morning and tosses the papers inside. He turns to Sandra and bows dramatically. "My lady."

"Careful, kid," Jude growls, but we all know he's joking. Mostly.

Sandra giggles as her hand disappears inside the hat. She takes out one of the scrunched papers and reads the name on it. "Oh! I love this. Okay."

He turns to me, holding out the hat. "Allie Cat."

My heart races as I reach for a piece of paper. It's not that I want to pick up the one with Travis's name on it or anything, but a few days ago, I saw the most perfect socks with bears on them, and I would die if I saw boss man wearing them.

My fingers shake slightly as I unfold the paper, and I don't focus too much on the way my stomach drops when I see Jude's name. I like Jude, and weirdly enough, I know exactly what to get him.

I give Charlie a nod. "I'm good."

He moves on to Jude, and when he gets to Travis, the tank-sized man shakes his head. "I'll get the last one."

"You sure, boss?" Charlie arches a questioning eyebrow. Travis doesn't repeat himself. "All right."

When he reads the name on his paper, he chuckles and passes the hat to Travis. I'm not ashamed to admit I watch his face like a hawk as he grabs the last piece of paper and unfolds it carefully. But his expression gives nothing away.

"Remember, we're working with a fifteen-dollar budget, so no need to go over-the-top. We'll do the gift exchange on

Christmas Eve after closing time. Any questions?" Charlie asks, but nobody has any. "Cool. And keep your Secret Santa, well, a secret."

He winks at me, and I shake my head in amusement. He really isn't subtle at all, so I'm guessing his piece of paper has my name on it. Knowing him, he'll get me some carrot cake for laughs. I wouldn't complain.

Sandra gives my arm a squeeze as she passes me by. "See you tomorrow, dear. Have a good night."

"You guys too." I wave at her and Jude as they disappear into the dark street.

Charlie comes up to me before leaving. "My friends and I are getting together this weekend after work," he says with a hint of hopefulness in his voice, as if we both didn't know what my answer was going to be. "It's gonna be chill, on a pub by the lake. I'd love to see you there."

I give him an apologetic look. "Char..."

"Come on, Allie Cat. It's almost Christmas." His excitement doesn't wear off, which is impressive, given how I always turn him away. "Unless you have other plans?"

My eyes travel past Charlie and land on Travis, who is busy cleaning the already-clean counter. He's not looking at me, but I know he's listening.

"I don't," I tell him truthfully.

"Does that mean you'll think about it?"

Will I actually think about it? I can't remember the last time I went to a party—in fact, I don't think I ever have. Not a real adult one anyway. Not a party I wanted to attend.

In the past, I've made plenty of against-my-will appearances at social gatherings and get-togethers my parents forced me to put on a fake smile for, but I don't remember ever enjoying myself at any of them. Probably because every word I said, every move I made, had to be measured and perfect for the camera.

"Allie," Charlie singsongs.

I blink. "Um, sure. I'll think about it."

"That's what I wanted to hear. See you later—text me. Bye, boss!" he throws back at Travis, who, to nobody's surprise, doesn't answer. None of us take it personally at this point.

Charlie leaves, but his proposition stays right there, festering away in my heart. Maybe, for once, I should say yes and see what happens. He won't force me to stay, and if I don't drink, I can take my car and leave whenever I want. If not, I can always call a taxi.

I'm thinking about it. I really am. It has the potential to become the worst idea I've had to date, but it won't hurt to try. Right?

My head and my heart are still toying with the idea when all the lights go out, reminding me that Travis and I are the only ones left at the bar. I grab my bag and watch how bear-man swallows the distance between us, heading for the door.

"Ready to go?" he asks, which catches me off guard for some reason. He's barely looked in my direction—let alone talked to me—since we saw each other at the grocery store yesterday.

"Yep."

We don't speak as he locks up, and he doesn't utter a single word as he follows me to my car. It's parked just a couple of streets away, but I'm not dumb enough to shoo him away when he offers to walk with me at night. Why he does it, though, escapes me. He usually just waits until I get inside my car, watching me from a distance.

I give him a genuine smile as I unlock the car and toss my bag on the passenger seat. "Thank you for walking with me."

But of course, he says the very last thing I expected him to. "Didn't want you to walk here all by yourself. Could be dangerous."

Forcing myself not to think about the warehouse, I ask, "In Bannport?"

The last crime to make it to the local newspaper was a robbery attempt at a gas station eight months ago, and nobody was injured because the attacker was just some college kid from the next town over who wasn't even armed.

"Dangerous people exist everywhere," he says, as if he's just read my mind.

"I know that," I concede, anxiety starting to climb up my chest. *Not now.* "I'll be more careful next time."

Having been in the military for years, I know he must have seen some heavy stuff. And... well. It feels good to know someone besides Jada and Paul cares about me like this. It's a nice feeling.

If I expected him to leave after that, he doesn't. Instead, he places one massive hand on the roof of my car and scans every inch and corner of the street as I get inside. Once I'm in the driver's seat, he shuts the door for me.

I roll down the window just enough to say, "Thanks, Travis. See you tomorrow."

He doesn't lean down to meet my eyes, so I don't see his face when he answers, "Drive safe, Allie."

I don't shiver at the way that gruff voice says my name. I'm just cold because the window is down.

Liar.

What's new?

Chapter Nine

I DON'T KNOW WHAT I'M DOING HERE.

When I texted Jada about coming to the pub, we both thought it would be good for me to get out of my comfort zone for a little while. If I feel unsafe or uncomfortable, I can always leave and never attend another party again. Easy.

I didn't notice something was wrong immediately. Charlie greeted me with an eager hug and said how excited he was that I'd come. He ordered me a drink and then introduced me to a couple of his friends. They were nice enough and didn't seem to know who I was, which put me at ease.

That is, until I remembered the reason why I've always avoided parties and large social gatherings like the plague.

Phones. Phones everywhere.

Pointing at faces, at drinks, at bodies, at every single corner of this place.

Breathe in, breathe out. Again. And one more time.

It doesn't work.

I hide myself in the shadows, as far away from everyone as I can without looking like a creep, and keep my head down. My fingers tremble slightly around my drink, and I hate myself for being this way.

"Hey," a feminine voice says, loud enough for me to hear it over the music. When I look up, a long-haired brunette is standing in front of me with a smile. I remember her from earlier—Charlie's friend Lola. "You're Allie, right? I'm terrible with names."

I give her a nervous smile in return. "Yes. And you're Lola?"

She nods. "Sorry for disappearing earlier, but one of my friends was having a crisis in the bathroom," she explains. "She broke up with her boyfriend last weekend, and she's not doing well." She leans in and whispers, "He's here tonight. *With another girl.*"

I wince. "I hope she's okay."

Lola shrugs and takes a sip of her drink before she says, "We're all plotting his demise as we speak. You can participate if you want."

Something unknown but not entirely uncomfortable settles inside of me.

Growing up, my friends were scarce. At school, my class-mates had the wrong idea about me and my life. I'd never felt a genuine connection with any of my so-called friends, never felt included in boy talks or the usual teenage gossiping session. Not really.

I was always the freak. My parents made sure of it.

So the fact that this stranger is talking to me as if we've known each other for years, the fact that she approached me because she wanted to... I might sound pathetic, but I don't know how to act or what to say. What would be appropriate? What would be considered awkward?

Just be yourself is what Jada would advise me to do.

Sometimes, it's not so easy.

"So, you work with Charlie?" she asks, a teasing smirk on

her lips. "Tell me he's not as annoying at work as he is outside of it."

I let out a genuine chuckle. "I wouldn't say he's annoying. Dramatic, though? Every minute of every hour."

"Gotta love him as he comes." She takes another sip of her drink, and I mimic her. "Charlie told us he invited you to our parties a few times."

Her voice doesn't hold any accusations, but my shoulders still tense up. "Yeah. I... I'm not big on parties. I wasn't going to come today."

"What changed your mind?"

I decide to be honest. "A friend convinced me." I omit the fact that said friend used to be my teacher because that would lead to many questions I'll never be ready to answer.

Lola gives me a conspiratorial smirk. "Is he here tonight?"

I frown. "He?"

"The friend who convinced you."

"Oh, no. She's a woman, and she doesn't live in the area."

She looks genuinely confused by that, which confuses me even further. "I just assumed... I'm so sorry."

"It's fine," I assure her. "Why did you think it was a guy friend?"

"I shouldn't have, I'm sorry," she apologizes again, her big eyes pleading. "It's just that there's a guy over there who hasn't stopped looking at you since you got here, and I thought..." Her eyes widen. "Do you know him? If you don't, don't worry. You can stick with me and my friends, and we'll call the police or something. I'll drive you home."

Her words come out so fast, it takes me a second to process everything she's saying.

A guy is looking at me?

My eyes find his a second later, as if a magnetic pull had worked its magic on me.

"I know him," I tell Lola. "He isn't a creep or anything, don't worry. But thank you so much for offering to help."

"Of course. That's what us girls are for," she says with firm conviction. "You can still hang out with us, by the way. Or if you want to go talk to your friend, that's all right too. Just come find us if you need us, yeah?"

Maybe her sweetness should overwhelm me, but instead I can't wait to tell Jada about it in the morning. *I made a friend.*

I give her a genuine smile. "I will. Have fun with your friends."

She winks. "And you have fun with yours."

I don't know about that.

Sitting in a corner booth alone and hidden in the shadows, Travis doesn't look like he's having a lot of fun. As I walk toward him with no clear plan in my head, I wonder if he's waiting for someone. If he's waiting for a woman. He doesn't strike me as the partying type, so why else would he be here?

I let myself fall on the seat in front of him and set my half-empty drink on the table. He's nursing a bottle of water, which only confuses me further. Who comes to a pub alone and doesn't order a drink?

"Hey, Travis."

He tips his head. "Allie."

I'm very aware of the people around us. Their phones, their cameras, pointing in so many directions at once, it's impossible to tell if I will be in the background of any of their pictures. The mere thought makes me want to run away, which prompts me to swallow down the rest of my drink. I might need another one.

That, or a distraction.

For my liver's sake, I choose the latter.

"Are you here with someone?" I ask him, the alcohol letting my tongue be a little more loose than usual.

I'm a lightweight, and whatever they put in that drink is

doing what it's supposed to. The chances of embarrassing myself in front of the only man I've felt a sliver of attraction for in the past decade are at an all-time high.

"A couple of friends." A pause, in which I ignore the way my shoulders sag with relief that he didn't say *a woman*, and then he asks, "You?"

"Charlie invited me, but I haven't seen him in a while."

Maybe this is the alcohol talking, or maybe I've officially gone insane. All I know is that, before my brain can process what I'm about to do, I stand back up and tell my boss, "Let's go. I want to kick your ass at darts."

"Darts?" he repeats in that gruff voice I'm not used to hearing outside of The Lair.

"You've played before, right?" We have a dartboard at the bar along with a pool table, but I've never seen him play either.

He doesn't answer. Instead, he maneuvers that enormous body out of the booth and takes a step forward until his shadow is cast over me. I'm met with a chest so wide, it stretches the material of the long-sleeved dark T-shirt he's wearing.

"You're asking me if I've played darts before?" He tilts his head to the side, a silent challenge glinting in his eyes.

This is new. I've never heard Travis sound almost playful.

I smirk, not breaking eye contact. "Well, have you?"

A low chuckle escapes him. Travis shakes his head as if he can't believe my question, and I swear this is the most amusement I've seen him show in a year.

He gestures to the back of the pub. "After you."

I don't see Charlie or Lola on my way to one of the dartboards at the back, but I do spot Travis's friends, including Josh, the birthday guy. Another group is playing pool nearby, but otherwise we are alone. The butterfly in my stomach is extremely aware of this fact.

"Want to invite your friends?"

But he shakes his head. "They're too busy trying to go home with a woman tonight."

And you aren't?

I remind myself once again, heart racing, that Travis's love life is absolutely none of my business. I'm probably saving myself from heartbreak by not prodding, too.

"All right. Let's throw a dart to see who starts," I suggest, grabbing all the darts and giving him half.

My boss stands tall, his eyes never leaving mine. "You go first."

"I don't mind going second."

"I insist."

Does he have to be so considerate all the time? First walking me to my car, then stocking pads and tampons in the bar's restroom, and now this? I'm aware that this is probably just basic decency, but I'm used to less. Way less.

When I told him I would kick his ass, I wasn't messing around. For someone who didn't play darts once growing up and only got into it thanks to a cheap board from the grocery store, I'm pretty amazing. The evidence lands on the outer ring.

My smug smirk doesn't go anywhere as I look back at Travis, whose own smile is almost nonexistent, but I think I see it. "Impressive."

I beam at his praise, but my pride doesn't last very long. A moment later, Travis's dart hits the bullseye with such minimal effort, I would believe him if he told me he was the International Dart Champion.

The worst part is, he doesn't say anything as he moves behind me, giving me space to throw my second dart. He knows I'm not going to kick his ass anytime soon, and he's enjoying every second of it.

The look I send him over my shoulder is nothing short of dirty. "Traitor."

He chuckles again, which must mean he's truly coming down with a fever. I don't think I've seen him this laid-back ever. "Come on. Kick my ass."

He's teasing me. Travis is *teasing* me.

"Oh, I will." I won't, and we both know it. But because I have a thing for embarrassing myself, and my lips work faster than my brain, I blurt out, "How about we make this more interesting?"

He arches an intrigued eyebrow at that. "Interesting how?"

Shut up while you can, Allie.

He's your boss.

"How about..." My heart is beating so fast, I'm afraid he might be able to hear it. "If I win, you'll have to wear one of my bracelets for a month. I'll make you one." I show him my wrist, where the tiny beads of my white-and-pink handmade bracelet glint under the dim light of the bar. "Deal?"

He gives me a curt nod. "And if I win?" he asks as if he already knows that's going to be the case. He might not be wrong.

I shrug. "I don't know. What do you want?"

"Nothing."

"Don't be boring."

"I'm not boring."

"Only a bit."

"Fine." He shifts on his feet. "If I win, you'll tell me why you dye your hair brown."

My mouth turns dry. I knew Travis was going to think something was up when he saw me trying to hide the boxes of dye the other day, but that didn't mean I expected him to actually bring it up. And still...

I don't want to lie anymore. I've done it enough times, and with every big or little lie, a part of me withers.

But I can't just tell him the truth. I *can't*.

I'm not lying because I think it's fun or because I'm bored and want attention. Trust is a luxury I can't afford anymore, and even though I know Travis, I don't *know* him. I can't risk it.

"Are you sure you want that to be your prize?" I ask, begging my voice to sound nonchalant. I don't think I'm too successful.

"That's what I want," he says with no hesitation.

I force a smile and fidget with my dart. "All right."

Maybe I shouldn't agree to something I don't want to do, but the knowledge that I can always lie about it calms me and makes me nauseous all at once.

Why do I have to keep hiding? I reached my destination. Maine is where I wanted to be. Wasn't I going to start anew?

I promised.

As I position myself in front of the dartboard, I realize it's too late for that. Every person I've met in Bannport who I care about—Charlie, Jude, Sandra, Travis—knows a version of Allie that isn't real. Not fully. If I told them the truth, they would never see me in the same light. They would never forgive me, would never trust me again. I can't back down now.

Anxiety gets the best of me, and my dart lands on the thirteen double ring. Not bad, but not my best. When I turn to Travis, his face has no traces of smugness anymore.

I give him a weak smile. "Your turn."

Travis takes my spot in front of the dartboard and throws his dart toward the wall.

He turns to me. "Oops."

Oops—

What the hell is he doing?

"You did that on purpose." I cross my arms, pinning him down with a glare that isn't at all intimidating. "It doesn't count. Do it again."

"Okay."

Another dart hits the wall.

"Travis," I warn.

"Allie." He sounds bored.

This man. "Fine. If this is how you want to play, let's play."

I'm not mad at him, only confused. Why would he miss on purpose, like he wasn't acting all cocky a minute ago?

Whatever. If he wants to be childish about this, I'm game. My next dart hits a neon sign with the words "Drink your sorrows away" on the wall. His lands straight on the sticky floor.

A minute later, all our darts are scattered everywhere *but* the board.

"That was a shit game," I tell him, although I haven't had this much fun in a while. Who knew throwing darts at the wall with my boss would help me get my mind off things?

He only shrugs those wide shoulders and gestures at the board with his bearded chin. "Looks like you won."

"What?"

"I hit the bullseye, but you scored more points overall," he clarifies. He swallows the distance between us, those molten eyes landing on my wrist. On the bracelet around it. "Green is my favorite color."

Green. "Like your eyes."

I realize my mistake a second too late. There's no use in hoping he didn't hear me because the look he's giving me tells me all three words were loud and clear. Not once in fourteen months have I seen his eyes look like this—dark, intense, like they're trying to pierce my flesh.

I overstepped. It was a weird thing to say, and I—

"You can use white too," he says, his voice sounding a lot throatier than before. Or maybe it's just my deranged head. "So it matches yours."

My tongue feels like sandpaper, and I'm not sure even the shortest of words could come out if I tried.

A ridiculous thought pops into my head—did he lose on purpose so I would make him a bracelet?

Or did he notice my awkwardness about the hair dye and regret his prize choice?

Both?

As we make our way back toward the front of the bar, Travis stays close. He isn't touching me but remains a comforting presence by my side.

Charlie spots us then and, to my surprise, doesn't bat an eye at me and Travis being together.

"Hellooooo," he drawls. That explains it—he's drunk out of his mind. "Allie, my favorite girl ever. Are you having fun?"

I can't help but smirk. "Not more than you."

"Boop," he says as he boops my nose. "See? I told you coming was a good idea." When his smile turns playful and his eyes glaze over, I can almost sense what he's thinking before he says it. "Coming is always a great idea. Don't you agree, boss?"

I burst out laughing at how ridiculous this conversation is, which makes Charlie laugh too. I don't think he knows why we are laughing in the first place, which makes me laugh even harder.

"Did you come today, boss?" Charlie asks next.

But Travis, to no one's surprise, doesn't find any of this funny.

"Charlie," he warns.

"Hey, I'm not working," he argues. "Am I not allowed to be your friend when I'm off the clock?"

"I don't befriend my staff."

If Charlie is affected by Travis's words, he doesn't show it.

Me, though? That's another story.

I don't befriend my staff. But he plays darts with them?

"Aw, don't be so mean. We are all friends. Although maybe

some more than others." He wiggles his eyebrows at me, as if there's an inside joke I'm not privy to.

"All right. Enough." Travis cuts him off. His hand lands on my back, guiding me forward. "See you tomorrow. Don't come to work with a hangover."

Before Charlie can answer, Travis is already directing us toward the exit. A moment later, we are met with the cold night air, and Travis drops his hand from my back. "Do you want to go home or go back inside?"

I don't befriend my staff. Why am I still so hung up on his words? This isn't new information. He might act a little less like an asshole to Jude and Sandra, but they aren't super close either. Making friends at work isn't his thing, and I get it, but...

"Yeah, I'll just..." I point to the dark parking lot. "My car is right there. You can go back to your friends. I'll see you tomorrow."

I don't look back to see if he's following me, but I don't need to. His heavy footsteps echo behind me until it's impossible to focus on anything else.

Why is he doing this? Making sure I get in my car safely *every single time* doesn't align with his "I don't befriend my staff" policy, and it only confuses the butterflies in my stomach even further.

Just as I'm about to open the car door, his voice breaks the silence of the parking lot. "Don't forget my bracelet."

I give him such a small nod, I don't think he sees it. "I won't. See you tomorrow, Travis."

He will get his bracelet because I don't break my promises, but when it comes to Travis, I shouldn't forget where we stand. If he doesn't befriend his staff, then I shouldn't try to befriend my boss either.

Chapter Ten

I WAKE UP WITH A START.

My first thought is that someone is inside my apartment. But after a moment, my eyes adjust to the darkness, and I can't see any shadows or hear any sounds.

One quick glance at the clock on my nightstand tells me it's past six in the morning. My head pounds despite having had only one drink last night, and my body feels like someone beat me up in my sleep. I already know it's going to be a long day.

I rub my eyes with the heel of my palms and stay quiet, double- and triple-checking that nobody is inside my apartment. When it becomes obvious that I'm simply paranoid, I put on my running gear, desperate for some fresh air.

Twenty minutes later, I still feel that familiar anxiety clawing at my chest despite the cold breeze hitting my face. *I didn't sleep well, that's all. Nothing's wrong.*

In an effort to calm myself down, I take in Bannport's breathtaking lakeside as I run. With its green rolling hills looming in the distance, every corner of this small town looks like one of those paintings you see at an exhibition and wish you could live inside of.

Bannport Lake sits in all its blue-gray glory, the surface undisturbed by boats or animals. The trees around the shore are eerily still, too, without the wind to sway them. No matter how often I take in this view on my way to work, its beauty never ceases to make something in my chest come alive.

Once I've calmed down enough, I make my way back to my apartment building. I'm fiddling with my keys when my phone goes off inside my jacket. In the time it takes me to open the door, get inside, and lock it, it doesn't stop ringing.

I can't explain why, but the second I see Jada's caller ID on the screen, I know something is wrong. Very wrong.

"Hi," I answer quietly. "Everything okay?"

"You didn't read my text?"

"You texted me this morning?"

"Look at it, please."

The urgency in her voice makes my heart pound too fast. Putting her on speaker, I quickly find the text app and click on the links she sent me while I was out running.

A man tried to abduct a young girl in her own home yesterday. Fingers are pointing at the child's mother, who shared pictures of their front porch with her 300K+ followers just hours before it happened.

Investigative journalist George Eden speaks out on child abduction case and social media: "Something similar happened years ago with Allison Buccieri. The internet never learns."

No.

No.

This is a nightmare. Only a nightmare.

It can't be anything else.

But I blink, and the articles are still there. Still real.

Still talking about me.

Buccieri.

I haven't heard, seen, or spoken my last name in six years.

Changing it to Smith was a no-brainer, considering how many Allison Smiths there were in the world. But I should've known fleeing Los Angeles didn't mean I'd also flee society's memory. This George Eden guy certainly hasn't forgotten about me.

"Are you still there?" Jada's voice breaks through the fog in my brain.

My hands shake as I hold my phone tighter. "Y-Yes."

I scan the article for more information about me when I come across a quote that empties out my lungs.

**"I would love to interview Allison Buccieri,"
declared Eden on his show. "The way she
vanished off the face of the earth can't be
coincidental. I think her sharing her experience would give people a much-needed wake-
up call when it comes to showcasing children's lives on social media."**

When I spot an old picture of me with the long blonde hair I'll never have again, I close the tab.

"Stay with me. Take a deep breath," Jada instructs. I do as she says, but I don't feel any better. "I scanned the internet this morning and saw nothing else about you, okay? This is all there is for now. I'm only telling you because you asked for updates if there ever were any."

I did, and I don't regret it. If people are talking about me, that means I could be in danger. Knowing what's being said can help me take control of the situation and prepare for different outcomes.

"Jada…" I start, but I have to stop to take a deep breath. "W-What if they find me?"

"Doxing is a crime," she reminds me. "Nobody will reveal your location. Not that they have any way to find you in the first place."

I should've left Bannport when I had the chance. What if it's too late now?

As if she could read my mind, Jada says, "Don't run away, Allie. Not again." There's a frustrated edge to her voice I haven't heard in a long time. "If you leave, you let your parents win. They don't deserve to have control over your independent adult life after everything they put you through."

At this point, my entire body is shaking so hard, I have to lower myself to the floor and sit down. "Jada…"

"No, Allie. *No.* I love you, and every time you run away, you hurt yourself a little more. Tell me I'm wrong."

I can't.

I can't tell her that because we both know she isn't.

"People have talked about you and your family before, remember? When…when the warehouse happened, and then after you stopped appearing on their social media. Nothing happened then, and nothing will happen now. They'll move on soon. It's natural for people to bring up your name when something so similar happens, but you're not in danger again."

Jada has always been my voice of reason, a life raft I can cling to when the tides threaten to drown me. She was there for me at my worst, as my teacher and as the only responsible adult in my life. I owe her everything, and I know she's right about this. But anxiety knows no reason, no boundaries, and so I keep spiraling.

"Why are you running away, Allie? What's the point?"

My eyes fall on my running shoes, and a shaky laugh escapes me at the irony of it all. No matter how fast I try to get away, my thoughts and memories are always there, ready to punish me.

"I just wanted to get away," I mutter. "From my family, my past, everything."

"I get that, and I don't blame you for it," she says. "But why do you keep doing it?"

It hurts to swallow. "I'm not running away now."

"But you're thinking about it."

"It's just…" I let out another shaky breath, pulling my knees against my chest. "I just want to live a calm, happy life, away from everything. I don't want to get caught up in drama. I just want to be left alone, Jada, and this media attention could ruin that."

"Oh, honey. You deserve a calm, happy life more than anyone else I know. And you *will* get it. But sometimes we need to be a bit brave in order to get what we want. You should take this article as a wake-up call and start living your life unafraid of the future," she says. "Worrying and running away won't fix anything. You've been doing that since you left California, and it didn't change this outcome. It won't stop people from talking about your case. So you might as well start living that calm, happy life now, Allie. Live your life for *you*."

"I don't know how to do that," I confess quietly.

"And that's okay, but it's time to figure it out. Step-by-step."

Living without fear. I must have done it at one point, but I don't remember what it feels like anymore.

Not after the warehouse.

Chapter Eleven

Age 12

THE SUN WAS SHINING THE DAY I GOT KIDNAPPED.

I remember every detail from that day—the three pancakes I had for breakfast, my little brother's temper tantrum before leaving for school that morning, the A-plus I got on my math test, and Marie complaining about her ruined skirt on our way out of school.

"I'll make my mom send her the dry-cleaning bill, I swear," she seethed, staring at the white yogurt stain on the front of her pleated skirt.

Eloise had accidentally knocked it over during lunch—and profusely apologized—but Marie couldn't let it go.

"Yogurt stains can't be that hard to remove," I offered lamely.

The truth was, I had never washed my own clothes, so I had no idea how stains were removed. I just didn't want her to feel bad.

But Marie kept cursing Eloise while trying to remove the stain with her nails. Under the scorching summer sun, I tuned her out and kept walking down the stairs that separated the main school building from the parking lot—and I smiled to myself, knowing nobody was waiting for me.

After a couple screaming matches, I'd finally convinced my mother to let me ride the school bus with Marie. I was old enough, and all the cool kids in my grade were doing it. We'd agreed I'd carry a cell phone with me at all times in case something happened, and that I wouldn't use it for anything else in case the battery ran out. I was only too eager to agree.

That's why I was surprised to hear a feminine voice calling my name when Marie and I stepped out of the front gate of the school.

"Allison! Sweetie, wait."

My steps came to a halt. With a frown, I stared at the blonde woman rushing out of a modern black car. Her smile was a mix of worried and awkward. I didn't recognize her.

"Do I know you?" I asked her.

Her hair looked too shiny and yellow, almost fake. She wore office clothes—nothing that would make her stand out from other businesswomen in the city or give me any clues about her identity.

"I'm Claudia, one of your mom's friends," she explained.

Does Mom know a Claudia? I wasn't sure.

"So sorry to bother you, sweetie." Claudia took a step closer. "Your mom sent me to pick you up and drive you to the hospital. Your brother was in an accident, and he's in the ER. I'm so sorry, but we have to hurry up."

My mouth turned dry. Johnny had been in an accident?

"Um, I need to take the bus," Marie quipped awkwardly, walking backward in the opposite direction. "Bye."

I couldn't pay attention to her.

"How do you know that?" I asked Claudia, my voice laced with skepticism and fear while my mind raced with worried thoughts about my brother.

Johnny has been in an accident. Johnny is in the ER.

"She knows I work a couple blocks away, so she sent me to pick you up. She and your dad had to rush to the ER with Johnny. He hit his head and was bleeding a lot, from what she told me."

Despite Johnny being only five years younger than me, we weren't super close, but I still loved him. Of course I did. The ER always meant bad news, and I didn't want him to die.

But my feet wouldn't move. Something in my stomach turned with an emotion I couldn't put a name to. Terror, yes, but also something else.

Among the fog in my brain, I scrambled for any reminders of Claudia and found none. My mother had many friends, and my twelve years were long enough to meet them all. Or at least to have heard of them.

"I-I don't know you," I stammered, holding on to my back-pack straps a little tighter.

Her chuckle took me aback. "Don't be silly, Allison. I was at your house just last week. I helped your mom replace those black shelves in her dressing room."

That made me pause. My mother *had* replaced some dark shelves for white ones in her massive dressing room after complaining that it altered the feng shui of the room. Whatever that meant.

There was no way for Claudia to know that unless she'd been there.

"Come on, sweetie," she urged me, putting a cold hand on my arm to walk me to her car. "Your parents are waiting. They want you to be there for Johnny."

I took a step forward, then another. The closer I got to the car, the more my stomach clamped, and the more nauseous I felt.

Something wasn't right.

"Wait." I stopped again. It earned me a frown from the woman, but I pressed on. "If you're really my mother's friend, when's her birthday?"

"August 12," she replied easily, as if the answer was foolishly obvious.

"What food does she hate the most?"

She answered with no hesitation. "Bananas. She likes the flavor—vegan banana bread is one of her favorite sweet treats—but she can't stand how soft the flesh is. Makes her gag."

"What's her favorite color?"

"Red, but she currently has a thing for leopard print. Reminds her of her young days."

That... was true. All of it, even the leopard print thing—she had just ordered a new leopard coat online two days ago.

"I know you're worried, but I promise it'll be all right." Claudia's smile was reassuring as her hand landed on my arm again. Her fingers held me a little tighter. "Just come with me."

My throat worked a swallow on its own. "I-I should call my parents."

"You have a phone on you?" Claudia asked. When I nodded, she gave me another patient smile. "You can call them in the car. But we should really be on our way, Allison. It's very urgent. Johnny was very badly injured. He might not make it."

The voice at the back of my head telling me something about this wasn't right, telling me to run, got drowned by her last words.

He might not make it.

Claudia led me to the back seat with a hand on my backpack before sliding it off my shoulders when I sat down on the sticky leather.

"Is your phone inside your backpack?" she asked softly.

I gave her another nod.

"Very well."

She shut the door with a little more force than I expected, making me flinch. I watched through the tinted windows how she rounded the car, threw my backpack in the trunk, and climbed onto the driver's seat.

Claudia wasn't smiling anymore. She adjusted the rearview mirror, touched a few buttons on her console, and suddenly a partition appeared between the front and the back seat. It looked like one of those plastic screens I'd seen in limousines in movies. Why did she have one?

Soon after she started the car, a male voice boomed through the speakers.

"You got her?" an angry, mean voice asked.

It didn't sound like my dad.

"Yes. I'm on my way," Claudia replied in a cold tone so different from the calm, patient one she'd used with me just a moment ago.

Despite my throat feeling like I had nails stuck in it, I managed to ask, "Are you talking to my parents?"

I knew the answer. Not so deep down, I knew this woman had lied to me. I knew I was in more danger than I could ever imagine. But a part of me wanted to believe it was all in my head. That the male voice belonged to my dad, but somehow the car speakers made it sound a little different.

And then Claudia chuckled.

"Oh, sweetie. You made it so easy."

My heart took a dive. "You're taking me to the hospital?"

"Nah."

Tears started brimming in my eyes, and I held on to the door handle. As if it would lead to safety. As if we weren't speeding down a highway. As if I could get out.

"L-Let me go," I stammered, yanking the door handle to no avail.

Her eyes met mine through the rearview mirror, all traces of friendliness gone from them.

"Should've thought twice about getting in the car with a stranger, little girl."

This couldn't be happening. Not to me. This only happened in the news and in movies. This couldn't be real life.

"Let me go!" I screamed to no one, because no one was there to help me.

Kidnapped. I was being kidnapped.

I kept yanking at the door handle, screaming, crying, and hitting the partition screen between us. Nothing broke but me.

Breathing became an impossible task. I cursed myself for not having kept my backpack with me. I could be calling the police right now, begging them to come help me, even though I had no idea where we were or where we were going.

I didn't know how long she drove for or if we were still in Los Angeles. It could've been twenty minutes or two hours; I spent every second trying to get out of that car and blaming myself for being so dumb. Not getting in a stranger's vehicle is a basic survival skill, something a little kid would know. How could I have fallen for it?

But she knew about my mother. Intimate details no one who wasn't close to her should've known. I didn't think she was her friend anymore, but I was still confused as to how she knew about her aversion to banana flesh and her dressing room shelves. Maybe she knew my parents somehow?

The car stopped. Looking out of the darkened window, I could barely make out the outside of some industrial area. Nobody else seemed to be around, but there were a few cars parked in the front. No noises either—not that I would hear much inside a vehicle.

Something in me unexpectedly settled then. Calmed when it shouldn't have.

I didn't fight it. I'd already neglected my inner voice once today, and it had led me here. It wasn't going to happen again.

My stomach dropped as Claudia—was that even her real name?—got out of the car. When she opened my door, her hand wrapped around my arm in a tight, hurtful grip, and she dragged me out of the back seat.

We were outside of a warehouse. Mold clung to the walls, and from here I could tell it was mostly empty except for dozens of pallets and containers grouped at the back.

What if she handcuffs me and puts me in one of those?

What if she does something worse than throwing me inside a container?

I knew I had seconds to save my life. That woman, whoever she truly was, had no intentions of ever letting me go back home.

When she stopped to peer inside the warehouse, I saw my chance.

With adrenaline shooting through every inch of my body, I kicked Claudia's knee. *Hard.*

She gasped and doubled, releasing her grip on my arm. Maybe she wasn't expecting me to fight back so aggressively, but I didn't stay behind to double-check her shock levels.

I ran.

I ran faster than I'd ever ran in my entire life.

I didn't know where I was, or where I was going, or if Claudia was coming after me, or if someone else who was working with her had their eyes on me.

I just knew I'd die if I stopped.

Then I saw it—a fence.

If I had been older, taller, more athletic, maybe I could've jumped over it. But I barely reached five feet, and even from a distance, I knew attempting to climb it would slow me down too much. I knew Claudia would catch up to me.

"This way!" her familiar voice bellowed, not far from me.

Every ounce of me wanted to panic in that moment, to cry, to *scream*, because I had managed to escape only to be abducted again, and that wasn't fair.

I have to fight. I can't give up.

Gravel dug into the bare skin of my legs and arms as I lay under one of the cars parked at the front. There was no other place to hide, no exit, and I knew if I entered that warehouse—even if only to hide—I wasn't going to get out.

From under the car, I saw Claudia's heels reach the gate where I had been standing just seconds before. They turned in all directions as she looked for me. Moments later, a pair of dirty sneakers attached to gray jeans joined her.

"Did you seriously fucking lose her?" the man shouted.

"She *kicked me*," Claudia shot back. "She couldn't have gone far. Search the inside."

"While you do what?"

"I'll check if she jumped the fence and is roaming the streets. If she stumbles upon those fucking pigs, we're done."

The man grunted something under his breath I didn't catch and jogged out of sight. I lay very still, barely breathing, barely moving my eyeballs for fear of attracting her attention.

Claudia punched some kind of code on the gated fence, opening a small door. She shut it as soon as she got to the other side, unknowingly locking me inside the warehouse lot again.

And I waited.

I waited for hours under that car for some kind of miracle to get me out of there alive.

I could hear distant masculine voices, which told me I wasn't alone, and someone would see me if I moved. Claudia came back some time later, shouting that I'd gotten away, that the police would come at any second, and that they needed to leave.

My stomach sank. If they were leaving, that meant someone would take this car. And as I saw it, I had two options—to get run over and die, or to be found alive and then killed anyway.

I shut my eyes and begged my tears not to choke me up. I couldn't make any noises. Not that it would matter, because just then I heard a voice shout, "Check the cars at the front!"

I was dead.

I was going to die at twelve years old at an abandoned warehouse somewhere, and nobody would ever find me.

I was never going to see my parents again. My siblings, Johnny and baby Cindy, either. I was never going to play with Milo again. I was never going to attend Mrs. Jada's classes, to feel the beach sand between my toes, to try on new shoes I'd end up not buying, to go on hikes and complain within ten minutes that I was tired, to play mermaids at the pool, to jump on the trampoline to see how close I could get to the sky, to read a book under my blankets with a lantern, to laugh or smile or sing or grow up or fall in love.

My life was going to end today, and there was nothing I could do to change my fate.

I'd never been a religious person, and I still wasn't then. But in that moment, with my eyes closed and my body curled in the fetal position under that car, I made the universe a promise.

If you let me get out of here safely, if you let me live, I'll make it up to you. I promise to make the world a better place. I promise to try even harder than I was going to try before. I promise you won't regret letting me live. I promise. I promise.

But the universe or God or whatever sentient or insentient being controlled our fate—if such a thing could be done in the first place—didn't listen to me.

"I found her!"

Gravel pierced my skin as someone yanked me from under

93

the car. The man with the dirty sneakers and the gray jeans grabbed me by the hair and *pulled*.

"You little shit," he snarled, his smoky breath hitting my face. "You thought you were smart, huh?"

Claudia rounded the corner. Her impatient eyes set on me for no longer than a second before she turned to the animal manhandling me. "Get her in the van."

"No!" I screamed, thrashing against his grip on my hair. I didn't care if he ripped it all out, if it hurt so bad that more tears filled my eyes. "Let me go!"

"You're not going anywhere." He yanked harder. "Do as I say, or this will get a lot more unpleasant for you."

I didn't listen.

If I was going to die, I was going to fight until my last breath.

"Help! Please help! I'm a child! Help!"

"Shut the fuck up," Claudia hissed. "Van, *now*."

"No!" I tried kicking him like I'd done with Claudia, but he stepped away just in time.

When he started dragging me toward the warehouse again, I *screamed*. A bloodcurdling scream, high-pitched, louder than any other sound that had ever left my mouth.

It sounded as inhuman as I felt.

The man covered my mouth, but I bit his hand so hard, I tasted blood.

And then I screamed again because they were going to kill me no matter what I did or said.

I screamed.

Again.

Again.

I screamed until the silent promise I'd made under the car reached the sky. Until it answered in the form of a police patrol car, stopping on the other side of the warehouse fence.

"*Shit*," the man grabbing me hissed.

My ears started ringing.

I kept screaming.

I couldn't stop.

Two police officers got out of the car, guns pointed at us.

I promise. I promise. I promise.

* * *

I woke up at the hospital two hours later.

When a police officer came by to get my statement, she asked me why I got in the car with that woman. I told her she knew private things about my mother no stranger should've known. She gave me a sad, pitying look, asked me a few more questions, and wished me a speedy recovery.

The next day, I found out that Johnny hadn't been in the ER.

There had been no accident.

My mother didn't have any friends named Claudia.

When I left the hospital soon after that, I saw myself in the news.

I saw myself everywhere.

Tragedy hits the Buccieri family.

Child of influencer family gets kidnapped. How much of our personal lives should we share online?

Online.

I wasn't allowed to go on the internet other than to do schoolwork, and even then, someone had to supervise me. I knew my mother posted videos and pictures online because she always said that was her job, but what did that have to do with Claudia?

That afternoon, I took her phone while she was in the shower and saw everything.

Photos of me, of Johnny, of our baby sister, Cindy, all over the internet.

Photos of our home, our bedrooms, our vacations.

Of the shelves she had recently replaced.

Pictures of me in my school uniform, holding certificates and awards with the name of my school.

Pictures of Johnny playing rugby, going fishing with our father, with his own certificates.

Pictures of Cindy's toy room, of her playing dress-up, of her covered in bubbles in the bathtub.

Our lives for millions of strangers to see.

My body turned cold. Was this how Claudia knew about my family? Because my mother talked about it online?

It wasn't until years later that I brought up Claudia to Jada and asked her what had happened that day. Not what the news had speculated on, but what had *actually* gone down.

Jada didn't look too keen on telling me at first. But after I insisted, she finally admitted, "After they were arrested, the police told us she was part of... of a ring of some sort."

"A ring," I echoed.

By that time, I was old enough to understand what that word meant in that context.

But I wanted to hear it from her. From the only adult I could trust.

"Why did they come for me?"

"They knew your parents had money, so maybe they wanted that. Your mom... Well, she made it easy for them to find out all kinds of information on your family to gain your trust."

Nausea climbed up my throat. "What kind of ring was that woman part of?"

Jada lowered her gaze. "Child trafficking."

The ground opened beneath my feet. My soul turned cold.

I understood then. All of it.

The danger I'd been in. What could still happen to me if I didn't save myself.

Because nobody else was going to do it for me.

Chapter Twelve

"Do you want to know who my Secret Santa is?"

I arch an unamused eyebrow at Charlie as he polishes some drinking glasses next to me behind the bar.

"I distinctly remember you telling us to keep our Secret Santa a secret," I remind him.

"We don't count, Allie Cat. We're best friends."

Jada's words hit me again.

Sometimes we need to be a bit brave in order to get what we want.

She promised to keep me updated on George Eden and any other articles that could arise in the upcoming weeks, but so far nothing new has come up. It doesn't ease the anxiety clinging to my chest every second of every hour.

I also can't deny that our conversation opened up something not entirely comfortable in me.

What do I want?

That's a question I haven't allowed myself to answer in a long time. Before, what I wanted was to get away and start anew. But now that I've done that—or I'm trying to—I want to find a further meaning to my existence. A meaning that includes a bit of that calm and happiness I've always longed for.

I look at Charlie, Jude, and Sandra, who have treated me with so much kindness from the start, and I find that I want to get closer to them. I want to go out with Charlie and his friends, tag along with Jude and Sandra to visit their grandson, experience new things.

My gaze shifts to Travis, who's tidying up the bar before we close for the night.

And fine, I want to get closer to him too. He's still my boss, and he'll never be interested in me in the same way I'm pathetically interested in him, but it doesn't matter. When we played darts a few nights ago, I had a great time. And I know he did, too, if only because Travis is never where he doesn't want to be.

I'm not ready to tell any of them the truth. Maybe I'll never be. But I'm ready to take a small step toward that calm, happy life I so desperately crave.

"We *are* best friends." I finally concede what my heart has known for a long time now, earning me a smirk from Charlie. "But I don't want to know who your Secret Santa is. It takes the fun out of it."

"Boo." He puts away a cocktail glass. "Now that I think about it, you're right. I don't want to tell you."

"See? You needed three seconds to think it through."

"It's going to be an epic gift, so I'd rather make you wait to see it," he says. "But you can tell me yours."

"Nice try."

"Worth a shot."

Some of the weight in my chest lifts every time I interact with any of my co-workers, which is as social as I get these days. But I remind myself nothing good will come out of rushing my process, so I pat myself on the back and count this small step with Charlie as my win of the day.

Minutes after Charlie disappears into the changing room, my boss's unmistakable voice sends a thrill down my spine.

"Don't forget my bracelet."

Heat climbs up my cheeks, and I shift my gaze to my sneakers. I don't know what's harder to believe—that I was bold enough to suggest making him one of my bracelets, or that he seems eager to have it.

I give him a smile. "Green and white, right?"

He dips his chin once, and that's all the answer I get. With another smile his way, I turn around to put away some bottles of alcohol before my shift ends.

Humming a song under my breath, I'm not paying attention to my surroundings—which explains why I don't hear him coming until he's right beside me.

"I'll take care of that," Travis says, carefully taking a heavy bottle from my grip.

My heart somersaults, warmth seeping into my skin when his fingers brush my much smaller ones. "Oh. Thanks, but my shift isn't over yet. I've got this."

"You'll finish sooner if I help you."

He doesn't sound gruff or mean when he says it, yet his voice doesn't leave room for arguments. And honestly? This week has been so mentally exhausting, I won't say no to a bit of help.

Together, Travis and I put the remaining bottles away. We don't speak, and I keep humming because he doesn't seem bothered by it. Charlie is the first one to leave, then Jude and Sandra until we are, once again, the last ones at The Lair.

I'm zipping up my jacket, ready to face the cold outside, when he says, "I'll walk you to your car."

I'm shaking my head before he finishes his sentence. In a teasing voice, I say, "Thanks, boss man, but I don't want you to spoil me so much."

The hardness in his face doesn't go anywhere. "It's late and dark."

"And I've been on my own for the past six years, taking care of myself. I'll be fine."

My admission catches him off guard. Maybe someone else wouldn't have noticed the way his eyebrows shoot up the tiniest notch, but I do. I notice everything about Travis, even when I don't want to.

"Okay," he concedes after a pause. "You're right."

I'm not sure he sounds that convinced, but I appreciate his faith in me being able to take a forty-second walk to my car without getting kidnapped.

That last thought sends a bolt of anxiety straight to my chest.

What happened with Claudia—or whatever her real name was—has never, not once, stopped haunting me. How she knew everything about my family so easily, how she managed to fool me. If I hadn't screamed like a maniac, I wouldn't be here today.

What if it happens again? What if there are more Claudias out there who want to hurt me?

It's just the article, I tell myself. It's brought all my daunting memories back, including the most traumatizing thing that has ever happened to me. But realistically, I know I'm okay. Their ring got dismantled. My mind is being my worst enemy today, that's all.

And yet, after waving goodbye to Travis, I nearly sprint to my car. The cold wind pushes back my bangs and makes me shiver despite my many layers of clothing. The streetlights are my only companions, and for a moment, I regret not having said yes to Travis.

But I can't depend on him. On anyone else. I'm okay on my own—

My thoughts skid to a stop when I reach my car and notice that the window behind the driver's seat is rolled down.

"What the hell," I mutter, frantically glancing around, but there's nobody here.

I unlock my car and search inside, my mind going a million miles per hour. Did I leave the window down? But why would I do that when it's so cold outside? Maybe I accidentally pushed a button or something?

Heart racing, I inspect every corner until I've tripled-checked that nothing has been stolen. Not that I keep anything valuable in here, but I do have a jacket in the back seat with a twenty-dollar bill inside one of the pockets, and the money is still there.

This makes no sense.

The thought of running back to The Lair and asking Travis for help crosses my mind for all of two seconds before I tell myself I'm catastrophizing. The most logical explanation is that I left it down by accident. There are no signs of a forced entry outside or inside the car—I checked compulsively—and there's nothing missing.

I'm safe. What are the odds of getting kidnapped twice? And what motives could anyone have now?

Taking a deep breath, I start the engine.

I'm not in danger. This incident has nothing to do with kidnappers or George Eden's interest in interviewing me, and everything to do with the fact that I've been distracted this week. Only that.

Just like I've been for the past year, I'm still safe in Bannport.

Chapter Thirteen

I spoke too soon.

Red-and-blue lights wake me up at four the following morning.

Confused and groggy, I drag myself out of bed with a blanket around my shoulders and peek outside my window. The sight of two police officers sobers me up like a bucket of ice-cold water.

Maybe it makes me the nosiest neighbor in my building, but not knowing what's going on will eat at me later. Especially after what happened to my car's window last night.

What if both are related?

A prickle of anxiety travels the length of my spine when I open the front door and see the old lady who lives in the apartment next to mine.

"They didn't take anything?" one of the police officers is asking her.

She shakes her head, adjusting her glasses. "I was woken up by a loud sound inside the apartment. I yelled at them, and they ran away. When I checked, they had tripped over one of the chairs in the kitchen."

Someone had broken into her apartment?

Out of the corner of my eye, I spot other neighbors watching the scene unfold from their doors.

"How many of them were there?" asks the other officer, a woman with a ponytail.

"I don't know." My neighbor shakes her head. "Two, I think? Maybe three. What I could tell is that they were men."

"All right. We'll open a case file and let you know if there are any advances," the officer says.

"I just don't understand," the lady keeps going. "Why break in if they didn't steal anything?"

"Maybe you scared them away before they could take anything," the male officer suggests. "By the sound of it, they don't seem to be experienced burglars. We'll keep an eye out, don't worry."

She harrumphs, "Not sure about all that."

I shut the door, having heard enough.

Someone broke into the apartment next to mine just hours after I found my car window rolled down. The two might not be connected at all, but my growing anxiety is telling me to run in the opposite direction of this town.

Not safe. Not safe. Not safe.

But I don't want to leave Bannport. I don't want to let fear take control of me now that I'm finally free.

I let out a frustrated groan and rub my eyes with the heels of my palms. I couldn't possibly go back to sleep now—I'm too paranoid.

Maybe this is the sign to get myself that additional lock I've been meaning to install for ages now. Or I could move out.

Where to, though, I have no clue. I think about the last time I browsed for rentals in Bannport—too expensive, vacation homes, farms. I wouldn't mind the extra land, but it's outside my budget.

Deciding I'm in no mental state to make decisions right now, I lock the front door and head for the shower, all while telling myself that these recent events have nothing to do with me.

* * *

"You look like shit."

Don't I know that.

"Thanks, Charlie."

"Rough night?" he asks as he passes me by to grab some peanuts for one of his tables.

It's four in the afternoon, and our shift is nowhere near close to ending, but luckily only five tables are occupied. Sundays are a slow day, and we get to go home earlier, which is the only thing keeping me on my feet right now. I'm too tired to exist.

"Something like that," I mutter.

If the past six years have taught me anything—my whole existence, really—it's that waiting until my problems become big and ugly to solve them isn't smart. I should tackle them while they aren't making too much noise.

"Hey, Char."

"What's up?"

"Do you know of any rentals in the area?" I ask him, hopeful. "They don't have to be super close to the bar or anything."

He purses his lips as he thinks about it. "What's your budget?" I tell him. "I might know someone, but I'll have to check with him."

My chest lightens up at that. "You do?"

"Yeah, I'll text him later. It's one of the guys from the gym. He mentioned something about moving into a bigger apartment next month, and maybe his landlord hasn't rented his old one to anyone yet. I'll tell him you're interested."

"Oh, Charlie." I struggle to wrap my arms around him from

the other side of the bar, but I manage to squeeze him. "You're a lifesaver. Thank you so much."

I feel his laugh in my ear as he hugs me back. "No problemo, Allie Cat. I can't promise a happy ending, though."

The playful tone of his voice isn't lost on me.

"You're out of control."

"Speaking of—"

"Get back to work."

I let go of Charlie and turn to bear-man only a few feet away, glaring at me—at *me*—with eyes so scorching, they would be burning a hole in my skin if they could.

"Sorry, boss," Charlie apologizes, never losing that lopsided smirk. "Was just giving Allie some good news."

"Save it for after your shift," he barks a little louder than normal, the harshness of his voice surprising me—and not in a good way.

Travis never raises his voice, so what the hell is his problem?

The Lair is pretty much deserted, I was just giving Charlie a quick hug, and—most importantly—our patrons don't care. They all know us by name, joke with us, and even invite us for drinks sometimes. They sure don't care about the staff hugging each other for two seconds during a slow shift.

Bannport is a laid-back small town, but it's clear that some of its residents aren't.

"What happened to you?" Travis asks when he turns to me, a disapproving notch between his brows. "You don't look well."

I remind myself he isn't worried about me. He doesn't give a crap and is only asking because my lackluster performance might be affecting his business. I don't think I've been sloppy today, but what do I know? He always has a reason to be grouchy, so maybe I'm breathing the wrong way and it's bothering him.

"I didn't have the best night's sleep is all."

It isn't enough for him. "What happened?"

Too tired to dilute the truth, I tell him, "Someone broke into the apartment next door, and it freaked me out, so I slept very little."

The notch between his eyebrows shifts from annoyed to something else. "Come again?"

"There was a break-in—"

"Are you hurt?"

"What? No." Why would he even think that? And why does the butterfly in my stomach open a curious eye at his concern? *Go back to sleep. Or better yet—die.* "It had nothing to do with me."

"Where do you live?"

When I rattle off my address, something in him shifts. My throat feels like someone has stuck cotton balls inside it as I watch the tension in his wide shoulders rise, those green eyes darkening as if bathed in shadows.

"Travis," I start, my heart hammering in an uncomfortable way, "what the hell is going on?"

Slowly, he lowers his head and uses that intense stare to pierce into mine. And then he says the last thing I expect him to.

"You're moving the fuck out of that shithole."

What. Is. Going. On?

"Excuse me?" I must have misheard him. There's no way he's *ordering* me to move out.

"You're moving out," he repeats.

An unpleasant feeling of disbelief clings to my chest. "Says who?"

"Says anyone with the slightest damn bit of common sense."

Oh, he's serious about this.

Despite the pool of anger bubbling in the pit of my stomach,

I keep it together long enough to ask him, "Can we talk in the changing room?"

Travis must sense the edge in my voice because he agrees. A moment later, he closes the door to the changing room and turns to me with the same stoic expression I suspect he's had his whole life. But imagining a grumpy baby Travis doesn't bring me the slightest amount of amusement today.

"What the hell are you doing?" I hiss.

The deep breath he takes next personally offends me. "Allie."

"Travis."

"You live in a dangerous part of town."

I frown. "What?"

"You live on King's Avenue?" When I nod, he continues, "There's a known point for drug dealing nearby. Some fucked-up shit."

I'm not imagining the frustration in his voice as he runs a hand down his face and mutters, "Goddammit, Allie."

I let my arms rise and fall to my sides. "What now? Why do you even care so much in the first place? Why are you angry with me and behaving like a total ass?"

The words have barely left my mouth and I already regret them.

This isn't me. I don't know when I turned into this defensive, ready-to-pounce woman, and I don't like her. This isn't the person Jada and Paul fought so hard for, the girl they raised because her own parents refused to live in the real world.

"I *care*, Allie, because I lost both of my parents to the same kind of shit they do in that area."

My heart plummets to my feet.

I open my mouth once, twice, to say something, but only his name comes out. And it's so faint, I don't even think he's heard it.

108

He's not looking at me. Those eyes that have captured my attention far too many times are now glued somewhere behind me. The space between us seems to stretch with every passing second.

He ends up breaking the silence. "I didn't mean to raise my voice at you or be an ass. I'm sorry."

"It's okay," I concede.

"No, it's not. I shouldn't have treated you like that."

"We're both agitated. Let's... let's just forget it."

He doesn't say anything to that. Instead, he asks, his voice gentler, "Why are you living there?"

"Well, first of all, I didn't know it was a sketchy area. I never saw or heard anything. Not even on the news." It's the truth. There's a weird atmosphere to my building's surroundings, sure, since it's pretty much deserted with no local shops or tourist attractions, but I've never felt in danger until last night. "And there are barely any apartments for rent here, but Charlie is going to ask someone he knows. I may be able to move out soon."

He gives me a slow nod. "Okay. I'll ask around too."

Once the tension of our fight leaves me, I ask him something I maybe shouldn't. But it's been eating at me since it happened, and I can't take it anymore. Plus, there's something about Travis that makes me feel safe and listened to. If I asked him for help, I know he'd say yes.

"Do you think it's possible for someone to open a car window from the outside without breaking the glass or damaging the rest of the car?"

He blinks. Then blinks again.

"Why do you want to know?" he asks, slowly.

I try not to wince. "Last night, I found one of my car windows open. But nothing was stolen or vandalized, so maybe I accidentally left it like that. I don't know."

"Someone broke into your car."

It's not a question.

"Maybe not."

But I'm not sure.

"You should've called me right away," he grunts. "Allie, this is some serious shit."

"No, it's... it's just in my head. I must have left it down and don't remember. I promise I'm fine. I don't feel in danger."

Most of the time. The possibility of my apartment being broken into haunts me. Not because I have anything of value they could steal, but because I was finally starting to feel safe in my environment. If someone ruins that...

They won't. I'm safe. I'm fine.

"Not feeling in danger and not being in danger are two very different things," Travis says, that worried notch between his brows still in place.

He has no idea how well I know that.

"I'm walking you to your car every night from now on. Not up for discussion," he declares, and I find myself not wanting to fight him on it.

After a few moments of silence, I know the conversation is over. I also know I have to move out, and I will. But for now, the only thing I can do is go back to the front and earn the paycheck that will allow me to find somewhere else to live.

Maneuvering around his huge body, I reach the door of the changing room. Before I leave, I glance at my boss over my shoulder. "I'm really sorry about your parents, Travis."

I wasn't expecting a response, and I don't get one. He gets nothing else from me, either, before I go back to work.

Chapter Fourteen

Not feeling in danger and not being in danger are two very different things.

Travis's stupid words keep ringing in my ears all throughout my shift, as I picked up some groceries earlier, and now again as I slice my chicken breasts to make chicken tikka masala for dinner. They aren't stupid because they lack intelligence, but because deep down—and, fine, not so deep down—he's right, and it bothers me to no end.

I'm the stupid one. Even if I didn't know it was a sketchy area, I should've researched my surroundings more thoroughly. I've been so busy trying to build my life back up that I forgot maybe, just maybe, I deserve better than a mold-infested apartment in a dangerous part of town.

So when my phone rings as I get the rice ready and I spot Charlie's name on my screen, I hold on to my last sliver of hope.

"Hello?" I put the phone on speaker and go back to finishing up my dinner.

"Greetings, my dearest friend. I bring news."

I put some rice and chicken onto a plate. It smells so good, I could cry. "The good kind, I hope."

There's some shuffling in the background before he says, "Of course, Allie Cat. Worry not."

"I'm listening."

"My friend's landlord still hasn't found anyone to rent the apartment to, so I told him you were interested. I'll text you the address so you can make a visit tomorrow morning. You're free, right?"

"Yep." I don't have to be at The Lair until four. "Thank you so much, Char. You're really saving me here."

"Hey, that's what friends are for."

He says it so easily, it takes me aback for a moment.

Friends. I have *friends*.

"Lola told me she chatted with you at the pub," he says, a hint of a smile in his voice. "I knew she'd love you. She told me to ask you for your number because she wants to hang out with you sometime, if that's okay."

I hesitate. Years ago, I promised myself I wouldn't stop until I got to the opposite side of the country to start a new life. Bannport isn't the place I had pictured as my home, but it has become the place I want to be in. The community I want to remain part of.

Don't I deserve to start anew like I said I would?

"Allie? You there?"

I expect the guilt to come when I say, "Sure," but it never does.

"Cool. You guys will have fun. Not as much as you have with me, but still."

The chuckle I was about to let out dies in my throat when the doorbell rings.

"Charlie, I have to hang up." Someone is at my door, and suddenly I can't feel my legs. Nobody ever comes here. "Tell Lola to text me. And thank you again for the apartment thing."

If he says something else, I don't hear it. My eyes zero in on the front door as my mind spirals with endless possibilities.

My parents have found me is the first thing I think of, but that's impossible. I've covered my tracks well for the past six years. Unless... unless Mindy, the woman I thought had recognized me at The Lair, told them about me.

The doorbell rings again, and I curse under my breath. I think of not answering, but I know I won't sleep a wink tonight if I don't find out who is outside my apartment. With my pulse in my throat, I tiptoe toward the door and peek through the peephole.

Only to see the last person I expected to come over.

I pull the door open, my shoulders sagging with relief, and stare into the eyes of the man who both confuses me and makes my heart beat faster than anyone else ever has before.

Travis's stoic expression doesn't go away. "Can I come in?"

I don't overthink it as I open the door wide enough for his massive body to pass through, then lock it behind me.

"Not that I'm not happy to see you, boss man, but what are you doing here?"

His hand moves, and I notice the plastic bag he's holding. "Got a lock for your door."

The butterfly in my stomach breaks free from the cage I'd shoved it into, proceeding to flutter all over my body, out of control.

"Do you want me to install it?" he asks, his eyes scanning mine.

He got a lock for my apartment. He came all the way here to give it to me because he knows I'm scared.

The lump in my throat doesn't let me speak. I can only nod.

"All right." He gives me one last unreadable look before taking out some tools from his plastic bag and getting to it.

I hurry back to the kitchen like a scared cat, my frantic

113

heart threatening to burst out of my rib cage. But I can't help myself and peek at the front door, where Travis is indeed putting some kind of high-tech lock on my door. This *is* real life.

"Have you had dinner yet?" I ask him, suddenly not wanting him to leave as soon as that lock is in place.

He doesn't look away from the lock as he asks, "Are you offering to feed me?"

My heart leaps. "What if I am?"

"Smells fucking good in here, so I'd say yes."

His easiness makes me smile despite my nerves. "I'll make a plate for you. Do you like chicken tikka masala?"

"I do." This time, he glances at me over his shoulder. The softness in his eyes turns my legs to goo. "Thanks, Allie."

Ten minutes later, there's a new lock on my door and my boss is sitting next to me on the couch, eating my food. How did my night turn into this?

"This is good," he tells me between bites.

My cheeks grow warm. "Really?"

He nods, wasting no time to eat another spoonful.

Satisfied with his reaction to my cooking, I sit back on the couch and try to finish my food without glancing at him every two seconds. We aren't talking, and the TV isn't on, but the silence between us isn't awkward.

When he empties his plate and I offer him some more, he gets up and says, "Don't move."

I try not to smile when he comes back with another plateful, but I fail spectacularly.

"Guess what." I wait until he turns to me with that stoic expression. "Charlie arranged an apartment tour for me tomorrow."

I grab my phone and show him the pictures of the apartment Charlie sent me earlier. It's a bit of a shoebox, but at least it's within walking distance of work. Most importantly, it's in a good area—I triple-checked. "What do you think?"

Travis takes his sweet time answering. "It's all right."

"That's it? Come on, boss man. Give me something else."

"It looks good. Who's renting it?"

I check the text Charlie sent me with all the info. "A guy named Robert Marcelli."

He hums, adding nothing else. I let him finish his second plate of chicken tikka masala in peace but don't waste a second as soon as he's done. "If you see something wrong with the place, I would like to know before I move there. I value your opinion."

"This is your choice to make, Allie. I don't want to boss you around."

"You're not. I asked."

He lets out a deep sigh. "There's nothing wrong with the apartment." A pause. "But I know who's renting it, and he's not someone you want to do business with."

I frown. "Charlie didn't say anything."

And he would have. I'm sure his friend would've complained about his landlord if he was that bad.

Travis slides me a look. "It's not men he has issues with."

Oh.

I swallow, my gaze dropping to the pictures on my screen. I knew it was too good to be true.

"Do you think he won't rent it to me because I'm a woman?"

It's ridiculous, not to mention pathetic. I can't believe some people still have such horrible mindsets. Cavemen, all of them, and not the good kind. Not the kind who throw you over a shoulder and—

Focus.

Right. Now is *not* the time.

"I could go with you."

Poker face, poker face, poker face. I'm not about to show him how those words have just made me lose the tight grip I keep on my feelings for him.

"Where?" I ask, because of course I do. Of course I have to make sure he knows I'm dumb.

But Travis doesn't react with an eye roll or a huff. "To see the apartment."

I shift on the couch and leave my empty plate on the coffee table. "Maybe I should cancel the whole thing. If you say he's a misogynistic asshole…"

There's the huff. "You can't stay here."

Now is my turn to let out a deep breath, my eyes focusing on the mold starting to eat at one of the ceiling corners in the living room. "I know, and I don't want to. I want to move out, but not if my landlord is going to be some creepy guy who will raise my rent or give me a hard time because I have boobs."

"No one's gonna mess with you."

"You don't know that."

"I'll break his goddamn legs if he so much as thinks about it."

I might have grown up with all sorts of privileges—a four-story home, yearly vacations to exotic places, quality food, access to prime healthcare, and the best schools, among other luxuries—but safety has never been one of them. My parents knew no boundaries. They sacrificed our privacy, *my* privacy, for money and attention, and now…

Now there's a weird feeling inside my chest, something Travis's protectiveness has lit up.

I scan his face for a moment. "Would you really do that?"

Maybe I should be cautious. When an ex-Navy SEAL threatens to break someone's legs, he probably knows how to do it. But Travis would never hurt me, and I could never be scared of him.

"In a heartbeat."

This is the same man who said he didn't befriend his co-workers not that long ago, and I shouldn't forget that. He just doesn't want to see me in danger—any good, reasonable person would feel the same.

I give him a genuine smile. "Thank you for offering to come with me, but I don't want to be a bother."

His chest goes in and out, and he relaxes against the cushions of my too-small couch. "If you were a bother, I wouldn't be here."

He has a point, but I'm still going to be a pain about this.

"You don't have to come with me." I don't want him to feel pity or think I can't handle my own stuff. "I've been living on my own for years. I know how to deal with difficult people."

I'm definitely not looking forward to trying to reason with a misogynistic ass, but at this point, I would do anything to get out of this place. *Almost* anything.

One of those massive hands moves to his head. He massages the short hairs at the back of his skull before letting out a long, tired breath. "I'm not saying you can't take care of yourself, but I want to be there. Consider me backup."

In the past, I would have given anything to have someone care for me like this. Then I grew a thick skin and nerves of steel and convinced myself I didn't need anyone to survive, not even Jada. Because, realistically, I was alone.

But I don't have to be alone anymore. At least, tomorrow morning I won't.

My head and my heart need a break from being on edge all the time. When Travis is around, it's like both can sign off for the day, as I let him take the reins. Unlike everywhere else I've worked in the past six years, at The Lair I don't feel watched or in danger. I don't feel the need to be on the lookout all the time.

Travis cares. He might not be the best at showing it, but he can't deny it.

I give him a sincere smile. "Thanks, Travis. The tour is tomorrow at ten. Does that work for you?"

His eyes are on me as he nods.

"Do you want to stay a while?" The question is out before I can stop myself. "I mean, if you have somewhere else to be—"

"I can stay," he says. "If you want me to."

Maybe it should freak me out that my boss is in my apartment right now, eating dinner with me. But it doesn't, not in the slightest, and I'm not ready to unpack why his presence calms me down to the point where I'm not worried about any break-ins anymore.

I'm going to see an apartment tomorrow, and I have a good feeling about it. This might be one of my last nights living in this part of town, and I refuse to focus on the dangers that might be lurking outside.

Travis is here.

"Of course you can stay."

We don't speak again as I turn on the TV and put on a movie. It's a romantic comedy, but if Travis hates it, he doesn't comment on it. I pay attention for about ten minutes before my eyes start getting too heavy to keep them open.

The last thing I feel before darkness takes over is the weight of something soft and warm being draped over me.

Chapter Fifteen

A SOUND INSIDE MY APARTMENT JOLTS ME AWAKE. IT'S faint, barely there, but I hear it.

Steps. Footsteps.

Claudia.

I shoot up, forcing my eyelids open, and bump my foot on the coffee table.

"Shit," I mutter in pain.

Someone's inside my apartment—

"You okay?"

I know that gruff voice.

Blowing out a breath, the sharp pain in my foot subsides as I rub it with my hand. "I thought someone had broken in."

The couch groans under Travis's weight as he sits. "Sorry I woke you up."

Between my hammering heartbeat and my throbbing foot, it takes me a moment to notice the steamy mug in his hand. I left a pot of coffee ready for tomorrow morning on the stove, and it makes me smile that he helped himself to some because it means he feels comfortable here. In my presence.

And then I notice the clothing item that is definitely *not* mine draped over my lap.

"Travis?"

"Mm."

"Is this.... Um, is this your jacket?"

"You looked cold," he explains.

I eye the blanket I keep in a decorative basket mere inches from his feet and decide to ignore the way my heart goes *thump, thump, thump* in my chest.

"What time is it?" I mumble, placing the jacket on the back of the couch.

"Around three."

I sit up, alarmed. "Oh my God, I'm so sorry. You probably wanted to go home. I'm sorry I kept you here."

But the huge man beside me grumbles, "Go back to sleep, Allie."

"But—"

"There's nobody waiting for me at home." Sadness and relief crash into me at once. "I have two dogs, but I keep the barn open, and their doghouses and food are in there, so they'll be fine. I have an alarm system and cameras. If you want me to stay just in case, I'll stay. But you need to rest."

"All right, but you need to sleep too." I'm proud of the authoritative tone of my voice. "You're working tomorrow."

"So are you."

It's too early to be doing this with him. "I slept a handful of hours. I'm fine."

"I'm fine too."

I raise an unimpressed eyebrow. "So, you're not drinking coffee to stay awake?"

"No."

"I've never seen you drink coffee before," I point out.

"I only have it for breakfast."

"And you're having breakfast at three in the morning?"

"Yes."

He's so full of it, I can't help my lips from twitching. "What if I stay awake? Will you go to sleep then?"

I know the answer before he says it. "No."

Because I'm very aware that we are not going to get anywhere if we continue down this path—and also because my sleep-deprived brain isn't thinking straight—I stand from the couch with a new resolve and disappear into my bedroom.

When I come back, Travis's eyes follow my movements with a face so straight, I couldn't read it if I wanted to.

I turn on the floor lamp by the couch, drop my bracelet-making kit on the coffee table, plop down on the floor in front of it, and announce, "We're making friendship bracelets."

Once more, I don't imagine the grunt that leaves the back of his throat. Bear-man, indeed. "I don't befriend my staff."

I ignore the stab-like feeling in my chest as I open the kit and look for the green beads I know I keep somewhere. "But you spend the night at their place in case there's a break-in?"

That shuts him right up.

The smug smirk on my lips remains as I conclude, "Friendship bracelets it is. Any objections?"

I'm sure he has many—too bad I'm ignoring them all.

I don't imagine the deep sigh he lets out. "I'm not making friendship bracelets with you, Allie."

The way I'm keeping this smile in place is probably breaking a world record or two. *Longer-lasting smile while your grumpy boss, who you have a massive crush on, breaks your heart.*

"Well, I'm not tired anymore, and you don't want to take a quick nap, so there's little else for us to do except look at the wall for the next five hours." I keep my voice light, hoping he doesn't notice the crack currently happening behind my rib cage. "There's nothing on TV, and I don't have cable, so unless you want to die of boredom…" I nudge the bracelet kit in his direction. "Come on, you'll make mine, and I'll make yours. We'll stop if you hate it. Pinky promise."

If my gut feeling is correct, Travis isn't going to pinky promise me anything anytime soon. He hasn't moved an inch from his spot, his back against the cushions.

"I'll pass."

Sure. No biggie. My heart isn't in shambles or anything.

"Okay." I try to keep my voice cheerful and unaffected, but this time I don't think I'm successful. I'm careful as I scoop up the beads I selected for him. "But I'm still making yours."

When he doesn't reply, I get to work. Grabbing the elastic cord, I tell him, "I need to measure your wrist."

He doesn't say a word as he holds out his wrist for me over the coffee table. And I don't focus on how thick his tanned wrist looks, or how many dark little hairs are on his arms, or how stupidly big his hand is compared to mine. Not one bit.

"Thanks," I mutter when I'm done, telling myself I can survive until the sun rises and Travis goes home.

I'm halfway done with the bracelet when he lets out a heavy sigh and sits forward, those stupidly hot forearms resting on his knees. His eyes are on me as he says, "Pass me that elastic cord stuff."

I don't say anything as I give it to him, unsure if he's really changed his mind or is just testing the waters. Instead, I tell myself I won't get upset for a second time if he decides this is bullshit.

"What colors do you want for yours?" he asks.

His eyes are on the beads and not on my face as I say, "Pink and white."

He shifts his attention to the elastic. When seconds pass and it becomes clear that he doesn't know what he's doing, I step in. "Here, let me help you."

My fingers graze his calloused palms as I take the cord from him. I wrap the elastic around my wrist, then cut it and give it back to him along with some tape.

"You can stick the tape on the end of the cord and fold it over so the beads stay in place. It should make it easier," I offer, giving him some beads as well. "I'm doing one green, one white, one green, one white. See? But you can do whatever you want."

Brow furrowed as if this were some kind of science experiment bound to blow up the whole block, my boss stays focused as he picks up a single bead between his thick fingers and stares at it. Just... blankly stares at it with so much intention, I can't hold in my chuckle.

He slides his eyes toward me. They look almost soft. "You laughing?"

My lips twitch. "No."

"Could've fooled me."

I nod toward his bracelet. "Off you go, boss man. This can't be harder than the Navy."

"Guess not."

Never in a million years did I think I would be making friendship bracelets with my boss at three in the morning, yet here we are.

I let Travis figure out the whole bracelet-making thing on his own. Beads keep slipping from his grasp, and he curses under his breath every time.

I've long finished my bracelet for him, but I don't want to leave him working alone, so I cut some more elastic bands and decide to make a few bracelets to donate this week.

"Why do you like making bracelets?" he asks out of the blue.

I keep working as I answer, "I've always liked arts and crafts, and this is easy enough. It takes my mind off things. I tried knitting once, but I was pathetic at it."

He hums. "I see."

Some may think it's too childish of a hobby for a twenty-five-year-old, but those who judge others aren't people I want to surround myself with. This makes me happy, and it's harmless, so who cares?

The streets outside are mercifully quiet, with only the low humming of my refrigerator to keep us company. We keep working in silence until he breaks it.

"Why do you dye your hair brown?"

I don't shift my gaze from the new bracelet I'm making, afraid of what he'll find in my eyes. And then I shrug, as if his question hadn't just undone me. As if my heart weren't beating a million miles per hour.

"It was time for a makeover."

We both know that's not the real answer, but Travis doesn't press. Until he asks, "Why are you here, Allie?"

I could play coy and be a smartass, tell him it's close to four in the morning, so where else would I be.

I could, and maybe I would have gone down that road a few months ago, but I'm tired of having to pretend I'm not authentic when that's all I've ever wanted to be.

"I needed a change of scenery," I say, my voice quiet. *Start with the smaller details, build it up next.* "I..."

But I can't.

My tongue feels too heavy, my throat is dry, and I can't speak. I can't—

I can. I absolutely can. It's all in my head.

Taking a deep breath through my nose, I keep my gaze on the bracelet. For some reason, telling him while not looking at him is easier.

"Where I grew up..." *No. Bad start.* "My family..." *Nope. Try again.* I clear my throat, hoping my voice doesn't sound as

124

unsure as I feel. "I wanted to be on my own. Find myself and all that. Get away from...from the pressure."

"You had a rough family life?"

His question takes me by surprise, if only because Travis never asks us anything about our personal lives. But he's asking about mine. About a past I don't want to remember because it still hurts too much.

"Something like that," I mutter, not wanting to elaborate. *So much for being authentic.*

He must pick up on my discomfort because his questioning stops. Silence falls over us again as I finish two more bracelets and Travis struggles with his. At one point, the sound of bike engines fills my apartment, and we both stiffen, listening, waiting, but nothing happens.

I relax. Travis doesn't.

"It's looking good," I tell him, nodding at his bracelet and hoping to distract him. Being alert all the time can't be good for him. "See? I told you it could be fun."

He grunts. "Never said this was fun."

"But is it?"

When he glares at me, I give him a knowing smile.

"It's not too bad," he concedes, which I'll take as a personal victory.

I'm not even a little ashamed to admit that when it comes to Travis, I will inhale every minuscule crumb he gives me as if it were a full meal.

But I've been thinking about something for a while, and I will take his questions for me as an invitation to get my fill too.

"Can I ask you something?" When he hums, I go for it. "Why were you buying all those toys the other day?"

He asked me about the hair dye, so it's only fair that I ask him about the toys.

I don't expect an actual answer or even a dismissal. When it comes to Travis, he's unapologetic about his own time—if he doesn't want to waste it, he won't. And sure, maybe he comes off as rude sometimes, but it's one of the many things I admire about him. I wish I could send certain people to hell as easily as he can.

So I'm not expecting it when he says, "For charity."

There goes my stupid, confused heart.

"That's amazing." The thought of Travis taking time out of his day and spending his money on kids warms my heart like nothing else ever has. "Why do you do it?"

Far more carefully than I've ever imagined he would, he ties a knot to secure the bracelet and grabs the scissors. "Do I need a reason?"

"You don't, but I'm sure you have one."

That big hand moves forward, palm up, as he passes me the bracelet. It doesn't look half bad, and I already know I'm never going to take it off. "Thanks, Travis. It looks amazing. Here's yours."

I pass it to him and will my heart to behave as he puts it around his wrist.

He mutters his thank you, sitting back again with—I'm guessing—zero intentions of making another bracelet. That's too bad—he's a natural. I'm not done with my bunch, though, so I focus my attention back on the one I'm making and decide to add a charm or two.

"I never got any Christmas presents growing up. I don't want other kids to go through that shit."

When I look up, his eyes are already on me. There's a layer of vulnerability in them that has never been there before.

"You have a big heart, Travis," I tell him truthfully. No matter how hard his rough exterior tries to conceal it, I can see right through it. "Those kids will have an amazing Christmas thanks to you."

He lowers his eyes to the ground. Is he embarrassed? He shouldn't be because this is the most adorable he's ever looked, and that's a word I never thought I would use to describe this mountain of a man.

"It's nothing."

"It's everything." I search his gaze. "What charity is it? I would like to donate something too."

He tells me the name, and I make a mental note to go to the shops in the next couple of days before Christmas week rolls around. I'm sure I can make a bunch of bracelets to donate, too, with different colors and charms.

I never got any Christmas presents growing up.

How devastating is that? It hurts too much to imagine a scowling little boy waking up on the most special morning of the year and not finding anything under the tree.

"I'm guessing you didn't have an easy childhood?" I wonder out loud, my voice turning softer.

After losing his parents, it isn't difficult to imagine why his childhood might not have been the best.

Those thick fingers scratch the side of his neck, a telltale sign that he's uncomfortable. But he still answers, which I appreciate more than he'll ever know.

"My parents passed when I was a kid, and I went to live with my uncle. He didn't have much, so I didn't have much. I don't blame him for not getting me anything for Christmas. Having food on our table was our priority. It wasn't until after I enlisted and started sending him money that things started looking up, and he opened the bar."

My heart is beating so fast, it can't be healthy. Travis is opening up to me about his past. I don't understand why he's trusting me with it, but I'll take it—I'll take any minuscule piece of information about him and treasure it forever.

"I'm sorry you had it rough." My voice turns quiet in the

darkness of the living room. "But thank you for telling me about it. If it's any consolation, you've turned out pretty good, and Uncle Neil seems happy. You're both great men."

He says nothing to that. My phone shows it's already past four in the morning, and I'm still wide awake, which means another tiring day at work looms ahead. Just great.

As I finish my next bracelet, this one with a butterfly charm, I ruminate about Travis's confession. He's the most closed-off person I've ever met, yet he's told me about his troubled past. He *chose* to share those things with me. I know I don't owe him anything in return, but...

Would it hurt to tell him why I'm here? Would he start treating me differently if I...

Of course he will.

I've been lying to him for a year. He'll hate me.

I swallow, but the uncomfortable lump in my throat doesn't go anywhere.

We chat about easy, casual things for a bit after that, and then I get cozy on the couch with a book while he watches a Western movie on TV. And when the clock hits seven in the morning, Travis heads home to take a shower, promising to be back for the apartment tour.

I let out a deep sigh as I lock up behind him, regret swirling in my stomach.

Chapter Sixteen

When Travis told me he was going to come back for the apartment tour, I didn't think he was going to drive me there. That may be why I'm now standing in front of him, confused.

I hike my bag higher on my shoulder and play with my car keys in my hand. "You don't have to drive me, Travis. I've got my own car."

"Not the point."

The look he gives me leaves no room for arguments. But because I haven't slept well and my brain isn't functioning as well as it should, my voice takes a teasing turn, and I say, "Careful, boss man. I might start thinking you tolerate me after all."

"I more than tolerate you, Allie."

My heart fills with adrenaline. What does *more than tolerate you* even mean?

"Come on, get in the car."

Does it mean Travis *likes* me?

I should probably fight him a little more on the car thing, but after two nights in a row of getting barely any sleep, I'll be happy to let him take the wheel today—literally.

Travis starts the car once I get inside. "Where to?"

When I rattle off the address Charlie sent me last night, he only nods and drives away. I sit back in the passenger's seat, taking in the interior of Travis's pickup truck for the first time. It smells clean and isn't full of shopping tickets and coins like mine is.

"Did you get any more sleep after I left?" he asks.

I need to know who took my grouchy boss and replaced him with this—dare I say—caring man who drives me places and asks about my sleeping habits. *Stat.*

"I didn't, but I'm not that tired." And because we are apparently on friendlier grounds now, I ask him, "And you?"

He shakes his head, eyes on the road. "Did you eat anything for breakfast?"

"I thought about making an omelet, but I got lazy."

I check my phone to see if I have any new texts from Jada, but there's nothing. Nothing from Paul either. I decide to wait until I check the new place to tell them about me moving. They don't know about my car or the break-in next door, and I don't want to alarm them when I'm fine. Mostly.

According to the map on my phone, the apartment is at least ten minutes away from my place, so when not even three have passed and the car stops, I slide my confused eyes to Travis, a silent question in them.

"You can't start the day on an empty stomach." He gestures with his chin toward the small bakery he's parked in front of. "Let's go."

With far more ease than I would've expected given his massive size, he's quick to exit the truck, but I pause with my hand on the handle. Is he about to buy me breakfast?

"Travis, wait," I call out. His truck is so tall, I have to use the footboard to get down. My boss stops, looking at me over his shoulder as I reach his side. "We don't have to stop. I'm really not that hungry."

"You've barely slept, and you have a long day ahead. A muffin won't kill you."

He's right, a muffin won't kill me—but his sudden concern for me might.

Travis opens the door to the bakery, says good morning, and holds it for me so I can follow him inside.

"What do you want to get?" he asks me, wallet in hand.

I'm about to tell him once more that he doesn't need to buy me anything, that I'm genuinely not that hungry, and that I won't pass out if I wait until lunchtime, but then I see a three-layer carrot cake and shut my mouth again.

The old lady behind the counter smiles at me, her eyes kind, as I say, "I'll have a slice of carrot cake, please."

"Excellent choice." She beams before sliding her gaze toward my boss. "How about you, Travis?"

She knows him?

"I'll have the usual. Thank you."

The usual? He comes here often?

I turn to him as the woman gets our food ready and ask him exactly that.

"Barbara is a friend of my uncle's," he explains.

I'm assuming Barbara is the woman behind the display full of goodies.

"I didn't know you had a sweet tooth, boss man," I tease him.

But it's not him who answers.

"Crabby as he might be, he can't resist my chocolate muffins," the woman says, a loving smile touching the wrinkly corners of her lips. "You must be Allie."

I give her another smile in return. "It's great to meet you."

"Likewise, dear. My name is Barbara." She passes two

brown bags to Travis as well as two steaming plastic cups of coffee and sends me a knowing look. "I hope this one isn't giving you much trouble at work. We all know how he can get."

I steal a quick look at Travis, but his face remains as cold as ever, unaffected by Barbara's amicable jab.

"He's all right." I drop my voice on purpose. "Most days."

She laughs, shaking her head. "Sounds about right. Gotta love all his rough edges."

"All right," my boss interrupts, placing the money on the counter. "Thanks, Barbara. I'll see you soon."

She gives him an amused look. "I'm dropping by Neil's on Friday. Don't be a stranger."

He nods in response, and I wave at her, following him out the door. "Have a good day, Barbara."

"You too, Allie."

I don't realize it at first, but when I do, I come to a halt right outside his pickup truck, my hand freezing on the door handle.

"Travis?" My mouth feels too dry, but I push through. "How did Barbara know who I am?"

She can't possibly know about my family. She doesn't fit the demographic.

He opens the passenger door for me from the inside, then passes me one of the paper bags after I sit down. "She knows everyone I work with."

Oh. *Oh.* That makes sense. But that means he talks about me, and I don't know how that makes me feel.

My shoulders sag with relief, and I stick my nose inside the bag, smelling the deliciousness. "How much do I owe you for this?"

"You fed me dinner last night. We're even."

I could fight him on this—and I'm about to—but then I notice the white-and-green beads around his wrist, matching the pink-and-white ones I'm also wearing today.

He's wearing my bracelet. He doesn't hate it or think it's silly.

One would think my slice of carrot cake—that comes with a cute plastic fork and everything—and my coffee would keep me busy during the trip, right? Wrong. So, so wrong.

Because as soon as Travis pulls into traffic, my eyes land on the beaded bracelet around his wrist again. Unable to help myself, my attention shifts from his wrist to his hand, to those thick fingers wrapped around the wheel, and my pulse quickens.

I've never been attracted to someone's hands before, and it's...definitely something. I wouldn't call Travis's hands beautiful, or at least not in the most conventional sense of the word. They aren't smooth or delicate but calloused and rough.

It doesn't help that I've seen him lift heavy boxes at The Lair with those hands and fix doorknobs and faulty furniture. His are capable hands. Hands with a kind of scorching warmth I've felt against my body, even if only for a fleeting moment that probably meant nothing to him.

This is just an infatuation that will lead nowhere. I know this, and I'm okay with it. Really. I'm not so delusional as to think my thirty-seven-year-old boss could ever feel anything for me.

So as Travis pulls into the parking lot of the apartment building, and I gulp down the remains of my coffee, I tell myself I'm allowed to daydream about his hands from time to time, but that I should stop before my heart becomes even more invested.

"Is that him?" I ask Travis when I spot a middle-aged man pacing back and forth in front of the building's entrance, dangling a set of keys in his hand. His jeans are worn and dark, matching his puffer jacket. I'm assuming he has long hair since it's pulled back with a tie. Nothing about him looks familiar.

He kills the engine. "Yeah."

We exit the car at the same time. As Travis throws my bag and our empty coffee cups in the trash, I make a beeline for this Robert Marcelli guy.

Mistake number one.

"You Allie Smith?" the man in questions asks, and not exactly in a nice way.

But I nod, my smile not faltering because I need to move out and won't jeopardize this opportunity. There are no other long-term rentals available within my budget right now, so it's either this or I risk being robbed.

"It's nice to meet you."

He doesn't say it back. "I need to be somewhere else in fifteen, so hurry up."

I blink.

"I'm sorry," I start, unable to hide my confusion. "We can reschedule if you'd like. My friend said you'd be free—"

"No rescheduling," he interrupts, making something anxious and ugly sit at the pit of my stomach. "You either like it or you don't, darlin'. I don't have all day. Let's get moving."

My feet stay rooted, not moving an inch. Robert's back is turned to me as he struggles to unlock the door, and I feel him before I see him.

"Who the fuck are you talking to like that?"

Robert freezes, then unfreezes a moment later as he turns to look at the menacing presence at my back. Travis is standing so close, I feel his body heat against my skin, lighting it on fire.

"Ward." By the way he says it, one doesn't need to be a genius to know the man who probably *won't* be my future land-lord isn't a fan of my boss, for whatever reason. It no longer surprises me that everyone knows everyone in small towns. "You with this chick?"

This chick.

My eye twitches.

And just like that, even if this were the last available apartment in the whole of Maine, I decide I would rather set up camp in the changing room of The Lair than see or speak to this clown ever again.

"You know what? I don't think this place is for me after all," I say loud and clear. I'm proud that my voice doesn't quiver, that my shoulders don't drop as Robert's face surely does.

"You kiddin' me? You didn't even see it," he argues.

"It's not the apartment I have an issue with."

Mistake number two.

Robert's expression morphs into something ugly and mean —something I haven't seen in six years. I fight against making the connection with all I've got, but the way his lip curls reminds me so much of my mother, I take a step back.

This man has no power over me. He isn't her.

Robert opens his mouth. "You b—"

"Careful how you speak to my girl."

The air whooshes out of my lungs.

My girl.

Me... Travis's girl?

When I feel him take a step forward, I snap out of it. I appreciate that he's standing up for me, but we don't need to send anyone to the hospital today.

"Thanks for your time." I send Robert my fakest smile, and I hope he isn't stupid enough to open his mouth again.

When his gaze travels to the ready-to-pounce beast behind me, and I see that throat working a heavy swallow, I know he isn't.

Travis waits until I'm in the car before he moves, his attention still on Robert. If he says something else to him, I don't hear it—not like my head has much space left anyway after those two words.

My girl.

135

He probably means I'm his girl as in part of his staff. I shouldn't overthink this.

Travis is a protective man. He always makes sure I get to my car safely and has come to my rescue several times in the past year when I've had to deal with difficult patrons. He even stayed the night on my minuscule couch to make sure I was safe if anything happened. Being an ex-Navy SEAL, protecting must be second nature to him. I'm not special. He does this for everyone—especially if they are under the average height and don't look particularly strong or menacing. He's only looking out for me like any other good person would.

"You didn't threaten him, did you?" I ask him when he slides into the driver's seat. I arch an unamused eyebrow when he doesn't answer. "Boss man, we can't jeopardize The Lair's reputation for something silly."

"Nobody talks to you like that and gets away with it, you hear me?"

I don't know how to respond to this version of him. The version that openly cares so much for me.

I more than tolerate you, Allie.

"We'll figure something out," he adds, pulling out of the parking lot. "You're moving out of that shithole."

I don't have the energy to tell him I'm not too sure about that.

Chapter Seventeen

Age 15

I chewed on my thumbnail, my eyes glued to the front door. My parents left for the vet with Milo, our dog, but it had been over two hours, and I was getting sick to my stomach just thinking—

Don't.

He's going to be fine.

Our nanny, a blonde-haired hippie my mother found on some website, walked into the living room with Cindy in her arms and gave me a pitying look. I liked Faith—she was cool—but her attention was making my skin crawl. Because if she was looking at me like *that* instead of being her reassuring self, it could only mean one thing.

The weight of a ton of bricks pushed down on my chest, making it difficult to breathe.

"Can I have string cheese?" Johnny asked her.

He sat on the couch, his attention on the tablet resting on his knees as he played a racing game.

My brother had always loved cars. Picking all his toys apart and rebuilding them faster than a ten-year-old should be able to was his thing. He used to say he wanted to be a mechanic when he grew up, but he changed his mind to mechanical engineer when our mother said it would be more prestigious.

"Sure, Johnny-boy." Faith beamed, but there was no hiding the worried gleam in her eyes. "I'll get you some."

She still hadn't come back with his string cheese when the front door opened. My mother, my father—

My stomach sank at the missing presence.

"Where's Milo?"

My mother didn't look at me, fishing for something inside her purse instead.

It was my father who said, his voice void of any tact, "He died."

Two words were all it took for my heart to crash and burn.

Died.

My best friend, our family dog of ten years, was *dead.*

"W-Why?" My hands started shaking, and my eyesight got blurry. "You said he was okay."

Milo had been throwing up nonstop for the past two days, but my parents had said it was just a bug, and he'd come back from the vet feeling better. I didn't think I would never see him again.

"He died?" Johnny asked, looking up from his tablet. There were no tears in his eyes. "Oh. Well, he was really old."

I resisted the urge to yell at him that ten years wasn't that old, that his age didn't matter anyway. Milo *died.* We'd never get to play with him again or feed him treats or jump with him in the pool. He was gone forever.

As I looked at the dry faces around me, I wondered with no short amount of rage if I was the only one who cared. Faith had left to play with Cindy in her bedroom, my father was scanning the fridge, Johnny took his racing game to the garden, and my mother was fiddling with her recording camera.

Is this a joke?

I went up to her. "Was Milo scared?"

Despite my tears, I was able to see her distinct frown. "How am I supposed to know that, Allison? He was a dog. He didn't know what was going on."

Wetness rolled down my cheeks. "You didn't say he was going to die."

Die. The word tasted bitter in my mouth. Ugly, dirty, poisoned.

She kept adjusting the settings on the camera. "We didn't know he was that sick. He had a tumor in his throat, and the vet said he wouldn't live much longer anyway."

I sniffed, not caring about the snot running out my nose. "I wanted to say g-goodbye."

She rolled her eyes. "Dogs don't understand human behaviors. It wouldn't have made a difference."

Her cruel words sliced my chest open wider. And then she poured salt into the wound by pointing the camera at herself.

The rapid way in which her demeanor changed from cold to distressed was... pure evil. There was no other way to describe it.

"Hi, everybody," she started in that fake voice she always used whenever she wanted to invoke sympathy. "I have some sad news today."

She took a deep breath and shut her eyes, pretending to rein in tears that weren't there.

"Our precious boy Milo passed away today," she told the camera. "He'd been with us for ten years, so we're all very upset right now. You probably can't tell, but I've been crying nonstop in the car on our way here, and I've only just forced myself to stop so I can film this for you guys."

Her words sounded practiced, calculated. Why was she pretending to be sad in front of the camera?

"Please send your prayers our way." She sniffed, dabbing at

invisible tears under her eyes with a French-tipped finger. "It was so sudden, we couldn't say goodbye how he deserved. Allison is very upset, as you can imagine. Allison, come here—"

"*Stop.*"

It took me a second to recognize my own voice. It had never sounded as cold and cruel as my mother's.

She glared at me over the camera, her stare murderous, while she kept aiming it at me. "Behave, Allison. Tell the people how you're feeling. I have to edit this video for tonight."

"You're not even crying," I accused her, rage swirling inside of me. My hands started sweating when I balled them into fists, my tears falling. "Stop pretending to care when you *don't*. And stop filming me. I don't want to be on camera right now. I *never* do."

She rolled her eyes like I was some big inconvenience. "This is my job, and the very thing that pays for those expensive concert tickets you love so much. Now let me film this, or you won't be getting any dinner tonight."

Before I knew what I was doing, I snatched the camera from her grip and sprinted to the other end of the living room.

"Allison!" she bellowed after me.

"No!" I shouted back, using the dining table as a buffer between us. "You're a *liar*. You don't care that Milo died or that you couldn't say goodbye. You weren't even crying. And I don't want to be in your stupid videos. Stop forcing me!"

"What's all this yelling?" my father asked as he walked into the dining room. His voice was calm, too calm, like he didn't really care and was only stepping in to fill some kind of father-peacemaker quota.

"Your daughter won't let me do my job," my mother spat out.

"I never consented to being part of your job," I bit back.

"*Consented,*" she mimicked. "Some big word that is, huh?

You think you're doing something here? You're *my* daughter, and you'll *consent* to whatever *I* say."

"That's not how it works." I looked at my father, knowing this was a lost cause. "You know I'm right. I shouldn't have to be in the videos if I don't want to."

I got kidnapped because of it.

That was something we never talked about in our family. Ever. As if the worst day of my life had never happened. I wasn't even sure Johnny knew about it.

"Just give your mother the camera, Allison," he said in an almost-robotic voice, once again confirming he didn't care about my feelings or decisions. "Those videos you don't want to be part of pay for all the nice things you have, so behave."

"You heard your father. Stop being an ungrateful brat and cry for the camera."

And cry for the camera.

I was ready to throw the camera across the room and smash it into pieces when my anger subsided unexpectedly, and a sudden realization arose.

I didn't want to be here.

With my family. In this house. In Los Angeles. In California.

I wanted nothing to do with the life I was born into. Absolutely nothing.

Cry for the camera.

Taking advantage of my momentary distraction, my mother snatched her camera from my grip. But I wasn't expecting her to grab me next by the back of my hair, forcefully dragging me down the hallway.

"I warned you," she snarled, gripping my hair tighter.

I gasped, her actions taking me back to that man. To the warehouse. "Stop! You're hurting me."

She only did after pushing me inside my bedroom and shutting the door.

"You'd better stay there until the morning, or you'll go without dinner for a whole week," she shouted from the other side.

I didn't react. Didn't yell back. Didn't say anything at all.

Claudia can't hurt me anymore. I'm safe.

But was I?

My eyes drifted to the laptop on my bed, and something lit up inside of me. Something that shouldn't have felt as right as it did.

Sitting on the ground, I kept stealing quick glances at the door to check that my mother was truly gone. And then I typed in what I hoped would be the beginning of the end.

Farthest state from California.

Chapter Eighteen

"I'm so sorry, honey."

I'm fine. I'm totally fine.

"She posted it last night in response to George Eden's statement, but from what I've seen, it hasn't made any major headlines yet."

I was an adult when I left California—a very young one, sure, but over eighteen, nonetheless. And I made it abundantly clear that I left on my own and why in that video.

What I decide to do or not do with my life should be no one's business but my own. But it never has been.

I don't want to ask her this next question, but I won't be able to relax today or sleep tonight if I don't. It's been three days since Travis stayed the night, and I don't think I've managed to sleep more than four hours a day, which means I look and feel like a zombie.

So even if I don't want to know the answer, not really, I still ask, "What did she say?"

When I cut ties with my parents after I left Los Angeles— and mentally long before then—I told myself I wouldn't waste

143

another second thinking of the two people who exploited me for their benefit.

But I soon learned that the past never leaves, and pretending it isn't there causes more damage than healing.

So, I decided to let out my frustrations about my family in the privacy of my journal, just a couple of times a week before bed, and that would be it. Yet I broke my own promise over and over again the first year I left, unable to unglue myself from online spaces I shouldn't have been in.

The second year, Jada saw right through my bullshit and promised she would be on the lookout as long as I stayed away. It was hard at first, but nowadays checking on my parents is at the very back of my mind—thanks to Jada and Paul and their unyielding resolve to keep me posted with the most relevant stuff.

My former teacher lets out a deep breath. "Do you really want to know?"

I think of the sleepless nights that await me if I keep wondering how bad it actually is instead of coming to terms with this shit show. "Yes."

My phone buzzes with a text, and I put it on speaker as I open the image Jada attached to our chat. I scan my mother's words, so fake and measured that I can't comprehend how she still gets a paycheck from this.

"What do you think?" Jada asks the question of the century.

Now's my time to sigh. "She's full of it. That's what I think."

Nothing happened to Allison. She had a happy and healthy upbringing, and she loved us very much. When she turned eighteen, our daughter was free to make her own deci-

**sions, and she chose to not be a part of this
life anymore. Her dad, siblings, and I have
nothing to do with this decision, as we have
always supported her and given her love. I
am distraught by the unfounded rumors that
this family mistreated Allison in any way or
was to blame for the terrible thing that
happened to her when she was twelve.
George Eden's speculations are nothing but
malicious. Legal action will be pursued
against anyone who seeks to harm our
family during this difficult time.**

Bullshit. All of it.

How dare she pretend nothing was wrong after putting me
through hell for most of my childhood and every single day of
my teen years?

After humiliating me in front of millions of people?

After her narcissism got me kidnapped and nearly sold to a
trafficking ring?

"She knows they're in the wrong," Jada says, but I doubt it.
My parents were the true definition of narcissistic and, by the
looks of it, still are. "You don't have to listen to all this media
circus. Your parents won't change, and the rest of the world is
just nosey. You're safe."

"It's not that I feel physically threatened." Maybe I do, but
that has everything to do with the car and the break-in and very
little with my family. "It's more... mental stuff."

"You're still on the fence about therapy?"

She's been pushing me toward it for a long time, but how
can I be honest with a therapist without giving myself away?
My life isn't exactly an easy one to explain.

"I'll consider it."

It's what I always tell her, and she hasn't been buying it for years.

"Allie.... Therapists are sworn to secrecy. They won't go to the press unless they want their licenses and livelihoods taken away, and trust me, nobody wants that."

It makes sense in my head, it truly does, but...

"I mean it, Jada—I'm thinking about it. I know I need therapy, and I promise I'll get there." Someday. "Just give me a bit more time to settle in Bannport, yeah?"

Because fifteen months aren't enough?

"I trust that whatever you decide to do will be the best thing." Even though she clearly disagrees with me on the therapy thing, I know she means her reassuring words. She always does. "I'm just looking out for you, honey."

"I know, and I love you so much for it. You are the best. I hope you know that."

Her chuckle eases some of my tension. "I love you more, Allie. Recess is about to end, and I need to go back to the students, but you take care, okay?"

I smile, remembering my math classes with her. They were the absolute best. "Have a good day today."

"You too, honey. We'll talk later."

My anxiety will only worsen if I don't get out of my apartment right now. Getting in the car is a no-brainer, and I consider stopping at my favorite deli on my way to The Lair as a little treat for not having lost my shit yet.

The bar closes on Wednesdays, but I know boss man will be there doing all sorts of things he shouldn't since it's also his day off. So that's why, twenty minutes after ending my call with Jada, I knock on the door of The Lair holding two takeout bags.

"Travis," I call out. "It's Allie."

I'm not sure why coming here was my first instinct. Maybe

because looking at the bracelet on Travis's wrist makes me feel better about life.

His confused frown is the first thing I see when he unlocks the door.

"What are you doing here?" he half grunts. Because of course he does.

I don't allow his foul mood—his usual mood—to deter me. Today has the potential to become one hell of a shitty day if I don't turn it around now.

"I brought you lunch," I tell him with a smile, showing him the bags.

His green eyes travel from the bags to my face, then back down. I know he can smell those chicken parmesan sandwiches because I've been salivating since I got them ten minutes ago.

"Can I come in?" I ask, in case my intentions weren't clear enough.

In usual Travis fashion, he answers with a grunt but doesn't shut the door in my face.

When I enter the bar, I spot a bunch of open notebooks, sheets of paper, pens, a laptop, and a calculator in one of the booths.

My math-geek heart leaps. "Is this what I think it is?"

"Accounting?"

"Do you need help?" I ask him as I place the takeout bags on an empty table.

Travis walks up to me, the warmth of his body seeping into mine. "You're into that?"

"Are you really asking if I'm into *numbers*?" I roll my neck. "This is my jam, boss man."

The eyebrow raise he gives me is one of muted amusement. "You're good with numbers?"

It's not surprising that he forgot about my résumé. My previous experience in customer service probably did it for him, and he didn't pay attention to anything else. So, I remind him, "I've got several certificates in finances and accounting."

Over the last six years, I've been trying to keep an active mind by doing things I enjoy. Hobbies like bracelet making, and this. As soon as I got my first paycheck, I saved up until I could enroll in an online accounting course. For the first time in far too long, I felt useful, like I wasn't wasting my life away.

I got my last certificate—my sixth one—five months ago, and Travis has just given me the perfect chance to let my inner math nerd loose.

"If you ever need help with the bar's accounting, just let me know," I offer, not bothering to hide the hopeful gleam in my voice. "I can sign an NDA or whatever you need."

He looks at me with intent. "Yeah?"

"I'd be happy to help."

"Accounting is a pain in my ass," he deadpans. "You're good at this?"

He's really considering this. Somebody pinch me.

"I can help you today so you can see for yourself," I decide, feeling giddy inside about the possibility of doing some real work with years of piled-up knowledge. "Free of charge, of course."

"You're not doing all this for free."

"Just this one time. Think of it as a trial exercise. If you want me to take care of the bar's accounting from now on, we'll settle on a rate."

His nod is short but convinced. "Works for me."

If Travis were literally anyone else, I would hug the hell out of him right now. He has no idea how much this little task means to me. To my mental health. To my self-confidence.

I spend the next hour crammed in a cushioned booth with Travis, my elbow grazing his bicep as I shift through all the documents and have a massive brain orgasm.

Eventually, he grabs the bags I'd set on a table earlier and sniffs inside. "You brought your lunch with you?"

I don't look up from the calculator. "Our lunch."

As if he suddenly didn't understand the English language, he repeats, "Ours?"

"I figured you hadn't eaten anything, but if you don't like chicken parmesan sandwiches, I'll just have yours for dinner later."

"I like them." A heartbeat passes. "Thank you."

Travis? Easily agreeing to me managing the bar's accounts *and* buying him lunch all in the same day? He must be coming down with a fever.

After heating up the sandwiches in the oven, we eat in silence as I think of ways to make the accounting easier since he's doing everything manually. No wonder he hates it.

"Would you be willing to get a computer software for it?"

Travis shakes his head. "I couldn't figure it out."

"You're old, but you're not *that* ancient."

That earns me a glare, to which I respond with a smirk.

"I'd rather keep using my books," he says, ignoring my jab.

"Okay. I can see you're very methodical about cash accounting, but it can get tedious. How often do you go over the accounts?"

"Every Wednesday."

"How about inventory?"

"Daily."

His organizational skills don't come as a surprise. In fifteen months, he's never been late to work, has never sent out checks a day later than usual, and The Lair is pretty busy every day. It wouldn't be if his managing skills sucked.

"You seem to have everything figured out," I observe out loud. One look at the bar's numbers and I can see we are making great profit, too, so his methods work. "If you want me to take care of the accounting in the future, just teach me how you do it, and I'll adapt. No biggie."

I catch him flexing his hands under the table. I still can't believe he's wearing my bracelet. A bet is a bet, I suppose.

"You'll really do it?" he asks. "I don't want to overwork you."

"You won't be doing such a thing. I'm a math geek, so you'll actually be doing me a favor. I'm in my element here. Most people get a headache just thinking about finances and account-ing, but I love staying focused like that. It soothes me."

I've never considered finding an actual job in accounting because I don't think I'm qualified enough. Sure, I've got several certificates under my belt—straight A's in all of them—but I can't compete with people who went to actual college for it.

So maybe that's why my heart leaps at Travis's next ques-tion. "What's your rate?"

"I'll have to think about it," I say, wiping the sudden sweat on my hands on my leggings. "When do you need an answer?"

"Whenever you're ready."

Okay. This is happening. I'm not freaking out.

"I'll give you an answer before next Wednesday." Once I calm my nerves, I'll need to do some research to avoid rattling off a number that is totally ridiculous. "Thank you for this, boss man. It might sound silly, but I'm really excited about it."

The small smile curling the corner of his lips is reason enough to send my poor heart into overdrive. "There's nothing silly about doing what you love."

I'm trying. I'm really trying. But it's like my boss—this older, grumpy, ex-military man with an intimidating exterior but a heart of gold—wants me to fall in love with him.

And I'm not convinced that I won't.

Chapter Nineteen

With the stress of the past few days, I'd forgotten about Charlie giving Lola my phone number until she texts me the following night.

UNKNOWN

> Hey Allie!!! This is Lola. Charlie said it was okay to give me your number, so I hope you don't find this creepy. Would you like to meet for coffee after the holidays or whenever you're free?? I can pick you up on your break from work. This is a very long text, sorry!!! It's okay if you don't want to hang out. Just let me know :)

Sitting cross-legged on my couch, I stare at my screen until it dawns on me that this is my life. That someone, for some reason, met me and thought I was *cool*. Cool enough to want to be my friend.

That's because she doesn't know who I really am.

I shake my head, willing the mean thoughts to go away. No matter what my mind tells me, I have the right to start over and to do it on my terms.

ME

> Hi, Lola! I'd love to meet for coffee this week. I get off work at three on Monday. Does that work for you?

I wait anxiously for a reply that comes only minutes later, my dinner from an hour ago jumping around in my stomach.

LOLA

> Yay!! I'm so excited. I know just the place, and you're gonna be OBSESSED with their carrot cake cookies (Charlie said you liked carrot cake, and I hope the idiot wasn't lying). I'll pick you up <3

A warm sense of belonging settles in my chest. I can't remember the last time I had a girlfriend, even though I've always longed for one of those tight-knit friendships I saw in movies and read about in books. I tell myself not to get my hopes up—I don't know her well, after all—but I can't help but nurse the good feeling I get from Lola.

ME

> He wasn't lying. I love carrot cake. Can't wait :)

Proud of myself for taking this step forward and not freaking out too much about it, I type a quick text to Jada with the news. I know she'll be proud of me too.

As I press Send, something happens.

Something I can't identify right away but know deep in my bones is bad. Really, *really* bad.

A deafening sound comes from the direction of my front door—a loud boom that freezes my body on the spot. For a second, I think maybe someone's knocking, but then I come to my senses—nobody knocks on a door as if they were trying to bash it down.

My spine stiffens, and panic wraps around my heart. I sit

very still and listen for any sound inside or outside of my apartment.

A minute passes. Nothing.

What the hell was that?

I'm about to get up to look through the peephole when it happens again.

The best way I can describe it is as if someone was throwing themselves at the door, trying to break it down.

My hands start shaking with adrenaline, but I remind myself that the last thing I need is to let fear paralyze me. If nothing else, I'm a survivor.

I'm alone at home, but maybe whoever is at the door doesn't know it. I won't make a sound, won't—

"Get it open, damn it," a male voice says, as if he were talking to someone else.

The metallic click of the lock fills the apartment. *They're trying to get in.*

With trembling fingers, I unlock my phone and dial nine-one-one, hoping that my dry throat allows me to speak. I crouch behind the couch, hiding in case they get in.

The man kicks at my door again as a voice on the other end of the line answers, "Nine-one-one, what's your emergency?"

I don't know how I manage to ignore it, how I tune everything and everyone out but this call. "T-There's a man banging at my door. He's trying to break in."

"Okay, ma'am," the woman answers in a calm voice. "What's your address?" I tell her. "Police are on the way. Please stay on the line until they get there."

"O-Okay," I stammer, crouching lower behind the couch.

Another loud bang, and I flinch. "P-Please." Tears prick the backs of my eyes, but I don't want to cry right now. I need to stay calm and strong in case something happens. "P-Police."

"They are almost there," the dispatcher assures me, but I'm pretty sure it's the standard answer. "Is anybody else with you?"

"No. I live alone," I whisper, hoping the man or men outside don't have some magical hearing.

The door rattles with another hit, and I shut my eyes, thinking this time it's coming down for real. By some miracle, it stands still.

Travis's lock.

It feels like a million years have passed when I finally hear, "Police!"

The relieved sigh I take next makes the tears come out, and I croak out, "I think the police are here."

"Okay," the woman answers. "Please stay on the phone until we make sure you are safe."

I'm wiping the tears away with the sleeve of my hoodie when there's a knock at my door, and the air whooshes out of my lungs again.

"Bannport Police," a man calls out. "We received a call from this apartment."

Still holding the phone to my ear, I check that it's really the police out there. Once I thank the dispatcher and hang up, I open the door to the same two officers who investigated the break-in next door.

The next twenty minutes are a blur. They question me about tonight's incident, and I spot at least another four officers making rounds up and down the hallway.

I knew it, yet my stomach still drops when they tell me there's a very high chance that whoever tried to get inside my apartment tonight were the same people who targeted this building a few days ago.

"I don't understand," I tell the officers, my voice still shaky. "I was inside. It doesn't make sense to break in when someone is inside, does it? D-Did they want to hurt me?"

They exchange a look that doesn't make me feel better.

"We'll send more patrol cars to the area and look up footage from all nearby cameras," the female officer reassures me. "In the meantime, is there another place you could spend the night? Someone you could call? You might feel safer somewhere else for the time being."

When they leave after saying-but-not-saying they can't do anything about the break-ins right now, I'm left with a sense of raw fear.

I knew I had to move out of here, but this is different. Because now I can't bring myself to spend one more second between these four walls that no longer form my safe place.

It's ruined.

Everything is.

Angry tears roll down my cheeks before I can stop them. Police don't seem to be in any hurry to find whoever is terrorizing this building. What if something happens before they find who has been breaking in?

What if someone tries to take me again?

As much as I try to ignore the connection, I can't help but think there's something very wrong and very strange about all this. Days after the George Eden article went live, I found my car window down. Now I'm convinced *I* didn't do it, not even accidentally. How would that even happen? Other than the one time I did it to talk to Travis, I don't recall rolling down my windows. I don't do it during winter—it's too cold.

Then, someone broke into the apartment next door but didn't take anything. Days later, they try breaking into mine. And if Travis hadn't installed that new lock, they would have.

I could be dead right now.

Maybe I'm paranoid, but what if someone is targeting *me*? What if Claudia's ring isn't truly dissolved and they're after me, fearing I'll speak out against them now that my name is on the news?

There are too many coincidences, and my gut is screaming that I'm not safe on my own anymore.

I don't know why I search for his number and dial it. All I know is that I feel in danger, and there's only one person whose presence can soothe me before I inevitably go into full panic-attack mode.

I tell myself that I'm being selfish for a good reason, that this is bad, and he'll understand why I'm calling at eleven at night, as Travis's gruff voice greets me from the other line. "Allie?"

"Hey, Travis. Sorry to bother you. I know it's late, but... could you come over, please? Someone just tried to break into my apartment."

There were times in the past fifteen months when I thought I had seen Travis look angry. As in, furious. It didn't happen often, but I recognized the signs—his face turned meaner, colder, harsher, and his massive body was shackled with tension. His jaw ticked, and his eyes boiled with a pool of simmering anger.

I thought Travis had looked angry when his friend put his arm around me that night and said all those nasty things. I thought he had been pissed off when I messed up the stock orders, or when I hugged Charlie, or when Robert Marcelli had almost called me a bitch.

Turns out I had seen nothing.

Travis knocks once, hard, and says in that husky voice, "Allie, open up. It's Travis."

As if I would mistake that voice for anyone else's.

I quickly check my phone and try not to react to the fact

that we hung up six minutes ago. *Six.* I have no clue where he lives, but his driving speed is impressive nonetheless.

I haven't opened the door all the way when I see firsthand how wrong I was about witnessing Travis's true fury.

Those military eyes scan every corner of my apartment, then my face. Assessing, looking for something I'm not sure he finds.

"Are you hurt?"

There's tension in his jaw and around his mouth, and he looks ready to pounce on any intruder.

"I-I'm not. I'm fine. Nobody got in."

If bear-man had been a dragon-man instead, he would've breathed fire right about now. "What the fuck, Allie?"

That earns him a slow blink. I open my mouth to ask him what I've done wrong now, but he beats me to it.

"I told you that you couldn't live here any longer."

Is he for real?

"I *want* to move out." He knows this. "You know I can't find a place, Travis. Why are you angry at me?"

When his eyes meet mine again, some of his tension seems to deflate. "I'm not angry at you."

I shut the door behind us. A few of my neighbors have gathered in the hall to discuss the break-ins, but I can't find it in me to join them.

"Sure looks like it," I accuse him. "Do you think I want to live here? That I want to be on edge all the time, waiting for the lucky day I get robbed? Or worse?"

I'm aware that my chest is heaving, that my voice is louder, and that I'm getting worked up, and I hate every second of it. I'm not scared of conflict, but I don't seek it either. And I hate that Travis thinks someone trying to break in is somehow my fault.

"Allie." His voice sounds softer, but I'm barely listening.

"Do you think I enjoyed calling the police and hiding behind my couch, hoping that my door held up?" My eyes travel to the ceiling, and I tell myself I'm not going to cry. I'm *not*. But my voice falls a second later, and so does the first tear. "I was so scared. I didn't k-know what to do."

Travis takes one step forward, then another. He holds out his arms, wrapping them around my shoulders. When my wet cheek meets the warmth of his chest, covered in an old shirt that smells of detergent, it finally dawns on me.

My boss, this intimidating man who stayed up all night in my apartment to make sure I was safe and wears a friendship bracelet I made for him, is *hugging* me.

"You're okay," that gruff voice says in a gentle tone I'd never heard from him before. "You were so fucking brave, Allie. I'm proud of you."

Another tear falls, then more. Maybe it's because I'm pressed against his chest and he can't see my face, or maybe it's because his hug feels like my only safe place right now. But I don't overthink it when my arms wrap around his torso, hugging him back.

And when he pulls me closer to his body, I don't overthink it either.

I let out a shaky breath. "They tried to... to..."

"Shh...." He buries his fingers in my hair. "You're safe now, sweetheart. I'm not gonna let anything happen to you."

My skin breaks out in a sea of goose bumps at the term of endearment, at the protectiveness of his words and embrace.

"I'm so sorry I spoke to you like that. I shouldn't have. I was so fucking scared for you, and I didn't handle it well." I feel the hand on my back rubbing circles up and down my spine, soothing me. "You did good, Allie."

I shut my eyes, begging the tears to stop, but I'm too shaken up to think straight.

Someone tried to break into my apartment while I was inside. What if they had succeeded?

"Look at me."

What would have they done to me?

What if the police had taken longer to show up?

"Allie, look at me."

A firm but gentle weight settles on my chin, and it takes me a moment to realize it's Travis's fingers, holding my chin up.

My eyes are so blurry, I might be imagining the soft look in his.

"I'm here, and you're safe. You're not alone anymore."

I blink, and more tears fall. I think my bottom lip might be trembling. "I don't want to stay here."

He nods. "Where do you want to go?"

I wish I had a place to call home, a safe space to run to when the weight of life falls on me. But I don't, I never have, and maybe I never will, so I'll settle for the next best thing.

"Can you take me to a hotel?"

Travis searches my gaze before he nods again. "Grab your things and I'll drive you. Yeah?"

I nod back as his warm fingers drop from my chin. Then I wipe at my eyes and try to muster as much strength as I can to start packing. There are only two hotels open during the winter season in Bannport, and knowing my luck, every room will be booked.

A few sets of clothes, all my underwear, my bathroom things, my shoes, my phone and charger, and all my cash later, I meet my boss at the door, from where he hasn't moved.

"You ready to go?" he asks gently.

When I nod again, he grabs the backpack and small suitcase I'm carrying. I let him, too tired to argue.

We don't speak as we walk to his car, the man who just

hugged me and glued all my broken pieces back together staying right at my back the whole time. A bodyguard.

Once I'm strapped in, he drives away into the night. At some point, he asks, not turning his attention from the road, "You doing okay?"

I give him an honest answer. "Not really."

As we drive through the quiet town, I reason that there's no point in telling Jada and Paul about tonight. I mean, technically nothing happened. I don't have a single scrape or bruise on my body, and nobody did anything bad to me. They don't need to know.

So I decide to keep tonight's events to myself—at least for now—as Travis pulls into a parking lot. I recognize this hotel from my first days in Bannport when I stayed here while I looked for an apartment. The rooms were clean and cheap, which is exactly what I need right now.

"This place work for you?" Travis asks me as he kills the engine.

"Yeah. Thank you for... for everything." Even if it makes my palms sweat a little, I add, "I've got it from here. You can go back home."

"All right."

But Travis doesn't leave my side.

And he doesn't go home.

Before I can argue, he books two adjoining rooms for the night and pays for them. Then he carries my bags to the elevator and gestures for me to follow him.

And before I can process what the hell is happening, he's handing me the key to my room and saying, "If you need me, give me a call or a knock."

I ignore the frantic beating of my heart and ask him, "Why are you doing all this for me?"

Because I don't get it. I really don't.

It's one thing to feel a bit fond of your employee—an employee he swore he wouldn't befriend—but *this*? Spending the night in a hotel when he has his own home just because I'm agitated and scared? This isn't normal, and I'm tired of wondering why he's going out of his way to help someone he doesn't owe anything to.

"I said nothing was gonna happen to you, and I meant it." Before the butterfly in my stomach can react, he adds, "I'll make a few calls tomorrow. See what apartments we can find in the area."

I think I nod. This is... this is too much, and it's happening too fast.

"I mean it, Allie. You need anything, you call me. Understood?"

I swallow. "Understood."

He dips his chin. "Try to sleep."

I nod again.

He looks like he's going to say something else but stops himself. The hand that's holding the key to his room flexes once.

"Good night, Allie."

Chapter Twenty

"COME AGAIN?"

I slide my co-worker and friend a look over my shoulder as I put away a bottle of whiskey.

Since it's Christmas Eve, we're closing down the bar a couple of hours earlier. Everyone is eager to go home to their loved ones—in my case, that means a quick video call with Jada and Paul. It may not sound too exciting, but it's more than enough for me.

Charlie, much like everybody else, can't wait to leave The Lair for the day. He invited me out for drinks with his friends, but I told him I needed to catch up on sleep. For once, it wasn't an excuse. When he asked why, I told him that I'm currently living in a hotel room because someone tried to break into my apartment.

Which explains the agape mouth and freaked-out look he's giving me right now.

"I'm all right," I insist. "I'm still looking for a place to live, but I'm sure something will come up soon."

A girl can dream.

When a somber expression takes over his ever-smiling face, I know I should probably not be so optimistic.

"Allie..." he starts before letting out a deep breath. "Shit, Allie. I'm so sorry that happened to you. I live with my parents and my two younger siblings, but you can have my bedroom if you want. Our couch is pretty comfortable, so no biggie. You don't have to pay for a hotel. That must be expensive."

My heart swells. "Oh, Charlie. Thank you so much for offering, but I can't do that." I reach over the bar and squeeze his arm in a friendly gesture. "I promise I'm okay. The hotel is cheaper than you think."

He doesn't look or sound convinced. "You said Travis is staying with you?"

There's no accusation in his voice, only curiosity and worry. Yet I feel my neck heating up, then my cheeks, and I lower my gaze to check something behind the bar that doesn't exist.

"He's staying in the room next door."

Non-fraternization policies aren't a thing in The Lair, clearly, as Jude and Sandra have been married for years. Still, nothing is going on between me and Travis besides maybe the beginning of an unlikely friendship. I don't want people to think otherwise.

"That's nice of him," Charlie says. "Have you hooked up yet?"

What. The. Hell.

Charlie barks out a laugh. "Don't give me that look. I was just asking a question."

"What kind of question is *that*?"

The traitor only shrugs. "You think I can't see the tension? Smell it in the air?"

Now I'm wondering if my good friend, this boy who crawled his way into my heart and refused to let the strings of our friendship go, hit his head when I wasn't looking. Because there's no way he just said that.

My heart is beating too fast to say anything other than "You're nuts."

"That's why you're all red?"

I palm my cheeks, feeling the warmth of my skin. "I'm embarrassed. You're insinuating I'm sleeping with the boss."

"I wasn't insinuating anything, Allie Cat. I'm just curious about your love life."

I don't think the glare I send him intimidates him in the slightest since he throws his head back in laughter.

"It's not funny," I say.

"But it is."

I don't know where Travis is, but if he comes out of nowhere and overhears Charlie, I will literally die on the spot.

"We haven't hooked up." I will my voice to sound steady as I look him in the eye. "In the past or ever. I'm not interested."

He shakes his head in amusement. "You're a little liar, aren't you?"

Something clogs up my throat, and I remind myself he doesn't know anything. He's only joking about Travis.

I force a smile. "Maybe I'll take you up on your offer and give some cockroaches a new place to live in your mattress."

His laughter sounds so honest, I can't bring myself to be angry with him. "You're a gem, Allie Cat."

"And you're a pain in my ass," I tease him, "but you're a gem too."

He raps his knuckles on the bar. "If you're done here, I think we can start with the gift exchange."

"Sure. Let me grab my present from the changing room, and I'll meet you here."

It takes us about fifteen minutes to get everything ready to close for the day, and then we're all standing together in the main area of the bar. It feels a bit like school, and it makes me giddy.

"There are a few different ways to play the game," Charlie starts. "Normally, we would put all our presents on one table, open the one with our name on it, and try to guess who it's from. But since we all want to get out of here ASAP, we'll do the shorter and slightly more boring version."

"Thank God," Jude mutters, making me chuckle.

Charlie's eyes land on me. "Allie Cat, the woman of the hour, will you do the honors and start the game?"

"Me?" I thought he would tell Sandra to go first or even do it himself.

"Yep. Who's the lucky bastard?" He slides his eyes in Sandra's direction and winks. "Or lovely lady."

"Kid," Jude growls under his breath.

I hold out my present for him, a shy smile on my lips. "This is for you, Jude."

His face lights up as he takes my gift. "Ah, I already know this is gonna be good. Thank you, Smith."

I pray that my smile doesn't waver at his nickname for me. "No biggie."

Just like I suspected he would, he takes one look at the T-shirt that says, "Proud husband of a freaking amazing wife," and roars with laughter. Sandra also laughs.

"This is perfect." He beams, putting his hand on my shoulder and giving it a squeeze. "Thank you. I'm changing into this as soon as I get home."

"The group chat would love a picture," I say.

"You got it."

Jude is next, and funny enough, his gift is for Sandra—a pair of shoes she's been ogling for a couple of weeks that definitely go over the budget, but we all agree it's okay because she's his wife. Plus, they couldn't be more adorable.

After planting a loving kiss on her husband's cheek, Sandra holds out the small bag in her hand in Charlie's direction. "For you, my sweet boy."

Charlie's eyes light up like a Christmas tree, but I'm barely paying attention. If I gave my present to Jude, Jude gave it to Sandra, and Sandra gave it to Charlie, that means... that means Travis could have a gift for me.

Not now, heart. Behave.

I'm brought back to the present moment by Charlie's loud hoot. "Oh shit! Literally."

When Charlie shows us his present—a roll of toilet paper that says, "This is the crappiest gift I could find," over and over again—I lose it. Everyone else laughs, too, and I think I even see the smallest hint of a smile on Travis's lips.

Charlie wraps his long arms around Sandra and gives her a loud kiss on top of her head. "Thank you, Sandra. I can't wait to wipe my ass with this."

After setting his precious roll of toilet paper aside, Charlie rubs his hands together and glances mischievously between me and Travis. "See, now the excitement will be lost because whoever I give my gift to will be the other person's Secret Santa."

"Just get on with it," Travis, who hasn't uttered a single word since we started, grunts.

Charlie puts his hands up in fake surrender. "Okay, okay." He reaches behind him and grabs a small box. "I hope you won't fire me for this, boss."

My breathing stops.

Travis is my Secret Santa.

I ignore the frantic way my heart is beating as he tears up the gingerbread-house-themed wrapping paper and is left with a plain white box. Then he opens it.

Travis blinks once, twice, at the mug in his hands. I can't

hold the laughter in when I read the message. "This is what a grumpy boss looks like" sounds about as accurate as a mug for Travis can get.

"I'm still on the payroll, right?" Charlie asks.

If I didn't have that grumpy-looking face memorized by now, I would've missed the slight upward tilt of the corner of his mouth and the way his stare goes a bit softer and more amused. But I don't.

"You're good."

"Amazing news for me. But sadly, I think we know who your gift is for, boss."

I'm not ready for Travis's eyes to find mine, and I'm not ready for how quickly he loses that easygoing inch of a smile. I'm pretty sure I'm not imagining the sudden tightness of his jaw either.

"Bring it on, boss man," I tell him with a smile. Maybe he's nervous about giving me a gift—as if he hadn't done much more for me already. But some people get all weird and awkward about giving or receiving stuff, so I understand. "I'll like whatever you got me."

Ignoring Charlie's hawk-like stare pinballing between us, I focus on my boss as he grabs a smallish box wrapped in plain red wrapping paper and passes it to me without a word.

I tear up the wrapping paper, and my heart leaps at the sight of a book of math riddles and a gift voucher for Barbara's bakery. "I love this, Travis. It's perfect. Thank you."

It really is. He knows math is my thing, and the fact that he remembered and put care into his gift makes my insides go all gooey.

As we make our way to the changing room, Jude thanks me again for the funny T-shirt, and I overhear Charlie telling Sandra how he can't wait to take a shit. Fun mental picture right there.

After our gift exchange, Travis disappeared somewhere, and I haven't seen him since. I don't know if he'll stay at the hotel tonight, too, but probably not. Nobody wants to spend the holidays away from home and their loved ones if they can prevent it, so I'd understand.

"Are you sure you don't want to come with us, dear?" Sandra asks me before they head over to their car. She knows I spent the holidays alone last year and that this one will be no different. "I promise it's no trouble. You like kids, right? Our grandson is coming over."

I give her an apologetic smile. "I love kids, and thank you so much for offering, but I'm fine on my own. Really. I don't celebrate Christmas anyway."

The look she gives me is so full of pity, I suppress a wince. "It'd be a pleasure to have you over for dinner. If you change your mind, just call me or Jude."

"Okay." She knows I won't, but I still appreciate her kindness. "Thank you again."

"Of course." She gives me another quick hug. "Take care, Allie, and happy holidays."

"Merry Christmas to you guys." I wave at her as she disappears down the street, following Jude and Charlie, who are chatting as they walk to their respective cars.

I'm zipping up my coat, ready to follow them, when an unmistakable voice stops me.

"Allie."

I turn to him with a smile. "Yes, boss man?"

The tight look on his face tells me what his words don't—he's done being my babysitter. And I'm fine with it, really. So what if knowing he was right next door allowed me to sleep through the night and not wake up drenched in my own sweat? Big deal.

He moves until the tips of his boots nearly graze my sneakers. "I have something else for you."

I frown. "What do you mean?"

Wordlessly, he reaches into one of his pockets and gives me a key.

If this were a movie and I had been watching it, I would've understood what that key meant right away. But because this is my life—a life I'm starting to doubt is even real—my mind empties.

My eyes are on Travis as I hold up a single house key between my fingers. They may or may not be shaking a little.

"What is this?"

Nothing, not a single thing in this world, could've prepared me for the words that leave Travis's mouth next.

"You're moving in with me."

Chapter Twenty-One

I THINK I KNOW WHAT'S GOING ON. WHEN I LEFT THE hotel earlier today, I must have slipped and hit my head on the icy sidewalk. Yeah, that must be it. Because there's no way my boss just told me to move in with him.

But two seconds of silence pass, then five and ten, and it hits me that this isn't the product of a head injury. This is my life right now. My *real* life.

I open my mouth and close it again, unsure of what to even say. That I can't accept? That he's lost his ever-loving mind? That I'll find a place soon?

We both know that won't happen. These past few days, I've asked around town in case anyone knew of any rentals, but I haven't had any luck. Overall, it's not looking promising.

"Travis—"

"You don't have to accept if you don't feel comfortable," he rushes out, and suddenly I understand why he looked nervous. I would think it's adorable if I wasn't on the verge of a mental breakdown myself. "I live alone in a farmhouse just ten minutes away. Three bedrooms, two bathrooms. I don't use nearly half of the space, and we both know you can't stay in that shithole any longer. The hotel isn't a long-term option either."

I work a swallow and beg my poor heart to calm down. "I don't want to intrude in your personal life or be a bother."

"I wouldn't have offered if I wasn't sure, Allie." It makes sense, but it also doesn't. My head is starting to pound. "You'll have your own bedroom and bathroom. We'll share the living room and kitchen, but I'm barely at the house."

A sudden urge to ask him where he goes and who he spends his free time with assaults me before I remind myself that I have no right to ask.

"Travis..." I shake my head and let out a deep breath that doesn't calm my nerves at all. "I appreciate how thoughtful you are, but I can't say yes. It's too much. I would be in your space all day, then at work too..."

His sigh, unlike mine, sounds more frustrated than nervous or tired. "How many times do I have to tell you? You're not a bother. I don't mind being around you, and I sure as fuck would rather have you protected under my roof than living at some goddamn apartment that almost got broken into."

I focus on that *protected under my roof* as if my life depended on it.

"It's only temporary," he adds, "until you find a proper place to live."

He has a point. He has many points, in fact, but I still can't say yes. I can't move in with Travis.

If the ground opened under my feet and swallowed me now, I wouldn't complain.

"What about rent?" I ask for some dumb reason. I don't want him to think I'm considering it because I'm not.

Travis crosses his arms over his chest and pins me down with one of his no-bullshit stares. "What about it?"

If this big, dumb idiot tells me I won't have to pay rent...

"How much would I owe you? Because I *am* paying rent in the very hypothetical case that I agree to move in with you temporarily. It's nonnegotiable."

He must recognize the determination in my voice because he says, "We'll agree on something."

"How much?" I press.

He rattles off an amount that is totally below the average rent price for this area, especially for a farmhouse, but I also recognize this is a battle I won't win. If I'm stubborn, he's stubborn times ten.

"What about bills?" I ask next, as if living with Travis didn't have the potential to become a terrible idea.

"The amount I just told you covers everything." My ass it covers everything—it's too low, and he knows it. "Consider it. You don't have to give me an answer now."

I shake my head, still unable to believe this is happening.

"I can't accept, Travis. I'm sorry. I'll just stay at the hotel until I find an apartment. I really appreciate what you're trying to do, but—"

"Allie," he says in a way he never has before. He sounds tired, defeated, and it makes me stop and watch him more closely. Those eyes matching the green beads around his wrist seem to turn a shade softer when he looks at me. "You can't live in a hotel forever. You know this."

There's no heat in his voice, no other emotion but exhaustion. And just like that, I know what the problem is.

"You don't have to stay next door anymore," I tell him, releasing him from his shackles. The smile I give him is meant to make my words sound more convincing. "I'm feeling much better now. You don't have to keep playing babysitter."

"You think I'm playing babysitter?"

Long gone is that soft Travis from a second ago, now replaced by his usual gruff self.

I have no clue what his endgame is. This hermit-man who doesn't even *befriend* his staff suddenly wants me to move in with him? I don't get it. And I'm tired of wondering.

"Why?" I ask him, ignoring his question. "Why are you doing this for me? Why are you going out of your way so drastically?"

He lets out a deep sigh, that huge hand moving to the back of his head before his eyes pin me down again.

"Because I want you to be safe at all times, goddammit. If anything happened to you..."

I hold my breath.

Travis shakes his head and drops his gaze. "I understand if you don't want to stay with me or think it's weird, but I'm not gonna let you deal with this alone. If you wanna stay at the hotel, let me pay for it."

At this point, the one butterfly I allowed in my stomach has multiplied so dramatically, there's no point in trying to count them anymore or tell them to go away—not when Travis opens his mouth and says things like that.

For my own sake, what I should do is thank him again and insist that he doesn't have to offer me a room at his place or pay for my hotel room. In a perfect world, I would be too scared to get closer to Travis and risk him noticing my feelings for him or asking more questions about my past.

But then I remember something else, something that weighs more than all those worries combined.

The night he spent at my apartment, awake just in case something happened, was the safest I've felt since I left California. And even in my parents' house, I would still be on edge after what happened with Claudia. They'd gotten arrested, but what if someone else came to finish the job? With how many pictures of the outside of our house my parents posted online, finding our address was child's play.

Maybe it's his size, his intimidating presence, or his military past—or all of it—but if I had to trust someone, just one person in the entire world to keep me safe, it would be him. Without a doubt, it would be Travis.

So would it really be that bad to stay at his farmhouse for a few days or weeks, until I can find my own place?

"Are you a hundred percent sure about me moving in?" I ask him carefully.

"Yes."

"A thousand percent?"

"Yes."

"A million percent?"

I finally get that grunt. "Allie."

"Promise me you won't kill me or sell my organs?"

If I had the slightest, tiniest doubt that Travis would hurt me, I would've kicked him out the second he knocked at my door the other day. Heck, I wouldn't be working here in the first place. He must know I'm only joking.

I'm not disappointed by his answer. "Your organs are safe with me. You promise your stubbornness won't kill me?"

"I don't think I can. My stubbornness is pretty deadly."

The fake-tired sigh he lets out next makes me smile. "You can move out of my place whenever you want to," he adds.

I appreciate his reassurance more than he'd ever know. "I'd like to see your house first, if that's okay."

"Of course. Does tomorrow morning work for you?"

"Tomorrow? As in, Christmas morning?"

"My uncle has plans with his friends, and mine won't be angry if I miss lunch. We can be done before then anyway."

Right. It makes sense. "Okay."

I stare at the small key between my hands, the key to my freaking boss's house. When I woke up this morning, this was pretty much the last thing I expected to happen today, but I can't find it in me to complain.

"Keep it," that gravelly voice says as he gestures to the key with his chin. "If you like the house, I'll help you move all your stuff."

I'm not stupid enough to turn down his help, even if I don't have many belongings anyway. But I'm stupid enough to have his words echo inside my head for the rest of the night.

Because I want you to be safe at all times, goddammit. If anything happened to you...

I might not survive moving in with Travis Ward after all.

Chapter Twenty-Two

It shouldn't surprise me that Travis spends another night sleeping in the hotel room next to mine. And when he knocks at my door on Christmas morning and offers to drive me to his farmhouse, I have to make a conscious effort to suppress last night's memories.

If anything happened to you...

He probably meant it in a *I don't want to look for a replacement because you're such an amazing waitress and accountant, so it would be a pain in my ass if you left* kind of way, and I should get over it.

Easier said than done.

On our drive, my head fills with all sorts of anxiety-inducing thoughts, such as how the hell I'm going to tell Jada and Paul that I'm moving in with my boss. And why.

"I forgot to ask you," Travis says after not uttering a single word during most of our drive to his house. "I've got two dogs. Is that gonna be a problem?"

"Not at all. I love dogs. What kinds of dogs do you have?"

"Both are Great Danes." He peels his eyes from the empty

road for a second and gives me a quick perusal. "They're not much shorter than you when they're on all fours."

The words *on all fours* shouldn't leave Travis's mouth ever again.

"Oh" is the brilliant response I give him, too focused on the heat climbing up my neck, all the way to my cheeks. *Stop. Am I fourteen?* But because that's not a socially acceptable answer, I add, "I hope they like me."

"They will," he says with so much confidence, it eases some of my nerves, but not enough that my heartbeat doesn't pick up when he pulls into a dirt road.

A couple of turns later, the trees give way to a massive farm-house with a barn, and my palms start sweating.

"This is the place," he announces.

His house looks modern, as if it had been renovated recently, and sits by the edge of Bannport Lake. On the horizon and across the water, acres of green land and rolling hills extend as far as the eye can see. It feels like being inside a painting.

No sooner has Travis parked his truck by the barn than I hear the barks.

My boss kills the engine and says, "Let me get out first and make sure the dogs aren't too excited."

Because they'll probably tackle me to the ground, I'm sure he wants to say. I wouldn't be opposed to such a sweet death.

Turning in my seat, I watch as two ginormous dogs come running toward Travis, now standing behind the car with his hands on his hips. He gestures with his hand, and both dogs slow their pace. They sit down a few feet away from their owner, tongues hanging from those cute faces, waiting for a new order.

I won't lie—that was one of the hottest things I've ever seen. Travis oozes authority and confidence on a normal day, but seeing him in his element, on his property, interacting with his dogs, is something else entirely.

When did it get so hot in here?

His knuckles tapping on my window bring me back to reality. "You can come out now."

I open the door slowly, careful not to startle the massive dogs. And when my feet hit the gravelly ground, I take in the most majestic creatures I've ever seen. Both have short black fur, but the one on the right has a bit of white on their snout, which is adorable.

"Oh my god. Aren't you some cute giants?" I look at my boss, whose eyes are already on me. "What are their names? How old are they? Are they boys or girls? Sorry, too many questions."

Is that a hint of a smile?

"Both are boys—brothers. They belonged to a friend of my uncle's, but he passed away three years ago, and I took them in. This one—" He points to the one with the all-black fur. "—is Buddy. His brother is Cooper. They're both five."

My heart swells. "Can I pet them?"

His eyes stay on me for a second too long before he says, "Come here."

I move slowly, trying not to startle them, until I'm standing with Travis. Buddy and Cooper look between their owner and me, probably questioning who I am and what I'm doing at their house. But their tongues are still hanging from their mouths, so they can't be too annoyed. I hope.

Travis puts a hand on the small of my back and guides me forward. "Let them sniff you. Not many people come by, aside from my uncle and a couple of friends, so they aren't used to company. But they're good boys."

He drops his hand, and I try not to feel too upset about it.

I also tell myself it's none of my business if one of those

friends is a woman or if they're more than friends. Instead, I focus on the two snouts sniffing my jacket. Travis wasn't joking —they're huge up close.

And because my heart was never meant to survive this man, Travis tells the dogs, "She's a friend, all right? Be gentle with her."

He *talks* to them. Also, me? A friend? Sure, we have friendship bracelets now, but I didn't think he took those seriously.

Also, what happened to *not* befriending his staff?

They don't react when I pet them—in fact, they ignore me a bit—which I take as a good sign. If they didn't approve of me, I guess they would growl or something, but they look as relaxed as they do with Travis.

"Want to see the interior of the house?"

The sun peeking through the clouds makes me squint as I glance up at him. "Sure. Are they allowed inside?"

Travis rubs their chins as both dogs try to lick his hands.

"Under normal circumstances, no. They are too big and knock everything down without meaning to. I keep the barn open, and their food, water, and doghouses are in there. But if there's a big storm, I'll allow them inside until it passes. They've never been too interested in coming inside the house anyway. They love it out here." He tips his chin toward the house. "Follow me."

I've never been inside a man's house before, so I don't know what to expect of Travis's. A bit of chaos, maybe a forgotten sock lying in the middle of the hallway. But the only word that comes to mind when I cross the threshold is...wow. Plainly and simply, *wow*.

Shiny wooden floors, cream-colored walls decorated with pictures of the Maine landscape, and spacious and sunny rooms meet my eyesight in all directions. There's a masculine air to his place that feels cozy.

"This is the living room." Travis stops behind the massive couch in front of a big flat-screen TV. Right next to it is the kitchen and dining area. "You can buy whatever food you want for yourself. If you don't want me to eat it, just let me know. You can eat my food if you want."

I try not to sound too awkward. "It's all right. We can share meals. I could cook for both of us."

He sends me an unreadable look over his shoulder as we move across the hall. "You're not my housekeeper."

I frown at his comment. "I never said I was or wanted to be."

Travis pauses in front of a closed door at the end of the hall. "You don't have to cook for me."

"What if I want to?"

"You don't have to."

"You didn't have to offer me a place to live, yet here we are."

I get one of those frustrated sighs that make him so endearing. "We'll see."

He opens the door to a sunny bedroom with white walls, flowy curtains, a big dresser, and a four-poster bed, big enough to have at least three people sleep on it.

"This is your bedroom," he says, as if I had already accepted his move-in offer. To be fair, after seeing this house, declining is becoming more unappealing by the second. "Let me show you the bathroom."

Conveniently, it's right next door. I peek inside and see a modern shower, a toilet, and a small sink. Everything looks and smells clean—no mold in sight, unlike my own apartment I haven't stepped foot in in almost a week.

"This will be your private bathroom," Travis says. "I never use it, but if someone comes to visit, they might."

"That's fine. You have your own bathroom?"

"It's attached to my bedroom."

"Fancy." I smile up at him. "You said there were three bedrooms?"

We pass by a door he doesn't open but lets me know is his bedroom, and we end the tour in the smallest bedroom across from his. When I look inside, I blink.

"It's empty," I say, as if he didn't live here and know already.

There's nothing here—not a bed, not a desk, not even storage boxes or a home gym. Nothing.

"Never got around to buying anything for this room," he explains, but there's a weird edge to his voice that tells me there's something else to it.

Even though I'm curious, I don't pry. Everyone is allowed to have their own secrets—I would know.

"So... this is your place." I steal a look at the dogs running outside through the window. When I turn to Travis, his eyes are already on me. "It's beautiful."

I cross my arms, glancing away from the first man I've ever felt completely safe around.

Would it really be so bad to say yes? I'd have my own bedroom and bathroom, and I'd sleep soundly every night knowing Travis is just down the hall and two massive dogs protect the property at all times. There's no way anyone would even dare think of breaking into his place.

Maybe hiding out in the lair with the big bear is exactly what this scared rabbit needs.

"What do you say?" Travis stands tall and imposing. My eyes land on the green beads around his wrist. "Do you want to move in with me?"

Chapter Twenty-Three

Age 18

"Are you one thousand percent sure about this, Allie?"

Under normal circumstances, Jada's frown would've made me rethink the whole ordeal, but not when it came to this.

"I've never been more sure about anything."

It was a quiet summer night on Jada and Paul's front porch, just a couple months after my eighteenth birthday. We were sitting in their rocking chairs, a small table between us. She'd made *pollo guisado* for dinner, then surprised me with my favorite salted caramel ice cream. My parents thought I was at a friend's house, and life was good for the first time in too long.

"Changing your name is a big decision," she insisted. "I will support you if this is what you want, but please think carefully."

"I have, Jada. For three years." In my sitting position, I drew my legs against my chest. "I want to do it. I want a new life away from my family and everything they did to me."

Reaching over the small table separating us, she grabbed my hand and gave it a reassuring squeeze. "I understand, Allie. I really do. You deserve a good life more than anyone else I know."

I shifted my gaze to the fairy lights on the porch, willing myself to keep the tears bottled up.

Grateful didn't begin to cover how I'd always felt about having Jada in my life. Her support, her guidance, and her love were the only reasons I managed to push through.

She had been the only adult to go out of their way to *really* check on me after Claudia. She hadn't agreed with my family forcing me to be in videos and pictures and knew how much it hurt me socially at school. After my kidnapping, she promised me she'd always be there for me even when she wasn't my teacher anymore—a promise she'd kept.

Jada and her husband were the only adults I trusted and felt safe with. Their spare bedroom had become my safe haven when I couldn't stand being at home. I spent most days there now that I was over eighteen and my parents didn't have so much control over me.

Which was why it hurt to say my next words.

"I also want to move away," I said quietly. "From California. Go somewhere far. I can't stand living here any longer. Not after...you know."

She gave me a sad but understanding smile. "Of course. You go on and explore the world in freedom. You'll always have a home here if you change your mind."

I nodded, my throat closing with emotion. "Thank you."

"Do you know where you want to go?" she asked. "My sister has a pretty big property in Dallas. I could ask her if she has a spare room for you. That way, you'll have your freedom, but also the safety of knowing somebody in a new city."

"I'd love that. I was thinking of leaving in a few months. Maybe next year. I want to plan things very carefully."

"Whenever you're ready, honey."

Night crickets and the wind chime on her porch were the only sounds for a while. I was deep in thought, feeling more confident with every passing second that changing my name and leaving California was the right choice, when Jada spoke again.

"You know," she started, "I have a feeling you'll come back."

That made me frown. "To LA?" She hummed, and I snorted. "No way."

"Never say never, Allie. I also have a feeling life will surprise you in very unexpected ways."

"All good ways, I hope?"

Her smile was soft. "In the end, they'll all be."

Chapter Twenty-Four

I'VE BEEN PACING IN CIRCLES AROUND THIS EXACT SPOT FOR what feels like hours, phone in hand, my mind working at a million miles per hour.

Realistically, Jada and Paul have to know about my new living situation—and I want to tell them. No matter how many times I tell myself my lies and omissions are my only way of surviving, it's starting to feel like an excuse rather than a real reason.

I want to do the right thing, the honest thing, and that is to unlock my phone, dial her number, and have this conversation. So why can't I?

The afternoon sunlight filters through the treetops and warms my face. Despite the cold, I take advantage of the sunshine of the second-to-last day of the year and shut my eyes, seeking its calm.

Just like he promised, Travis helped me move into his spare bedroom the day after I toured his farmhouse. I'm officially out of that moldy apartment, and I can say with full confidence that I'll never miss that place—good riddance.

Then I spent my first night here, under the same roof as

Travis but in my own space, and it was... weird but also oddly comforting. I fell asleep at three in the morning, too alert to fully relax when it was so calm outside.

For the past five days, Travis hasn't been in the house when I woke up. I don't know if he always gets up that early or if he did it on purpose so I didn't feel uncomfortable with him there, but I hope it isn't the latter.

For five days, we haven't talked much and barely saw each other outside of The Lair. At home, he's always out in the barn doing something while I eat dinner, and then I hear him come back when I'm already in my room.

I'm not dumb—I know he's avoiding me. I just have no idea why.

Still, this is the happiest I've been in a really long time. In part because I feel safer, in part because I accepted Travis's offer to handle the bar's accounting and love my new position, and in part because I met Lola for coffee two days ago.

Our coffee meet-up didn't last longer than an hour, but in that time, she told me about her little brother, the yoga classes she attends at a local gym and how I should join her, and growing up in Bannport.

She was curious about what it was like to live in Los Angeles, but luckily, she didn't ask too many questions—which meant my lies didn't get out of control. I was afraid she would recognize me, but nothing in her body language or actual words gave me that impression. We agreed to meet up again after New Year's.

Maybe my life is truly changing for good.

I spot Buddy and Cooper sniffing around the lake and decide I need to do this before Travis gets here. This is my afternoon off, and I plan to surprise him with homemade pizza when he gets back if he doesn't ignore me again, so this call has to happen now.

Taking a deep breath through my nose, I look at Jada's contact on my phone and remind myself this is the person who cares the most about me in the world. Of course, she's going to lose her mind a little when I tell her about my new home, but she'll come to terms with it. She'll support me, just like she always does.

Before that small window of positivity closes, I press the Call button.

"Honey?" The excitement in her voice makes me feel bad for what I'm about to tell her. "How are you? Did you have a nice Christmas?"

We video chatted that day, but my move was so recent, I couldn't bring myself to tell them the news then.

I swallow down my nerves. "Hi, Jada. I had a busy day with a rom-com and a few glasses of wine." That part is true. I made the most of my last night in that hotel. "How about you guys?"

I listen with a genuine smile as she tells me about their Christmas Day and how grown their nieces and nephews are. Jada and Paul might not have or want to have children, but they are the closest parental figures I have. I could never, not in this lifetime or the next, thank them enough for all they've done and continue to do for me.

"Paul finally got his electric bike for Christmas, so he can't complain," she jokes. "But we don't have plans for the New Year yet. I think we might end up having a cozy night at home. We aren't getting any younger."

I roll my eyes even if she can't see me, a smile on my face. "Please. You guys don't look a day over forty, and you know it."

I'm met with a genuine laugh. "Remind me to call you every single hour for confidence boosts."

"You know I'll be down for that."

"You're too nice, Allie. Do you have plans for New Year's?"

Lola and Charlie mentioned a get-together by the lake to

watch the fireworks, but I don't know if I'll go. "I might hang out with some friends."

"That sounds amazing, honey," she says, her voice soft and motherly and everything that is good in the world. "Are they good to you?"

"They're all really nice to me." I clear my throat and try not to feel like the most horrible person alive for what I'm about to do. "Jada, there's... there's something I need to tell you."

The mood shifts. As if she were right in front of me, I feel the tension radiating off her body. And when she asks, "What is it?" in that clipped voice I haven't heard in a very long time, I know I can't back down.

I've been thinking about how I'm going to break the news for days, and because I still have no clue what the best tactic is, I decide to be blunt about it.

"Someone tried to break into my apartment, and I had to move out."

Silence.

A heavy weight settles in the pit of my stomach, but I keep talking.

"I'm okay. They didn't get in. I know that doesn't make you feel better, but... yeah. I called the police, and they said they were going to deal with them, whoever they are. Apparently, I was living in a not-so-safe area, so they think someone drank too much or got too high and... you know."

I decide not to tell her about the car because I don't want to make her even more worried.

When she says nothing, I check that she's still on the other side of the line. She is.

"Jada?"

It takes another couple seconds to finally hear her voice. "That's... that's a lot to process, Allie. Are you okay? You said

188

you weren't hurt? Where did you move to? Do you want us to fly out there?"

"You don't have to come here. I'm fine, really. I was a bit shaken up at the time, but I feel much better now. I'm not hurt at all."

"Allie..." she starts. "Allie, are you sure you want to stay in Bannport?"

"Yes." I'm surprised by how quickly my answer comes out. It's honest too. "I do, Jada. I didn't expect to, but I feel at home here. I think... I think I'm starting to build a life here, a life I really like."

"Okay," she concedes. "If you think that's the right choice, you know we'll support you. We just want you to be safe, honey, and what you've just told me..." Another pause. I can only imagine what's going through her mind right now. "You never said where you've moved to. I'm assuming you're still in town."

"I've been apartment hunting for a while, but there's nothing available within my budget that isn't a holiday rental," I start, pacing around in circles again. The sun is about to set, and the air is getting colder, but I barely feel it—my heart is beating way too fast, and my armpits are sweaty. "I stayed at a hotel for a bit, but, um, Travis offered me one of the spare bedrooms at his farmhouse until I could find a place."

There's confusion in her voice as she asks, "Travis? I thought he was your boss. Or is he one of your friends?"

"Travis is my boss," I confirm.

"Is he... I thought he was married?"

The mental picture of Travis having an imaginary wife who is obviously a thousand times hotter, funnier, prettier, and smarter than I am makes me nauseous. But that is a problem for another day.

"He's single. No kids either." And then, for some stupid reason, I add, "It isn't weird or anything. I promise. He's a great man, and I feel comfortable here. It's only temporary. He didn't want me to pay rent, but I insisted."

"This is a lot to take in," she repeats, her words followed by a deep sigh. "Are you sure you're okay? I know you can take care of yourself, but do you promise you'll tell me if you need help of any kind?"

"I promise." I hope she can hear the honesty in my voice. "I'm really okay. Better than I've been in a while, in fact. I got a promotion at work."

Because of course I had to throw that in there. I don't know if I thought that would make her feel better about this whole mess, but at least she sounds interested and not so freaked out when she asks, "A promotion of what kind?"

My chest feels lighter as I say, "I offered to handle the accounts at the bar, and Travis accepted. I'm so pumped about this, Jada. All the online courses I took weren't for nothing after all."

"Of course they weren't for nothing. Even if you'd never used them, they helped your brain stay active, and you did something you enjoyed and are good at. That's just as important," she says, turning into the schoolteacher I miss so much. "We're proud of you, honey. Really proud of you."

Don't cry. "I love you guys."

"And we love you, but I'm still worried. Paul will be, too, when I tell him later."

I swallow the uncomfortable lump in my throat. "I'm truly okay now. Travis has two massive guard dogs, cameras, and he's an ex-Navy SEAL. I'll be fine. I feel safe here."

"That's all really good." There's a but coming. I feel it in my bones. "But I'm worried that living with your boss could compromise your position at the bar."

It's a reasonable concern to have—and one that has crossed my mind before—but I say, "This is only temporary. And

Travis... he's not the most social person, so I rarely see him at home anyway. We don't argue about laundry or dirty dishes or anything like that."

She doesn't sound too convinced. "Well, as long as you can keep your professional relationship separate, I suppose it will be fine."

"It will." And this time, I'm confident it's not wishful thinking. It's about time my life starts looking up. "I'm going to make dinner. We'll talk soon, okay?"

"Okay, honey. We love you, and please take care. I'll call you tomorrow."

"All right. I love you too."

There's no denying that Jada is worried—and I get why—but I also appreciate how much genuine trust she puts in me and my decisions. And it's that reminder that gets me through the rest of the afternoon as I put away some clean laundry and make two pizzas for dinner.

Some time later, the front door opens, then slams closed, and my boss walks in.

"Allie?" he calls out. When he comes into view, his frown is as deep as it can get. "What are you doing?"

All right, I'll give it to him—it's the first time he comes home, and he sees me sitting on his kitchen floor, watching the oven.

"Chilling."

He doesn't look amused.

"What are you doing?" he repeats, even though I've already answered his question.

"I'm making pizzas for dinner. There's one for you if you want."

Travis ignores that, his imposing body looming above mine, looking even bigger when he puts his hands on his hips. "Get up. You'll catch a cold sitting there."

"I'll be fine." I give him a small smile, hoping to get one in

191

return or—at the very least—a frownless expression. I get neither. "I'm watching them, so they don't get burned."

"They won't," he grunts. "Get up."

Travis holds out a hand in my direction. "Come on."

I try not to overthink it too much as I slide my much-smaller palm into his.

Once I'm on my feet, I let go of his hand before he does it himself and makes my heart do one of those uncomfortable drops.

"Dinner should be ready in ten. Are you hungry?"

I'll take his grunt as a yes. "You didn't have to cook for me."

"And you didn't have to offer me a room here, but alas. It's not like I'm being forced to do it, boss man. I'm doing it because I want to. I love cooking. It's relaxing."

"Don't call me that."

"Don't call you what? Boss man?"

"We're not at work."

I shrug. "Fair enough."

I watch as he takes his winter jacket off, his biceps flexing with the motion. "I'm gonna get changed."

He disappears down the hallway without another word, and I take a moment to breathe. In and out, and again.

Travis is his own person, and I like him just the way he is. Grumpy edges and all. I shouldn't expect him to do a one-eighty just because I'm now living here.

He doesn't come back until the pizzas are done, and I don't think I've struggled so much to take something out of the oven before. Not because these pizzas are particularly heavy, but because Travis is wearing sweatpants. Gray ones.

"Need help?" he asks as he enters the kitchen, making my cheeks grow hotter than the stupid oven.

"It's fine. I got it." I set one of the trays down and reach for the other one. "I hope you like pepperoni and cheese. I didn't get too creative."

He starts cutting the pizzas into small triangles. "Smells great, Allie. Thanks for dinner."

Is that my heart soaring a little? I think so.

"It's nothing. Where do you usually eat? I'll grab us some plates."

"You cooked. I got it from here," he decides. "The couch is fine. You can go sit down."

It hits me then, as I sit on the couch, that I've never hung out here. For some reason, I didn't feel like I was allowed to be in the living room even though Travis explicitly told me I could hang out in every room of the house except his bedroom—as if.

Travis comes back a couple of minutes later, carrying two plates full of pizza slices. He sets them on the coffee table and goes back to grab two glasses of water and some napkins. Then he sits on the other end of the couch, as far from me as he can without falling off the edge. I try not to let it bother me too much.

"Wanna watch something?" he asks, his eyes glued to the TV he's just turned on.

"Sure."

I don't know what I expected Travis to put on, but a sitcom wasn't it. Two episodes later, both pizzas are gone thanks to my boss's insane appetite. I mean, I get it—he has to sustain that ginormous body. I overheard him once saying he works out a few times a week, so it makes sense that he needs the energy.

Wordlessly, he gets up and carries our empty plates to the kitchen once we're done. And then he comes back, turns off the light, and sits back down on his side of the couch.

This is fine. Totally fine. We've just had a homemade dinner together, and now we're watching TV like friends would do. No biggie.

Did I mention he's wearing gray sweatpants?

The show we're watching is one of my favorites, but I find it hard to concentrate on anything but the man sitting only a few inches away. I steal the quickest glance at him, and I regret it only a second later. His sitting position is relaxed, both of his legs open. One of his hands is holding his head that is tilted to the side, and the other hangs loosely over his thigh. A thigh I bet would be more comfortable than this couch.

I don't want to climb into his lap. Get a grip.

It's late and dark, and I'm exhausted. It must be that. So when the current episode ends, I turn to Travis.

"If I don't go to bed now, I'll fall asleep on your couch and drool all over it, and neither of us wants that." Is that a tiny smile? "Have a good night, Travis."

He tips his chin. "Good night, Allie."

As I head for my bedroom, I can't help but do a little victory dance in my head. I survived tonight. I had dinner with Travis and behaved like a normal human being.

"Allie. Wait."

He's on his way to the hallway, only a few feet away, when I turn around.

"Yeah?"

Something weird happens next. Travis, the man who oozes confidence from every pore in his body, hesitates. He opens and closes his mouth once before frowning, as if he couldn't believe he's struggling with whatever he wants to say.

Huh.

But this is still Travis, which means he recovers quickly.

"There's a New Year's party by the lake coming up. A few of us are going."

This must be the gathering Charlie and Lola told me about. But why is he bringing it up?

"Would you like to come with me?"

With me.

I wasn't going to go, so what does it say about me that it suddenly sounds like the best plan in the world?

"You can say no if you have other plans," he says, voice all husky.

If he's dying to get an answer from me—which I doubt is the case—I decide to cut his suffering short.

"It sounds fun," I say with a smile. "I'd love to go with you."

He tips his chin once. "All right. Night, Allie."

I wave at him over my shoulder as I resume the walk back to my bedroom. "'Night, boss man."

When I hear him grunt in annoyance behind me, I don't hold in the laughter.

Chapter Twenty-Five

"WEAR SOMETHING WARM OR YOU'LL FREEZE TO DEATH," Travis tells me the morning of the New Year's Eve party.

I should've listened.

It's not that I'm wearing a tiny dress and showing my bare skin, but I underestimated how cold it was going to be. My puffer jacket, wool hat, and thick scarf are barely keeping me warm as I try my hardest not to chatter my teeth.

"It's cold as balls, isn't it?" Charlie comments before taking a sip of his mulled wine. He points at the makeshift tent whoever organized the party put over this area in case it rained. "It's not doing shit."

"It's really not," Lola agrees, puffing hot air into her gloved hands. I curse myself for forgetting my own gloves at home.

"Just one more hour until midnight." Charlie finishes his drink. "You'd be warmer if you drank something hot. Want me to get you something, Allie Cat? Maybe some mulled wine?"

I'm tempted, but I tell him, "No, thanks. I'll be fine."

If I got drunk and Travis had to drag me to his house, I would never recover. And I've already embarrassed myself in front of that man enough to last several lifetimes, thank you very much.

Speaking of my boss, I have no idea where he is. We left his farmhouse together, and I saw Uncle Neil and Barbara when we got here, but after Charlie and Lola spotted me and brought me into their friend group, I lost sight of Travis.

"Hey, guys." One of Charlie's friends—Tom—returns with a beer in hand and a mildly drunk smile on his face. I met him an hour ago, and he seems harmless enough despite the wink he throws my way. "Are you having a good time?"

He's a little older than us, said he works in the entertainment industry, and is visiting his family for Christmas. I tell myself there's no harm in talking to this guy even if he's a little flirty. Didn't I want to become more social? It could be my New Year's resolution.

"I can't feel my hands or my nose, but yeah. How about you?"

He smiles. "More than great."

"Leave my Allie Cat alone," Charlie says, but there's no heat in his voice. I think he's too drunk for that.

A slight breeze hits my face, and I give up on my fight to stop my teeth from chattering. I should've brought a freaking quilt. Or better yet, I should've stayed under the very warm roof of Travis's house.

"I'm just playing around," Tom says, sliding an arm around Charlie's shoulders as he chugs down his beer, his eyes on me. "You know that, right?"

I try my hardest not to wince. "Totally."

Tom opens his mouth to say something else, but he doesn't get the chance.

Something heavy and warm settles over my shoulders then, its weight so sudden that my heart leaps with panic. But Charlie is glancing over my shoulder and isn't exactly hiding his smile, so it must not be a serial killer.

"I told you to wear warm clothes."

I don't need to look behind me to know who that deep voice belongs to.

"I'm wearing warm clothes," I argue, a white cloud coming out of my lips.

My cheeks heat up—and not from the sudden warmth—when I notice my body has disappeared under a gigantic snow jacket that can only belong to one man.

"You've been shivering for the past hour," my boss says, all while keeping both of his hands on my shoulders. He must notice we're not alone because he adds, "Charlie."

"Hey, boss." My friend and co-worker glances between us with a playful glint in his eyes I could kill him for. "Did you come to take Allie Cat away?"

His fingers splay across my shoulders, so long that they reach the base of my neck. His touch isn't rough or demanding, but a steady presence that reminds me he's here. That he's got my back.

Or maybe I'm reading too much into it.

"Unless you want to stay," he tells me, his breath grazing my ear.

His thumbs start applying pressure in the back of my neck, massaging it. *Oh God.*

"Allie Cat?" Charlie eyes me with a knowing look, which makes me think he probably said something I didn't hear because my head is full of not-so-appropriate thoughts about the man at my back.

"I'll go with Travis for a bit," I manage to say, my heart beating so fast, I'm afraid the whole party can hear it.

It's Lola who gives me a knowing smile and says, "You guys have fun."

I don't imagine the hands that leave my shoulders to travel down my arms, only for one to settle on my back. Wordlessly, I wave goodbye at them and follow Travis into the throng awaiting the New Year.

We don't stop until we reach an area surrounded by food trucks and picnic tables. Sitting at one of them are Uncle Neil, Barbara, and a few of Travis's friends I recognize from that birthday party at the bar.

"Allie-girl." Uncle Neil throws his wrinkly hands in the air when he sees me, a huge smile on his lips. He gets up with more ease than I would've expected from a seventy-something-year-old and pulls me into a hug, away from his nephew's touch. "What the hell are you wearing? I'm not up-to-date with the latest fashion trends."

I smile and hug him back. "I'm afraid I'm not either. This is Travis's jacket."

He gives me a friendly pat on my cheek, reminding me of the grandfather I never met. "Is my boy good to you?"

"He's the best." I have no clue if Uncle Neil knows about my new living situation, so I don't bring it up. I lean in conspiratorially. "But he's a big grump."

The old man throws his head back in laughter. "Won't argue with you on that. You two sit with us. I'll get drinks."

Travis doesn't sit with me, instead choosing to stand behind my seat, his hands bracing on my backrest. The gesture feels intimate for some reason.

Barbara leans over the table and gives me a smile. "I didn't know you were coming tonight, Allie. Are you having fun?"

Snuggled in Travis's snow jacket, I spend the next hour talking to everyone from Uncle Neil to Barbara to some of Travis's friends and other people I don't know the names of. Everyone treats me like I've been part of their inner circle for years. They all want to know what Travis is like as a boss, which

I find funny because I know they expected some dirt, but I have nothing but good things to say about him.

Except that some days it feels like something crawled up his ass and died there, which gets me a bunch of laughs and a shoulder squeeze from the man behind me.

"The fireworks are gonna start any minute now," Uncle Neil says after a while, promptly standing from his seat and holding out a hand in Barbara's direction. "Let's move closer to the shore before it gets too crowded."

Something between worry and warning passes in his eyes when he looks at his nephew next, and I get a weird feeling in the pit of my stomach. But I brush it off, concluding that maybe it has something to do with Uncle Neil's health, and I don't have a right to ask about that.

Barbara clings to Uncle Neil's arm, both heading for the lake, and I can't help but go up to my boss and ask him the one thing I can't stop thinking about.

"Travis," I half whisper once I'm close enough. He falls into step beside me. "Are Barbara and your uncle... you know, a thing?"

He raises an eyebrow. "A thing?"

"You know what I mean."

"I don't," he says, but when I glance up at him, the corner of his lips is twitching upward. *Cute.*

I nudge his hard arm. "Come on. Give me a free pass to be nosey."

My eyes might be playing tricks on me, but I'm pretty sure that's a smirk on his face. "I didn't peg you for a busybody."

"I have my moments."

"You do, huh?" The weight of his hand moves up to my shoulder, the one furthest from him. And I don't overthink it too much as those long, thick fingers span around it, holding me against him as we walk. "She's his special friend."

"What does that even mean?"

"It means they're partners. My uncle says he's too old for girlfriends, and he doesn't want to get married." He drops his hand when our group stops moving just a few feet away from the water. "Does that satisfy your curiosity?"

"Kinda." And because I want to take advantage of one of his very rare playful moods, I gather the courage I didn't know I had and ask him, "What about you?"

His eyes remain on the lake, his head towering above everybody else's. "What about me?"

He's playing coy. Too bad my boldness is bigger than my fear of rejection tonight.

"Do you have a special friend?"

I'm not imagining the way his body leans into mine. "Why do you want to know?"

I've never been more grateful for the darkness as I feel my cheeks heating up. "I'm a busybody, remember?"

I tune out the loud crowd around us, too aware of the man beside me. A small eternity seems to go by before I get an answer.

"No special friends for me. Haven't had one in a while."

"Oh." I hate myself a little for being so relieved about this before I realize it wouldn't matter. Travis is my boss and landlord, and nothing is going to happen between us. Ever.

"I don't have any special friends either," I say because I want him to know this for some reason.

He takes me aback by asking, "What about Charlie?"

"Charlie?" That gets him a frown. "You think I'm dating Charlie?"

He slides me an unreadable look. "Maybe not dating, but something else."

He thinks I'm sleeping with him?

I fight the urge to gag. Charlie is like a younger brother to me. Just the thought of him like *that* makes my stomach turn. But on the outside, my stare is nothing but calm. "Why? Because I hugged him once?"

When Travis looks away again, I don't miss the tick in his jaw. "You seem close."

Why does he sound so serious all of a sudden?

"Am I not allowed to be friends with my co-workers?" I ask him genuinely. If I'm doing something wrong that could cost me my job, I would like to know. Although, knowing Travis, if my friendship with Charlie were a real issue, he would've already warned me about it.

"Of course you are," he says. "Forget about it."

I don't understand why he's being so weird about this, but I don't have time to ask because the first explosion of red and blue goes off over our heads, and everyone around us starts cheering.

Parents put their children on their shoulders, and couples start snuggling against each other. Travis's arm is still touching the side of my body, and even though he might not hear me over the fireworks, I still say, "Charlie is just my friend. We don't have feelings for each other. Trust me on that."

I feel his scorching stare on my face, but my eyes stay on the sky.

Travis says nothing else as the fireworks show goes on. I'm enthralled by the beauty of it and the sense of being part of a community, of being surrounded by so many people for the first time in so long. I don't remember the last time I welcomed the New Year like this, and now that I've had a taste, I'm not sure I'll want to spend another December 31 alone.

I watch the fireworks until I notice something.

Every time a firework goes off, Travis flinches. It's a small twitch of his hands, almost imperceptible, but I see it.

Knowing Travis, he'll probably brush me off if I mention it.

But when he flinches again, I decide his grunt of rejection will be worth it.

"Are you okay?"

That hard gaze slides down to me, and he gives me one single nod.

A nod that means nothing three seconds later when another explosion brightens the night sky and his hand twitches again.

Without thinking about the implications or consequences, I grab Travis's hand and give it a squeeze. At first, I think he's going to pull away. That would be the most Travis thing to do in this situation.

Instead, he starts tracing soft circles on my skin with his thumb every time a firework goes off.

The cold in my body melts away at the tenderness of his touch, at the fact that he's seeking my comfort.

And for the first time, I wonder if there's a chance—a very tiny one—that Travis feels the same for me.

Chapter Twenty-Six

I sneak yet another glance at Travis. To the normal eye, he might look and sound perfectly fine, but not to me.

It's not often that I feel proud of my obsession with my boss. Although *obsession* might be a dramatic way to describe it. What I feel for Travis is... more like a crush that has gone off the rails.

And now, as I hear him sniffle for the umpteenth time as he cleans the tables, one thing becomes impossibly clear.

"Are you sick, boss man?"

He throws me a look over one of his wide shoulders. "No."

I scrunch my nose. "Try again."

He turns that massive body in my direction, pinning me down with a diluted hardened stare that tells me without words that I'm right. He doesn't even have the energy to be his usual crabby self, and I find that more hilarious than it probably is. It's not that I'm happy Travis is sick, but it *is* ironic, considering he was the one bugging me about catching a cold at the lake two days ago.

"I'm not sick," he says in that gruff voice that sounds just a tiny bit raspier today.

I arch a don't-bullshit-me eyebrow.

Without me having to add anything else, his chest rises and falls with a heavy breath before he admits, "I'm low on energy, not sick."

This man.

"Okay. Well, let me know if your energy levels drop even lower, all right? I can drive you home and make you some energy-powering soup."

He throws me another one of his not-so-pissed-off glares, but our conversation ends there as we go back to work. And if he catches me checking on him every five minutes for the next three hours, he doesn't comment on it.

I pride myself on being a patient woman, always waiting for the other person to be ready to talk, ask for help, or whatever they need. But by the time our shift ends, I've had enough. Because Travis's eyes have gotten droopier with each passing hour, his skin looks an unhealthy shade of pale, and he's still wearing his snow jacket inside his house as he scans the fridge.

"Travis," I call out. He either doesn't hear me or is pretending not to, so I insist. "Travis."

"Mm?" He finally acknowledges me, closing the fridge without having grabbed anything. "You hungry?"

I sigh and take a step in his direction, the tips of my socked feet nearly grazing his boots he still hasn't taken off. "Are you going somewhere?"

"No."

"Then why don't you change into your home clothes?" Which consist of sweatpants, thick socks, and an old T-shirt—a far cry from the snow jacket, hat, and military boots he's sporting now.

He narrows those green eyes at me. "I'm going to."

"Oh, yeah? Before or after you admit you're sick?"

I'm expecting him to fight back like he's been doing all day.

"Fine," he grunts. "I might have a headache. It's nothing."

"It's not nothing." I go up on my tiptoes and snatch his wool hat from over his head. "Come on, big grump. Go change. I'll take care of dinner."

Of course he argues. "You don't have to. I can cook."

I let out another tired sigh.

"You know you're handsome, but—no offense—you look terrible right now. Seconds away from passing out due to exhaustion, if you need specifics."

Travis's eyebrows go up a millimeter. "You think I'm handsome?"

There's a hint of *something* in his voice. Something I can't pinpoint right away because I don't hear it often from him. Is he flustered? The base of his neck looks redder, but it must be the fever.

I toy with his hat in my hands, his familiar smell drifting up to my nose. It's intoxicating.

"Don't change the subject," I tell him, my own neck and cheeks feeling warmer than just a moment ago. And then, to make things worse for myself, I grab his arm and walk him out of the kitchen. "Go change and wait for me on the couch. I got this."

He lets out a deep, I'm-about-to-argue breath. "Allie."

"Please, Travis." I turn to face him, my hand still around the rough fabric of his jacket. "Don't fight me on this. You're sick, and I want to take care of you. Who's going to boss us around at The Lair if you're sniffling and feeling miserable all day?"

I don't think I'm imagining how his stare softens. And I'm surely not imagining how he grabs his hat from my hands and places it over my head.

"You're something else, sweetheart."

He disappears down the hallway before I can process what just happened.

Shaking my head, I head back to the kitchen and get started on my signature chicken soup. I can't get so bent out of shape from a simple gesture he meant nothing by. I'm only clinging to a fantasy world in which Travis also feels this zapping electricity between us every time we're close.

In an attempt to get it together, I start chopping ingredients on the cutting board. And when I hear the shower running, I only imagine Travis naked twice.

The soup is almost ready by the time his heavy footsteps make his presence known. I make a herculean effort not to glance at his sweatpants—Travis wearing them should be illegal —and notice he ditched one of his usual T-shirts for a hoodie. Headache, *right*.

"Smells great," he comments as he grabs two bowls from one of the top cabinets I can't reach and sets them on the counter. And I don't say it, but I truly appreciate that he always compliments my cooking.

"This is almost ready," I tell him. "Wait for me on the couch?"

When he doesn't fight me, I know he must be feeling like hell.

"Did you take something for your headache?" I call out from the kitchen as I serve the soup moments later.

"Took a Tylenol before my shower," he answers.

He's leaning forward on the couch, legs open in a wide stance, the remote dangling from one of his hands. He's put some sitcom on TV, and all I can think about is how unfair it is that he still looks this attractive while sick.

Careful not to burn myself with the hot ceramic, I grab one bowl of soup, set it on the coffee table in front of Travis, then go back to the kitchen for the other. I take my—his—hat off next, but only because the central heating is starting to make me sweat.

I give him a small smile as I sit next to him on the comfortable couch—seriously, I could fall asleep here every night—then feel how hopelessly my heart cartwheels when he smiles back.

"Are your taste buds working?" I ask him after he takes the first sip of his soup.

He arches a curious eyebrow. "Huh?"

"Your taste buds." I wrap my hands around my bowl a little tighter, seeking its warmth. "When I'm sick, I always lose my sense of taste. It's so annoying because all I want is to eat comfort food, but everything tastes like cardboard."

His low chuckle travels directly to my lower stomach. "My taste buds are fine."

"You're one of the lucky ones, then."

He glances at me for a beat too long. "I am."

We go back to our soups, sitting in a comfortable silence with only the TV to fill it until he asks, "What's your comfort food?"

I finish up my soup before answering, "Carrot cake."

He smirks again. "Of course it is."

"What is that supposed to mean?" I feign outrage.

"You took home two slices when we celebrated Sandra's birthday last year." *He remembers.* "And you ordered some at Barbara's not that long ago."

"Guilty. It's my comfort food *and* my favorite food."

"I thought comfort food was supposed to be something hot with a lot of cheese."

"Maybe. I mean, I wouldn't say no to some grilled-cheese sandwiches when I'm feeling miserable. But because I lived alone for a long time, there was nobody to make them for me, and I didn't have the energy to cook. Store-bought carrot cake always did the trick. I'm not picky."

The admission slips out, and I don't realize it until he asks, "How long have you been on your own?"

With a sudden lump in my throat, I busy myself collecting our bowls now that he's finished, and I stand. "Since I was nineteen."

I head back to the kitchen and force myself to relearn how to breathe as I rinse the bowls before putting them in the dishwasher. I didn't lie to him, so why do I still feel like crap?

Travis is openly looking at me as I leave the kitchen.

"Can you turn off the living room light, please?" he asks softly. "The darkness helps with my headache."

Silently, I do as he says and plop back on my designated spot on the couch.

"Why nineteen?"

My palms get sweaty, but I can't find it within me to not answer. "Remember how I told you I had a... a difficult family life?"

"Something like that," he tells me as he reclines on the couch, draping an arm around the back. His fingers are almost grazing the back of my head. "You told me, *something like that*."

How does he have such a good memory?

"Well, that's why I left at nineteen. I waited until I was old enough and felt ready," I explain, not surprised to feel out of breath. Will it ever get easier to talk about this? "I'm not sure if I've ever told you about Jada."

"Is she an aunt?" He frowns, thinking. "You talk about her when Sandra asks about your family."

"She's technically not family, but..."

"Blood doesn't always make family," he says. The light coming from the TV casts a glow on his face, which looks softer than usual.

I give him a small nod. "I know."

"Good."

"Jada is... *was* my schoolteacher," I tell him for the first time.

"For a long time, she was the only adult I could rely on. Her husband too."

Travis tilts his head. "You don't talk to your parents anymore?"

I shake my head.

I can tell he wants to ask more questions, but I appreciate that he doesn't. More than he knows.

"Well," he starts, shifting on the couch. The warmth of his hand seeps into my skin, and it's not even touching my hair. "You've got us now too. Everyone at The Lair."

My throat clogs up. I never expected to end up in Bannport, let alone to get close to my co-workers. But in a little over a year, we've become a unit that makes me feel like I belong somewhere for the very first time.

"I'm here for you guys as well," I mutter in the darkness. I hope he can tell I mean every word.

It must be the fever messing with his brain chemicals is what I tell myself when, just a moment later, Travis's fingers tangle in my hair. My heartbeat comes to a halt, only to pick back up with a brutal force as he starts massaging my scalp.

I have no idea what's gotten into him, but I don't question it. I lean into his touch, not surprised that my body relaxes at once because he has that effect on me. He's the only one who makes me feel safe enough to turn my brain off.

Drawing my knees to my chest, I close my eyes and *breathe*. I enjoy the here and now, with him, not thinking about my past or my future. Just him.

"Allie?" His quiet rumble pierces through my nearly asleep state.

"Mm..."

"You know I'm here for you, don't you?"

I open my eyes to find him staring at me with a kind of quiet softness that makes my breath hitch. And I nod, resisting the urge to climb into his lap and hide my face in the crook of his neck—he can't expect me not to want to do that when he says things like that.

"I'm here for you too," I tell him in a whisper.

He's gentle as he cups the back of my neck. "You can tell me anything. I'll never judge you. You got that?"

The lump in my throat makes a reappearance. "I got that."

"Good."

He closes the distance between us slowly. The next thing I feel are his warm lips on my forehead, pressing a lingering kiss to my skin.

"Good night, sweetheart. Thanks for taking care of my grumpy ass."

Chapter Twenty-Seven

It's a quiet afternoon at The Lair a week after Travis's sick day, and I'm distracted.

My forehead still tingles from Travis's lingering kiss, and my mind is still filled with questions about his behavior on New Year's. Why did the fireworks make him flinch? And why did Uncle Neil send him that warning look?

Travis is so imposing, so dominating, such a protector, it's strange to find out he's not invincible. That there's something out there that gets to him.

It's unfair for me to think this way. No matter how strong or brave, we all have weaknesses, and Travis is no different. I wish I'd had the courage to pry further that night, but the moment is gone, and I won't get it back.

I'm brought back to the present by the front door opening and Tom, Charlie's friend from the New Year's Eve party, walking in.

The bar is pretty deserted aside from two occupied tables at the back. Despite him being a bit of a flirt at the lake, I give him a welcoming smile as he approaches the bar, where I'm polishing some glasses.

"Hey, Tom. What can I get you?"

I don't notice his stoic expression right away. He was nothing but playful—and maybe a bit drunk—at the fireworks show, but there seems to be no trace of that carefree guy as our eyes meet now.

He looks at me with intent, as if he were analyzing my every breath, and leans over the bar in a way that feels too practiced. Like he's trying to appear nonchalant, but his body is too stiff to make it work. He licks his lips. "I came to talk to you, actually. If you have a minute."

I glance around the bar, knowing I can't use the *Sorry, we're too busy right now* excuse because there's almost nobody in here. Jude and Travis are taking inventory in the kitchen, so it's just me at the front—I could tell him that.

But then he insists, "It's kind of urgent."

"Sure." I force a relaxed smile. "How can I help you?"

"You're Allison Buccieri, aren't you?"

My ears start ringing, my hands get clammy, and suddenly I don't think there's enough oxygen for me in this bar.

"I'll take that as a yes," Tom continues, his eyes never leaving my face.

My fingers find the beads on my bracelet and start toying with them, willing the panic to die down in vain.

I need air.

I need to get out of here.

Quit. Flee. Start again.

"What do you want?" I blurt out, my voice quivering but quiet so Travis doesn't hear me. If he comes to the front and sees how tense Tom is making me, he'll have questions. Questions I can't answer.

Tom raps his knuckles on the bar, a casual gesture that poses such a vast contrast to my frantic heartbeat. "We don't want to bother you. We just want to know if you'd be willing to speak out on—"

"Who's *we*?" I cut him off. "How did you find me? Who *are* you?"

Blood drains from my face then, remembering that Charlie mentioned Tom worked in the entertainment industry. He never explained what his job was, and I'd been careless to not think anything of it.

"I work for George Eden," he says, confirming my suspicions. "We got a lead a while ago from someone on our team. Someone who came to The Lair and thought she recognized you."

"Mindy?" It comes out as a whisper.

The woman I almost killed because I gave her a burger with onions. The woman I *knew* had recognized me but hadn't said anything. How foolishly wrong I'd been.

"Yeah." Tom's eyebrows lift in surprise. "She was here on vacation and had an issue with her food, and... Anyway, not the point. Since my family lives here, I offered to talk to you during the holidays. George is fascinated by your case, and he'd like to interview you for his talk show. You flew under the radar for six years, Allie. That's no small feat."

And now it's ruined.

All my efforts to start anew, gone.

"Our audience would love to know why you left in the first place. Why you changed your name and your appearance. What happened with... you know, the kidnapping."

Before he finishes that sentence, I'm already shaking my head.

It was too good to be true. All of this—my job, my friendships, my new life.

Amid the chaos in my head, I realize starting over has never been a true possibility. Not when I could never, no matter how hard I try, escape a past that was broadcasted for millions of people to see.

"No."

One word. That's all I can manage as my throat closes and unshed tears collect in my eyes.

Tom sighs. "I understand this is hard to take in, but please hear me out. We only want your statement—that's it. We suspect something went down with your family that made you leave despite their claims that everything was fine. One doesn't change their name and physical appearance for no reason."

I shake my head again as the nervous tears falls. My head spins, and I brace myself against the bar so I don't pass out. *This can't be happening.*

"Leave. Please."

It's not a question or an invitation, but Tom persists. "Influencer families overexposing their children online is becoming a very dangerous issue. We're trying to bring awareness so that Congress considers new laws to protect children—"

I'm barely listening. I'm barely *breathing* as this stranger ruins my life and I'm helpless to stop him.

"Leave me alone. Please," I beg him, not caring anymore who sees me break down. "I left for a reason. I don't want to remember. I don't want to relive my kidnapping. You can interview someone else."

His eyes soften just a tad. "I understand. I do, Allie, but think about it. Your experience could help us move forward with Congress. You were kidnapped, and many people are convinced it had to do with your family sharing personal information online. The police never issued an official statement, and the rumors have gone in all directions. Any proof you have of parental abuse or neglect would really help our case. We're only trying to protect other children from going through the same thing."

I'm hearing the words, but my head and heart don't respond. They're stuck in the nightmare unfolding right before my eyes.

They found me.

The past six years, all the measured steps I took and sacrifices I made, have been for nothing.

"Leave," I say one last time, my voice shaking as badly as my hands. "I-I don't want to be part of this."

This time, Tom doesn't insist. His defeated sigh makes something uncomfortable roll in my stomach.

"All right." He reaches into his pocket and takes out a business card, placing it in front of me. "Call this number or email me if you change your mind."

I don't take it. I barely move, still shaking, as he leaves the way he came.

The sound of the door shutting behind him echoes in my head and buries the footsteps closing in.

"Allie?"

As if physically shaken by Travis's voice, I sober up at once.

I grab a nearby cleaning cloth to busy my hands so he can't see them shaking. "Hi, boss man."

When his eyes follow the movement, I know there's no way he's buying my nonchalant facade.

And when he asks, "What's wrong?" I confirm it.

"Nothing's wrong."

The lie feels bitter on my tongue, but I can't risk Travis asking questions. I said no to Tom enough times for him to get the memo. I don't think he'll come back to bother me again, so there's no reason for Travis to know why I'm so shaken up. What would I even tell him?

The truth, once and for all.

"Allie. Talk to me, please."

I shake my head and lower my gaze. "I'm fine."

He spots Tom's card at the same time I do, but he's quicker to grab it. He reads it once, twice, before his eyes land on me again. "A production company?" he asks slowly. "What is this doing here?"

"Just some guy."

"Did he bother you?"

I hate that my heart jumps at his protectiveness. I don't deserve him, this selfless man who always looks out for me when all I do is lie to his face.

"I'm okay, Travis," I insist.

He stays quiet for a moment, and I think he's going to leave until his gentle hand takes the cleaning cloth from my fingers.

"Your hands are shaking."

It's not a question, so I don't give him an answer.

Jude calls his name from the kitchen, but he doesn't move. Not for a moment, and not before he says, "We'll talk at home."

I don't nod or say anything.

On autopilot, I power through the rest of my shift, managing to remember everyone's orders despite my head circling back to Tom every two seconds. His business card ended up in the back pocket of my jeans, and even though I've thought of throwing it in the trash and forgetting about this nightmare, I can't bring myself to do it.

This changes nothing.

George Eden and his team can do whatever they want, but I, too, deserve to move on. I deserve to make my own choices— choices that don't involve revisiting a past that is ruining my present.

Any proof you have of parental abuse or neglect would really help our case.

Tom's words slice through my chest and refuse to let me breathe.

Because I do.

I have more than enough proof of the hell my parents put me through, but I will never be brave enough to show it to the world.

Chapter Twenty-Eight

Age 19

The plan was simple—pack the essentials, grab some cash I knew my parents kept in their joint home office, and get the hell out of there.

I had cleared everything else with Jada's sister, who'd kindly offered to rent me one of her empty bedrooms in Dallas for a fraction of the average rent cost in the area. And with the mechanic giving my car the green light for the long trip, I was only left with one last task. Arguably, the toughest of all.

The "get the hell out of here" part of the plan had been murky from the start, something I always seemed to have enough time to figure out later. Only that *later* never came around.

It was inconvenient, given that I'd be leaving this house the following day, and I still had no clue how. There was no *Running Away from Home 101: The Ultimate Guide* to help me through it, exactly. Playing it by ear had always been the idea—until I realized it wouldn't be as easy as walking out of the door and never coming back.

My parents, as much as they'd never had my best interest at heart, would've panicked if I'd disappeared into thin air again.

And when trying to run away from home, having the police called on me—and potentially finding me—was never the goal. I didn't need a social media circus with my name at the front either.

While Johnny was off at school, my father was at the golf club, and my mother was meeting some friends for one of her long brunches after dropping Cindy at day care, I lugged my suitcase all the way to my car in the garage. Then I sprinted back up to my parents' home office, entered the passcode to my mom's safe—her birthday—and took ten thousand dollars in cash.

As I stashed the money in the pocket of my hoodie, I told myself this was my only option. I couldn't afford to be tracked through my credit card—which my parents still had access to—and that money...

I'd *earned* it.

My parents had used my image without my consent for years—to advertise overpriced toys, fancy child-friendly cruises, tacky clothing brands, and everything else under the sun that gave them a fat paycheck in return. As far as I knew, none of that money was stored away for my future. Not a single penny. I'd recently turned nineteen, and neither of my parents had revealed they kept an overflowing, supersecret savings account for me.

So was it really *stealing* if I'd helped earn it against my will? Arguable.

Yet I still felt like I'd go into cardiac arrest during the minute it took me to grab the money.

The house was still empty when I finished, the only noise being the *thump, thump, thump* of my frantic heartbeat. I didn't get caught. No alarms went off, and no rabid dogs whose existence I never knew of chased me down.

Gripping the money tightly in my pocket because I couldn't

believe I'd had the audacity to do *that*, I allowed myself a moment to regain my breathing.

"Okay," I muttered out loud before I recited my mental to-do list for good measure. "I have gas, my things are in the car, Jada printed out the reservations for the hotel I'll be sleeping at tomorrow…"

I was forgetting something. That blank space in my list was nagging me like a pebble in a shoe, but I couldn't put my finger on it.

Was it my new ID with the name change? No, that was in my backpack, under my bed.

My credit card, then? No, I'd decided to leave that behind.

I frowned, annoyed. Then what—

A shiver skidded down my spine when my eyes landed on my mother's laptop, unassumingly lying on her messy desk.

The one thing I was forgetting wasn't something I wrote down in the first place. Without it, though, my escape would be for nothing.

My parents had never accepted no for an answer. They lived a privileged life, used to everyone catering to their out-of-touch needs—like that one time they made a point to remind a restaurant hostess how many social media followers they had, so why the hell would they have to pay for dinner?

They thought their fame made them untouchable. I knew better than to assume they'd be okay with me leaving with just a "Goodbye, don't contact me ever again" note. They would take it to the police and use their money and connections to find me despite me being over eighteen. They would turn to social media and announce my disappearance, hosting their own personal pity party.

I had to be smarter. I needed to make sure there was abso-lutely no way they could turn to the internet or the authorities.

As I kept glancing at my mother's laptop, my brain lit up with an insane idea. But what choice did I have?

The money in my pocket crinkled when I took a step forward. There was no way my parents would ever *think* of contacting me if I blackmailed them with...with...

I gulped, my conscience screaming in my head.

Make the video and get away forever, Allie. Before you run out of time.

Chapter Twenty-Nine

THAT TIGHT, UNCOMFORTABLE FEELING TOM'S VISIT LEFT clinging in my chest doesn't go away for the rest of the day. Not as I close up with Travis and Jude, not as I drive home, and not as I make dinner while Travis disappears who-knows-where. He said something about grabbing a couple things downtown, but I was barely listening.

Tom works for George Eden, who knows where I am. Who wants to interview me to... what, exactly? Expose my family? Why else would he ask for evidence of abuse or neglect?

I rest my elbows on the kitchen counter, head pounding. If I put my heart on mute and only listened to my head, I know what it would tell me—my parents didn't protect me growing up, so I don't owe them a thing now.

I shut my eyes because no, I don't want to go on national TV and talk about my past. I won't reach a happy, calm life by stirring the pot.

"Smells delicious in here," a deep voice says, shattering my train of thought.

A deep voice that doesn't belong to Travis.

Thinking of the time someone almost broke into my old

apartment, I'm about to grab a kitchen knife to defend myself when I spot a familiar figure with a huge smile on his welcoming, wrinkly face.

"What does an old man have to do to get a hug these days instead of stabbed?" Uncle Neil asks, taking his hat off and placing it on the back of the couch.

I'm sure the relieved breath I let out can be heard across the state. "I thought you were a murderer."

"No murders. I'm only here for some of that delicious food. C'mere, my sweet girl."

I can't help but smile as he wraps his arms around me. Out of the corner of my eye, I spot Travis shutting the door behind him. "I didn't know you were coming tonight."

He pulls away, keeping both hands on my arms as he gives them a friendly squeeze. "I was at the bar and invited myself over for dinner. Had to see that you were really living here."

My eyes find Travis's over his uncle's shoulder. "It's, um, a temporary thing while I find a new place."

"And how's that going? Any luck so far?"

If only I had looked at a single listing in the past three weeks. "It's not going too well, but I'm optimistic."

He pats my arm. "I'm sure Travis could use the company. Right, old man?"

I chuckle when Travis gives him a grunt.

"Dinner is ready," I tell both men. "I didn't know you were coming, Uncle Neil, but I think there's enough for the three of us."

"You didn't have to cook. I was going to order some takeout," Travis says, brows pulled together, as he walks into the kitchen. "But it smells fucking good."

I try not to beam at his praise. "Thanks."

"Sit down. I'll take care of everything," he says.

I follow Uncle Neil to the dining table and sit across from

him. Unlike his nephew, he doesn't need much to start an amicable conversation.

"So, Allie, Travis tells me you took over the accounting at the bar. I didn't know we had a nerd among us."

The way he says it tells me he's only teasing. I'm pretty sure I'm imagining the glimpse of pride in his eyes, but I run with it nonetheless.

As Travis sets the table and brings over the roast chicken I made, Uncle Neil tells me how he also enjoyed that part of the job back in the day, and how he would've liked to get a formal education in finance when he was younger.

Travis doesn't say much when he sits down with us, focusing on his meal instead, but I don't mind it. Uncle Neil talks enough for everyone and isn't shy with sharing embarrassing stories about younger Travis.

"He came home with his hair chopped off in odd places one day," he tells me. "Said he wanted to look like one of those rock stars from a magazine. Can you believe it?"

I throw my head back in laughter, mirth swirling in my chest as I slide my gaze to my brooding boss. "That's cute, Travis."

He only grunts.

Uncle Neil adds, "He was always a serious kid, but sometimes he did out-of-pocket stuff like that. It was those friends you had. Troublemakers, all of them."

Travis finishes up his food and takes a sip of water before responding, "Don't you think it's getting a little late, old man?"

Uncle Neil rolls his eyes. "All right, all right. You want some alone time with Allie-girl, I get it."

My cheeks heat up. "Oh, that's—"

"Damn right I do."

My heartbeat quickens.

Uncle Neil's smile doesn't go anywhere as his gaze pinballs

between me and his nephew. What he sees there, I'm not sure I want to know.

He leaves soon after that, agreeing that he's tired and wants to watch his favorite show in peace anyway before going to bed.

While Travis drives him home, I shut myself in my bedroom and grab my laptop. I know I shouldn't, but I can't get my conversation with Tom out of my head. Searching my name online is the only way to find out if damage has been done.

Allison Buccieri to speak out on family abuse? George Eden insists her statement could change the social media landscape.

Far from being scared, my blood boils as I read the headline. Because what *is* this? When did I agree to speak out at all?

I suppress the urge to call Tom and demand him to tell the truth, to say I want nothing to do with this. Or better yet, to keep my name out of their mouths. But when I spoke to Jada earlier, she advised me to stay calm.

"Headlines will mention your name in the upcoming days," she accurately predicted. "You know how the internet works. They want to bait people for clicks. Don't pay them any mind— that's what Paul and I are here for. We'll update you if it gets out of hand."

But I can't look away, frantically searching online spaces I shouldn't be in for more clues about George Eden's intentions. What if he reveals my new identity? My location?

Just the thought of a bunch of reporters waiting for me outside The Lair is enough to make me nauseous.

I'm about to click on another article that mentions my

family when a knock on my door makes me shut my laptop so fast, I may have shattered the screen. I'm too nervous to check.

"It's Travis," says that familiar voice I've come to associate with so many things—calmness, safety, butterflies.

I swallow. "Come in."

He's hesitant as he opens the door. "Can we talk? You're fidgety today. Anything happen that I should know about?"

It starts quiet, unsure, as if my brain can't decide if we're safe enough to let our guard down or if we need to keep hiding.

I'm so tired.

And so my heart takes the lead, just like every time Travis is involved, and against my better judgment, I break down.

It begins at the tips of my fingers, then climbs the length of my arms and up to my shoulders. My bedroom isn't cold, but my body starts violently shaking all the same.

"Hey." He kneels before me, eyes seeking mine. His voice is gentle but firm. "Talk to me."

My mouth is too dry, and my heart is beating too fast.

Because what could I even say to him?

That I've been lying to everyone since I set foot in this town?

That my real identity is at risk of being unveiled to the entire country on national TV?

That I don't know how to stop hating myself for all I've done and continue to do?

Travis is careful as he sets my laptop aside and grabs my shaky hands between his warm ones. "Breathe with me, Allie. Come on."

My chest heaves when I follow his command, and it takes me three tries to take a full breath.

"In. Out. Again."

His thumb starts rubbing soothing circles on my cold skin.

"That's it. You're doing so good, Allie. Will you breathe with me one more time?"

A tingle travels down the length of my neck, and I nod.

"Are you feeling better?" he asks after a few moments of silence that stretch in time because I can't find my voice. I manage to nod.

He stands to his full height, still holding my hands in his. "Come with me. I want to show you something."

Before I allow myself to overthink it too much, I use his strength to push myself up. Without letting go of his hand, I follow him out of the room. I'm not expecting to end up next door—in the only room of Travis's house that sits completely empty.

He wants to show me something... here?

Wordlessly, he shuts the door behind us and leads me to the opposite end of the room before sitting down on the floor. He tugs at my hand. "Come here."

The usual alarms that go off in my head every time I think of getting closer to Travis are gone. Slowly, I lower myself to the wooden floor until I'm sitting next to him.

I don't know how long we bask in the silence and darkness while I wait for my heart to calm down. With my head resting on the wall behind me, I turn so I can check on him. His eyes are already on me, his head in the same position as mine.

"Why did you bring me here?" I ask, my voice a whisper.

He hears me anyway. "For honesty."

A knife slicing an open wound hurt less than those words.

My voice sounds strained when I speak next. "What do you mean?"

What if he kicks me out for being a liar? We didn't sign any contract, so I'm sure he can do that if he wants to. And I wouldn't dare to argue because he would be in the right.

"There's a reason this room is empty," he starts.

Somehow, my heart knows it's going to break in the next few moments. I don't fight it.

"I enlisted in the Navy when I was eighteen to get some weight off my uncle's shoulders."

His voice has never sounded this somber. I don't like it at all, this dark pit I can tell Travis's mind has just crawled into. Fighting against the urge to drag him out of it, I hold my breath and listen to his story. One I never thought I would hear.

"I already told you my parents passed away when I was young." I nod, but he doesn't see it. He's looking at my hand, still wrapped in his. "I'd always been close to my uncle, so when he took me in, it wasn't a huge change. I already spent most of my time with him growing up."

I squeeze his hand. A silent cue that I'm here, and I'm listening.

"For a few years, we struggled to make ends meet. We could barely afford one meal a day for both of us." He takes a deep breath through his nose. "I started working at a car repair shop to help him pay the bills. It wasn't much, but at least we didn't go to bed hungry anymore."

In a quiet voice, I tell him with my heart on my sleeve, "I'm sorry you had to go through all that, Travis. You didn't deserve it."

I almost miss his headshake. "It's all in the past."

If there's anyone who understands that just because it's in the past doesn't mean the wound is healed, it's me.

"Enlisting was the obvious path after I graduated high school. I wasn't particularly patriotic, but at least my uncle would have one less thing to worry about." *Thing*. He isn't a *thing*. If my heart wasn't broken before, it sure is now. "I spent twelve years in the Navy, sending him as much money as I could. That's how he eventually opened The Lair. It did well, and our financial struggles disappeared shortly after."

229

"I'm sure your uncle is very proud of you," I tell him. *I'm proud of you.* "You changed both of your lives."

It's difficult to explain how my body is able to feel the shift around us. How the air thickens, how the tension rolls off his body in invisible but powerful waves.

"There was a cost. I've seen some shit in the Navy, Allie. Shit no human should fucking see."

All because he wanted to keep a roof over his uncle's head. Because he wanted to put food on his table. Because he wanted a better future for the one man who had always been there for him.

"I left after twelve years because I couldn't take it anymore. I've seen friends die before my eyes. Men who had families here, children, wives they couldn't wait to go back to. I've seen..."

He shuts his eyes, and I squeeze his fingers again. He brings both of our hands to his face, and I caress his bearded cheek as he leans into my touch, a heavy breath leaving his chest.

"I came back a different man." His whispered voice is rough, pained. And I won't, but I itch to climb into his lap and hug him until the horrors go away. "A detached, lone fucker who gave up on too many hopes he didn't know he had."

His chest shakes with a heavy breath. "I bought this place three years ago. I got a good feeling about it but thought it was too large for just me. I got it despite..."

Suddenly, I understand that this is who Travis has been all along—a sheltered soul waiting for the right moment to crack open.

"I used to want a family of my own. I didn't grow up with great parents, but I wanted to..." He runs his free hand through his short hair, exhaustion marring his face. "I don't fucking know. I didn't allow my parents or the shit they did and didn't do to define my formative years. I always saw my uncle as my only father figure, so it's not like..."

Travis isn't a man of many words, and this conversation only proves it. How the words get stuck in his throat, struggling to come out, to say what he wants to tell me.

I can feel the frustration rolling off his body, so I keep caressing his cheek and ask in a slow, gentle voice, "You wanted to be a dad?"

A sea of goose bumps breaks out on my skin when he nods. Why does the thought of Travis having children with some face-less woman make me breathless? I'm ridiculous.

After the hell my parents put me through, the idea of having children of my own wasn't appealing for a long time. But over the years, I started to realize I would never *ever* do to my kids what my family did to me. I might be a liar, but I'm not a controlling narcissist.

For the past couple of years, I've imagined what it would be like to start a family someday with a man who loves me and shares my values—values that don't include compromising our kids' safety for a check. But that man can't and will never be Travis, so I should tell my heart to stop beating so fast at the mere idea of a future I have no right to imagine.

It's surprisingly easy to forget about all those things when the reality of what he's just confessed sinks in.

He used to want a family. He used to want to be a father.

Used to.

"You don't want that anymore?" I ask, hoping he understands he doesn't have to answer if he doesn't want to.

"After I came back, the horrors I'd seen... I couldn't stand the idea of losing anyone I cared about. Still can't."

It's only now that what I should've realized from the start clicks—Travis never gets close to anyone because he's scared of losing them.

That's why he's a total grump at the bar. Why he would rather work than hang out with his friends. Why he hasn't been in a relationship for years. Because, if he allowed himself to build connections, he could end up hurt again.

"But you still bought a big house," I wonder out loud, my voice so quiet that I have no clue if he can even hear me.

Everything about him makes so much more sense now, the things he does and doesn't do. Every little thing.

For fuck's sake, Allie. Because I want you to be safe at all times, goddammit. If anything happened to you...

Didn't he say that to me when he was trying to convince me to move in with him?

I couldn't stand the idea of losing anyone I cared about. Still can't.

"I keep this room empty because I once hoped it would become a nursery, but I don't think that's gonna happen anymore."

The air whooshes out of my lungs.

"I can't bring myself to turn this into anything else. It doesn't feel right," he adds, his voice quieter than I've ever heard it.

"Travis..." I start, unsure of what I could even say to make his pain go away or if there is anything that could at all.

"I'm not telling you this because I want your pity," he says, a little bit of his usual grumpiness seeping through his words.

"I know that. But I care about you, and I don't like to see you hurting. You deserve to heal."

His thumb caresses my hand. "I'm doing better now that I'm in therapy."

I hate that my eyebrows rise in surprise. "You are?"

"For my PTSD, yes."

Jada's encouragement to give therapy a try echoes in my

head again, but I push it away. "That's amazing. I'm glad you're getting the help you need."

Even if there's still a gaping hole inside my chest from just sitting in this empty room. One that was meant to belong to the most important little person in Travis's life—a person he might never get to meet now.

No, don't cry. This isn't about me.

"What I mean to tell you is that I know you're hiding something," he says, stopping my heart with just a few words. "It's not my business, but I wanted to say that living an inauthentic life isn't fucking worth it. Not a single second, okay? If I had gone to therapy sooner, if I hadn't lied to myself for so damn long, saying that I was fine, maybe this room wouldn't be empty today."

I don't think I'm breathing anymore.

"I'm just gonna ask you one question, and you're gonna give me an honest answer," he says, sounding so serious that I can only nod. "Do I need to take care of anybody?"

My throat is dry. "What do you mean?"

"Is someone putting you in danger? Are you running away from people who want to hurt you?"

I shake my head, hoping he can hear the truth in my words. "It's not like that. I'm not in danger."

At least, I don't think I am. Sure, my apartment almost got broken into, and there was that weird thing with my car window, but nothing has happened since. I feel safe now, sheltered under Travis's roof.

He stares at me for so long, he seems frozen in place, but then he says, "You can tell me anything, Allie. I'll always be on your side, no matter what."

My lips part. The air shifts around us again, replacing the tension with a different kind of heaviness—one I'd read about before, seen in movies, but had never experienced. Never thought I would.

My hand on Travis's cheek stills. I hold my breath as he slowly turns his head until his lips press against the cold skin of my hand.

"I'm sorry I've been harsh with you," he murmurs against my skin. "I'm still learning how to let people in, but I'm not sure I'm doing a good job."

"You are. Thank you for opening up to me," I tell him. "You're my favorite person, Travis."

"And you are my weakness, Allie."

My body sizzles with anticipation as Travis presses another kiss to the back of my hand. So gently, so at odds with the facade he shows to the world.

"Travis..."

"Yes, sweetheart?"

Tell him. Tell him now.

My eyes drop to his mouth, unable to look away because we've never been this close before, and I want to... I want to—

The dogs start barking outside, making me jump. Travis curses under his breath, the moment shattering as he stands to look out of the window.

"What is it?" I ask, both alarmed and breathless. *We were about to kiss.*

He stays silent, glancing into the darkness as if it belonged to him. When a few moments pass and the dogs don't bark again, he says, "I'll check the cameras, but it was probably a fox or some other animal."

"Right," I mutter, silently grateful he can't see the blush on my cheeks. I stand back up with as much poise as I can muster, then awkwardly say, "I'll go back to my room. Thanks for... thanks for telling me everything."

His nod is short, stiff, and he doesn't look at me.

My stomach drops at his cold dismissal, but I tell myself it's for the best. Crossing the line with my boss and landlord isn't a good idea, no matter how badly my heart insists otherwise.

Chapter Thirty

The week goes by normally—or as normally as it can go after Travis told me about his empty bedroom, said I was his weakness, and almost kissed me.

It's during times like this that I wish I had a group of tight-knit friends I could vent to. Charlie is as close as it gets, but it would be weird to tell him I have a thing for our boss. Lola is a good friend, too, but I don't think we're there yet. And I don't talk about relationships with Jada, if only because my life has never been easy enough to allow those conversations, so I wouldn't even know where to start.

So, I do the next reasonable thing—check online forums.

Several entries under *Is it okay to have a crush on my boss?* suggest that yes, it's perfectly fine as long as I don't act on it because it could ruin everything. I also find not-that-encouraging explanations on the *Is it okay to be attracted to an older man?* forum, which leave me more confused than before.

Eventually, I reach the conclusion that maybe I'm just infatuated with Travis. That it's not a crush but a strong attraction explained by the fact that he's the first man who's shown mild interest in me. He's the first man I've felt safe with, which is making me confuse feelings of gratitude with love. Possibly.

Only that my feelings for him don't correlate with infatuation. They're too strong, too real, too rooted in my heart. *But what if I'm just seeing what I want to see?*

Several articles and forums suggest going on dates to test this theory. Maybe Charlie or Lola could introduce me to one of their friends that isn't a total creep. I haven't been on a date since...well, ever. I think it's time.

I'm twenty-five, for crying out loud. I've been kissed before, once, and it's not that I feel particularly self-conscious about not having had sex, but I can't exactly start a relationship with some unsuspecting man while I lie to him every day. But a date won't hurt, and it could be a good distraction from Travis.

If everything else fails, at least I will have pushed past my fear of socializing. Who knows? Maybe I'll make a friend or two in the process.

"Char?" I call out, knowing he can hear me from wherever he's crouching behind the bar.

"What's up, Alliegator?"

I set the broom aside and rest my elbows on the bar, getting on my tiptoes so I can look at him. He's putting away some napkins and straws. "Do you have any cute, single friends?"

"If this isn't an interesting request," he teases. "Why? Too chicken to admit you like the boss?"

My cheeks flush before I can help it. "I just... You know."

He stands and runs a hand through his blond curls. "Very eloquent, sweet cheeks. I do have a few cute, single friends who are into women. Want their number?"

"I was thinking maybe I could tag along whenever you guys hang out again? If you're okay with that."

"I'm sure we'll do something fun this weekend. Lola will be

there, and I'll make sure to invite my cutest and most available friends."

He throws me a wink before grabbing a dirty cloth from the bar and leaving in the direction of the changing room.

As I finish sweeping the floors, I try to convince myself that I'm doing the right thing by asking Charlie to set me up with one of his friends. There's no real pressure to meet anyone anyway. I'll just hang out with them this weekend and see how I feel about it.

"Allie?" Travis's unmistakable deep rumble asks right before I spot his massive figure coming toward me, a scowl on his hard face that looks meaner than usual. And that's saying something.

"What do you need, boss man?"

"Help me in the back. Bring the broom."

I do as he says, trailing behind him until he stops by the pool table.

"What are you doing?" I frown when he gently takes the broom from my grip.

"Sweeping the floors," he says, as if I weren't looking right at him.

I rest my lower back against the pool table. "I can see that. Why did you want me to come with you if you're only gonna make me watch?"

"Bye, boss!" Charlie hollers from the front, and I wave at him as he exits the bar. But before he's gone, the little shit winks and adds, "I'll get you a hot date this weekend, Allie Cat. Don't sweat it."

My cheeks redden, and my first instinct is to look at the man beside me. But Travis doesn't even lift his head. And why would he? It's not like my love life—or the lack thereof—interests him in any way.

I probably imagined our almost kiss too.

While he cleans up, I take a closer look at the pool table. I've never played before. My father had one in our basement, but I wasn't allowed to go near it because he didn't want me to break it. As if a child could do such a thing.

"See you tomorrow, you two," says Sandra.

I turn back around just in time to say goodbye to her and Jude.

It's not the first time Travis and I have been left alone at The Lair, so I don't think much of it until I hear the sound of the broomstick being placed against the wall. And then I feel his presence at my back, getting closer, warmer.

"Wanna play?"

I meet his gaze over my shoulder before turning around to face him. "I've never done it before."

His nostrils flare at the same time as my pulse accelerates.

"I can teach you."

Those words shouldn't sound so dirty.

"Okay."

Neither of us move. Eyes locked, I wonder if we're still talking about pool. But Travis doesn't flirt, and he most certainly doesn't flirt *with me*. He doesn't do innuendos or cheesy lines.

"Let's get you a cue," that raspy voice says before he walks to the opposite side of the table. "Come here."

His soft command shouldn't send a thrill down my spine, either, but here we are. My mind is lost, and for the first time, I don't care to find it.

Travis grabs one of the smallest cues and passes it to me. "You have no idea how pool works, then?"

My fingers brush his when I grab the cue. "I didn't even know this was called a cue until two minutes ago. I've been calling it a stick this whole time."

He shakes his head as he passes me by, not hiding his

amusement. "Let me get this ready, and I'll teach you how to play."

I'm not ashamed to admit that, in the next few minutes, I only understand 20 percent of the words that leave Travis's mouth. Maybe less.

"What do you mean I lost?" I frown after I make the first shot.

Well, technically, the second—the cue slipped from my grip on the first one, and I swear I heard a laugh behind me. I can't even be mad about it because I like the sound way too much.

The massive bear-man next to me has his body propped against the table, a smug look on his face I also can't be mad about.

"You sank the black ball," he explains.

"So what?" I scoff. "Doesn't that give me a point? I'll take a pity one if necessary. I mean, the aim of this game is to sink the balls into the holes." I pause. "Like, the pool balls into the pool holes. That's what I meant."

Kill me now.

Travis shakes his head in amusement. "The eight ball has to be the last one you sink. Otherwise, you lose."

"That doesn't feel right. Does that mean we have to start again?"

He places a hand on my shoulder and gives it a squeeze, the heat of his skin kissing mine through the thin material of my work shirt. "I'll bend the rules for you."

Okay. No big deal. We're talking about pool here. There are no other rules to bend.

"Solids are yours," he says as he leans over to keep playing.

In one swift movement, Travis hits the white ball, which then sinks two striped ones into different holes.

"It's still your turn now, right? Because you scored," I ask.

He sends me a smirk over his bulky shoulder. "You're a fast learner."

Travis sinks another ball before it's my turn. Even though my cue is shorter than his, I still have trouble positioning it between my fingers. I guess it's good that I've already embarrassed myself in front of him enough times to last me at least twenty years because I'm pretty sure I'm making a complete fool of myself right now.

"Okay. All right." I straighten my back and blow a strand of hair away from my face. "I got this."

I can't see his face, but I sure hear the smirk in his voice. "I know you do."

"Don't make fun of me, big guy."

"Would never dream of it."

I send him a dirty look that does nothing but make that smirk a little wider.

I lean over the wooden frame, but just when I'm about to go, my hand slips and the stupid cue ends up hitting the table with more force than necessary. "Damn it."

"Easy," Travis says. "Let me show you."

He sets his cue on a nearby table. I hear the sound of his military boots getting closer, one beckoning step at a time. And I don't hear it, but I feel his warmth as he positions that massive body I've ogled more times than I will ever admit behind mine.

He pushes my lower body forward with a gentle hand as I hold on to the cue. His body moves with mine, his left arm resting on top of mine as his fingers wrap around my own, holding the cue with me.

Then he whispers, "Follow my lead."

I can barely breathe as his other hand grabs the end of the cue, grazing my waist. And then he thrusts us forward, just barely, but enough to press our bodies together.

We hit the white ball, which then sinks a yellow one.

Neither of us seem to care.

"You got it now?" he asks in my ear, his voice low.

I can't form a single coherent thought right now, let alone recall what he's just taught me. Pool is at the very back of my mind.

Slowly, our bodies come back up. He takes one step back, making me instantly miss his close proximity.

"You sank one, so you go again," he instructs, his voice rough.

A shaky breath falls from my parted lips as I lean forward, targeting an orange ball this time. Somehow, I manage to hit the white ball, but it lands nowhere.

"You're getting there," he encourages me, his eyes on the table as he positions himself in front of the white ball. Easily, he sinks two striped ones. He goes again and again, as if he hadn't just stolen away my breath and my reason.

At some point, he must notice I'm not paying attention anymore because he asks, "You okay?"

No, Travis, I'm not.

I'm not sure about anything right now.

There are many things I dislike about myself—how effortlessly lies roll off my tongue, how much of a coward I am when instead I should show the world that it won't crush me, how my brain shuts down when my body is shackled with anxiety, and I lose all control over my mouth. And that's exactly what happens next.

"Why are you still wearing the bracelet?"

His eyes don't leave me, watching my every blink and breath intake. I don't lower my gaze either.

"You don't have to wear it anymore," I feel compelled to remind him when he says nothing. "The bet was one month. You can take it off."

His eyes shift to the white ball. He only has two striped

balls left to sink.

"I don't want to take it off," he says, simple as that, as he sinks both balls and wins the game.

"Why not?"

He doesn't answer right away. He doesn't say anything at all as he sets his cue on the pool table.

I don't move as I watch my boss, the same man who told me I was his weakness, start toward me. He doesn't stop until the tips of his boots graze my white sneakers.

He's close. So close, I can feel every inch of his warmth. So close, he may be able to hear the frantic beating of my heart.

His voice is low, hoarse. His eyes don't leave mine as he asks a question that I'm not sure I understand.

"You have no idea, do you?"

One of his hands hikes its way up, up, up, until the weight of his fingers settles on the nape of my neck. Fingers that start kneading my skin softly, as if he's scared to break me. My lips part at the possessive gesture.

"You have no idea what you do to me. Do you, sweetheart?"

His voice is charged with a kind of roughness I've never heard before. Not from him, and not from anyone else. Ever. It's a roughness that makes my heartbeat quicken, my stomach flutter, and the pressure between my legs grow heavier.

Travis is a whole foot taller than me, but suddenly his forehead is pressed against mine. Our proximity traps the air in my lungs, the words in my throat, and it kills every thought in my brain telling me to stop this before it's too late.

I should tell him that whatever this is, it's a mistake. Not because we work and live together and not because he's twelve years older than me, but because I'm too broken, and I don't know how to fix myself. If I even can.

"You really want to go on a date with some guy?" he asks

roughly as his hand cradles my cheek, holding me with gentle firmness.

"No," I tell him with every inch of honesty I have. "I don't."

I'm done lying to myself.

I'm done pretending that what I feel for him is infatuation or a mere crush.

Because the truth is, I've fallen in love with Travis. All in.

And I can only hope it doesn't end in heartbreak as I unapologetically grab the metaphorical reins of my life and take a step further.

My nose nuzzles his. My voice is barely above a whisper when I ask him, "You don't want me to go on a date?"

"Only if it's with me."

My heartbeat picks up when he uses those strong hands to hoist me up by the waist and set me on the pool table. He positions his body between my legs, his arms caging me until we're mere inches apart.

"Fucking hell, Allie," he rasps, forehead against mine, hands on my waist.

"What?" I breathe out, my eyes settling on his plump lips.

He shuts his eyes. "Tell me this isn't right."

I swallow. "I won't lie."

He opens his eyes to search mine, his gaze intense and scorching.

"Tell me this is a mistake," he says.

"This isn't a mistake."

He inches closer.

"Tell me to stop."

I can't.

I won't.

"Allie," he growls, bringing me impossibly closer.

And closer.

Every fear and doubt in my head dissipate. Maybe I'm being

greedy, taking what has never been mine. And maybe I should feel bad for leading Travis on when he deserves better than this, than me. But it's been way too long since I allowed my heart to beat for something. For someone.

And I need him to be mine in the same way I'm longing to be his.

"I don't want you to stop," I whisper against his lips.

My boss, the man who has taken better care of me than anyone else ever has, who shows me through his actions that I mean *something* to him, doesn't move an inch. He doesn't pull away, doesn't lean in either, and it sends my heartbeat into overdrive.

His heavy breathing mixes with mine, but it's not enough.

I need him closer.

I need *him*.

"Allie," he grunts.

His last warning.

My last chance.

The moment my lips touch Travis's, something in me shifts. It tears the beating organ in my chest apart, giving way to a new emotion I don't recognize.

I might have closed the space between our mouths, but the illusion of being in charge disappears quickly. Because Travis pecks my lips once, twice, before the beast in him lets loose.

The warmth of his hands seeps into my skin as his tongue explores mine. Our kiss starts slow, then changes to something less gentle. But his roughness is never cruel, never unwelcome.

A groan escapes the back of his throat as I wrap my arms around his neck, needing his body against mine more than I need my next breath. My legs curl around his waist, and suddenly I'm not on the pool table anymore.

The fact that Travis is a strong man has never escaped me. I just didn't know he could support all my weight with such ease, and now my mind is going places it should stay away from. My center being pressed against his hardness isn't helping either.

"Goddammit, Allie," he grunts when he breaks our kiss.

I don't think I've ever heard his voice sound huskier than right now, and it's not doing my aroused body any favors.

His hands move lower and lower and lower as his mouth descends on the sensitive skin of my neck and he cups my backside.

"You have no fucking idea," he whispers between kisses, his voice as hungry as his touch. "How badly I need you. Like the fucking sun."

"Travis..." I beg as he pecks my lips. What I'm begging for, I'm not sure—for him to keep kissing me, to hold me tighter, to never stop.

"Tell me what you need," he growls against the curve of my neck as I throw my head back to grant him better access. "Whatever you need, sweetheart, it's yours. I've waited long enough to kiss you."

It's at this moment that I realize I've missed all the signs. His heightened protectiveness, the unexpected way he opened up about his past and his fears. How have I not seen it before?

Travis cares about me. Just as deeply as I care about him. In his own quiet way, but he does.

He doesn't give me a chance to keep overthinking as he closes the space between our lips again, his tongue meeting mine. His movements aren't slow, and it shocks me that despite my inexperience, I can follow his pace with ease.

When he squeezes my ass, a whimper escapes the back of my throat. He meets it with a grunt of his own, sending the most delicious thrill down my spine.

"Travis..." My voice slips in between kisses. "I need—"

"Sorry, boss, I left something in—"

We pull away seconds before I meet Charlie's wide-open

eyes over Travis's shoulder. Whatever he was going to say next dies in his throat as he comes to the obvious—and correct —conclusion.

Travis's hands are still on my ass as he turns his head to look at Charlie, but he says nothing. Neither of us do.

Because Charlie has just caught me making out with our boss in the middle of the bar.

Did I mention my legs are wrapped around his waist and his hands are in a very inappropriate place?

I don't know what I expected Charlie to do, but it wasn't to point a finger at us with a huge grin on his face and say, "I fucking knew it."

Travis and I watch his smirk grow wider, clearly unfazed by having walked in on us.

"You know what? Good for you," Charlie says with a shrug. "It was about damn time anyway. Just tell me I can wear sneakers to the wedding because dress shoes make my feet hurt, and I plan to dance until you kick me out."

I'm about to pass out—or away. Likely one after the other.

"What the fuck are you doing here?" Travis demands.

My heart flutters as he presses me closer to his body, with no intentions of letting me go despite our current ordeal.

Charlie holds his hands up. "I forgot my keys in the dressing room. I'll be out of your hair real quick so you can... keep going."

With a smirk, he darts off toward the back.

Travis sighs, his chest expanding against mine. He's careful as he helps me down, and once he makes sure I'm okay, he presses a lingering kiss on my forehead.

But he says nothing after that and steps away. Not a "This shouldn't have happened" or a "We'll continue this at home." Yet I still muster a smile because I like Travis a lot, not only as a boss but as a person, too, and I don't want this... whatever that was to taint our relationship.

"I'm going to head out. I'll see you at home," I tell him, my head down as my cheeks grow warm.

I would be lying if I said I didn't want him to stop me before I left. To suggest we wait until Charlie leaves again so we can continue. But Travis only gives me a stiff nod and says nothing.

I'm fine. This is fine. He'll be awkward for a bit, and then we'll be fine.

Another lie.

Chapter Thirty-One

"Did you sleep with him?"

Someone is going to end up six feet under today. His name starts with *Char* and ends with *lie*.

"Stop it," I hiss, glancing over my shoulder to make sure Travis isn't listening. "Nothing's going on between us."

Charlie arches a blond eyebrow. It's past closing time, so it doesn't surprise me that he waited until now to interrogate me. "I literally saw you sucking face last night."

He keeps going, not waiting for an answer because we both know what he saw. "You can't tell me nothing's going on between you when his hands were on your ass and your legs were keeping him hostage. *Hostage*, Allie."

I let out a deep breath. "I know, but that was all that happened. We aren't... together."

He searches my gaze. "You like him, don't you?"

"I... may or may not have a tiny crush on him."

"A *tiny* crush?"

"All right, maybe a medium-sized one."

"A medium-sized..." He shakes his head. "You know what? As long as he doesn't have a medium-sized di—"

"*Charlie.*"

"Not that there's anything wrong with medium-sized dicks, but looking at how big he is, I would assume—"

"I'm done with this conversation," I blurt out, hoping my cheeks don't look as flustered as I feel. Yet heat swirls in my lower area all the same, recalling the feeling of Travis's strong body against me last night. Of the definitely not tiny or medium-sized bulge pressing against my stomach.

A piercing stab goes through my chest only a moment later. It's not difficult to sober up again when I remember Travis has been ignoring me for the past twelve hours.

I try not to take it personally. He told me about his past and how difficult it is for him to open up, so I get it. Really. The blame for this radio silence isn't entirely on him—I could've always brought up our kiss last night or this morning, but I didn't. Because if intimacy is tough for him, being brave is also hard for me.

Shaking my head to clear it of all sorts of distracting thoughts until I'm done with my shift, I turn away from Charlie.

And come face-to-face with a wall.

No, not a wall—a chest. A chest so hard, it can only belong to one man.

"Allie. Can we talk?"

Despite the confusion and nerves that have barely let me function throughout the day, I follow him to his small office at the back. I haven't spent much time here in the past few months. He doesn't either. There's not much in his office but a desk, a single chair, and tall bookshelves where he stores his accounting books. I don't close the door behind me, and he doesn't ask me to.

"What do you need?"

"You, Allie."

Our eyes lock.

I don't move an inch. I don't give him a reaction because I don't even know what to say.

This isn't how I expected this conversation to go, considering we didn't speak last night when he came home. And when I woke up this morning, his truck was already gone.

"Last night, I..." He runs a hand through his short hair, a telltale sign that he's overwhelmed. "I've never done this before, and I'm a fucking mess. Give me a second."

Panic grips at my chest, and I hate myself for it. Because if Travis is about to say what I think he's about to say, I don't deserve to hear it.

I don't deserve his love, not when I've been feeding him lies since the day we met.

"All right," he starts again, the intensity of his gaze almost unbearable. "What I meant to say is that you are my—"

"Travis," I interrupt him gently.

My heart is beating too fast, my head is screaming too loudly, and I've had enough.

Enough with the lies.

Enough with hiding a past I can't fix no matter how much I'm ashamed of it.

Enough with hiding my authentic self from the one man I want everything with.

I take a deep breath and hope my voice doesn't shake as I say, "Before you say anything, I need to tell you something important."

His expression remains open despite his slight frown. "Okay."

The thing about waiting too long to do something—something you know you *should* do—is that you risk running out of time to do it on your terms. You risk never getting the chance to explain things slowly, properly, allowing the other person to ask questions.

Every time I pictured telling Travis about my parents, my siblings, my kidnapping, and everything else, I imagined us having a private, calm conversation, after which he wouldn't hate me for having lied for so long.

I never pictured this.

"Allie?" Charlie calls out from outside the office. "Some people came asking for you, and they're, um, very insistent. I think you should come out."

There's a strange edge to his voice I don't have time to overthink. Travis gestures to the door with his chin. "Go. We'll talk later."

"But—"

He closes the distance between us and presses a gentle kiss to my forehead. Heat climbs up my neck as one of his hands places a strand of brown hair behind my ear.

"Later, all right?" he asks softly. "I'll wait."

"Allie." The urgency in Charlie's voice makes my stomach turn.

With one final look at the man who is willing to give me everything without asking for anything in return, I follow Charlie.

If I had to pinpoint the exact moment my soul dies, it would be the second I step outside Travis's office.

Standing in the middle of The Lair—a place that has been exactly that, my refuge, for the past sixteen months—a vicious shiver runs through my body and locks it into place.

"Allison."

No matter how much time passes or how far I run, I will never forget the voice I still hear in my nightmares.

My mother's voice.

A tremble runs through me, making my voice and my hands shake. "W-What are you doing here?"

I blink, just in case I've hit my head and I'm seeing things.

But the seconds pass, and my mother is still here, at The Lair. And so is my father behind her and my brother, Johnny.

I can't look away from him. I haven't seen him since he was fourteen. Now at twenty, it shouldn't surprise me that he towers over our father. He looks so much like him, too, with his dark hair and tanned skin, I almost do a double take.

Johnny and I have never been close. He either enjoyed our parents' social media circus or didn't care, while I fought to escape it with every fiber of my being. I was always deemed the difficult child, the problematic one, and eventually he started seeing me as such too.

Now, as his dark eyes pierce through mine, emitting nothing but hatred, it hits me that my own brother is a stranger.

"You know why we're here," my mother snarls, inching closer to me. "You thought a little hair dye and a change of name could hide you forever? *Please.*"

"Who's this, Smith?" Jude's voice joins in from behind me.

My pulse jumps.

"*Smith,*" my mother spits out, as if the word disgusted her. "You have these people fooled, don't you? Don't worry, sweetie, I'll let them know exactly who they're dealing with."

"What are you doing here?" I ask her again, stepping closer in an attempt to make her forget we're not alone. I'm not brave enough to look at my co-workers and friends, at the damage behind me. "How... how did you find me?"

It's my father who says, his voice as cold and detached as I remembered, "We hired a private investigator a while back. You might have hidden from the world, but you can't hide from your family. We knew where you were all along."

"W-What?" I stammer. Then, as if stuck by lightning, I count the people in front of me again. Three, not four. "Where's Cindy?"

"Your sister is at home," my father says. "We didn't want her to—"

Johnny cuts him off. "Stop giving her explanations. She left us and is about to sell us out for dirty money, for fuck's sake. Let's just take what we came for and get the hell out of here."

The fact that my younger brother seems to outright hate my guts doesn't escape me. But his words are what set off a loud alarm in my head.

I wrap my arms around myself because my body can't stop shaking. "I have nothing that belongs to you."

"You do," Johnny accuses. "We searched for it and didn't find it, but you've always been sneaky. You must have kept a copy for yourself. We want it gone."

My heart gallops. "What do you mean you searched for it? What is *it*?"

It hits me—the car, the break-in next door, the almost break-in in my apartment that made me move in with Travis.

But *no*. It would be insane to think my brother or my parents were behind that. It would mean they have been in the area for months, and that's simply not possible. I would've seen them.

"The video," my mother snarls, interrupting my thoughts. "You had no right to spew such lies about our family."

Lies?

"Delete your copy of the video at once and sign an NDA," my mother continues. "You may be our daughter, but we won't hesitate to take you to court if you so much as breathe a word to George Eden or his social-justice-warrior wannabes."

They think I'm going to expose them on TV?

Unlike the rest of me, my voice doesn't shake when I say, "I want nothing to do with you *or* George Eden."

Then I turn to my brother. To the boy-man I barely recognize anymore. "My car, my apartment..." My throat closes up. "Did you have anything to do with it?"

He doesn't need to admit it. And he won't, either, because we're surrounded by witnesses. But the furious, arrogant look he gives me is more than enough.

"We want the video," my father says. "Tell us where it is, delete it, sign the NDA, and stop this charade."

A weird calmness takes over me, like that day at the warehouse. And before I know it, I blurt out, "Or what?"

The air shifts from tense to downright hostile. For a moment, I wouldn't put it past my mother to throw herself at me and try to maul me like a wild animal—but then a heavy weight lands on the small of my back.

"What's going on?" Travis asks behind me, tension radiating off his body.

I take a small step closer to him, my body acting on instinct. It's only now, with Travis by my side, that I muster the courage to glance around.

Charlie's eyes pinball between me and my family as if recognition has finally dawned on him. When his look of betrayal becomes too heavy a burden to bear, I have to look away.

Unsurprisingly, seeing Jude and Sandra doesn't make me feel better. Jude is behind the bar, while Sandra is standing by the kitchen, their eyes on me. Jude can't stop frowning, and Sandra looks a second away from crying.

I did this. I never told them the truth despite my multiple chances. I've ruined everything.

"Who are these people, Allie?" Travis asks, his voice low.

"*These people* are her parents and her brother," my mother starts with no short amount of venom in her voice. "Don't think we haven't looked you up, *Travis Ward*."

"Let's talk outside," I manage to let out, panic dulling my

senses. They won't get Travis involved in this mess. They have no right to.

"Wouldn't you like that," Johnny sneers at me before sliding his gaze to Travis.

The two stay locked in a cold, cruel stare off, and my heart betrays me. For a moment, it folds in on itself, forcing me to conjure an ideal future in which my parents never put me at risk, in which my brother doesn't hate me, in which he only stares down Travis as part of an overprotective act because he doesn't trust anyone to take care of his older sister.

But then reality sinks in, slicing my chest open as it does.

"Get out of my bar." Travis doesn't need to raise his voice. It drips authority on its own. "Or I'll throw you out myself."

My mother snarls, "Are you threatening *a woman?*"

"*Stop*," I lash out, feeling like the world is about to collapse on me any minute now.

Pressure builds in my chest, and I know there's no getting out of this. There never has been a happy, calm life in the cards for me. And the worst part is, I can only blame myself for it.

I look at my mother, my father, my brother, and say goodbye to the people behind me for good. Because, after this, The Lair will no longer be my home.

"You *ruined* my life," I snarl, turning to my parents, tears gathering in my eyes. *I hate it. I hate them. I hate myself.* "You made money off me without my consent for years, exposed me to millions of strangers, and got me *kidnapped*. And you have the nerve to barrel into my life six years later, *demanding* I give back the only thing that protects me from you? How *dare* you?"

Through the tears, I think I see my mother flinch. But experience has shown me empathy isn't part of her emotional range, so I'm certain I'm only seeing what my inner child has always longed for—a caring mother who's capable of apologizing and righting her wrongs, no matter what it took.

My mother hesitates, but she picks herself back up quickly enough. "We know you stole that money. We saw it on the cameras and have it on tape. Ten thousand dollars is no joke, Allison. If you delete the video and sign the NDA, we won't press charges or reveal your new identity to the press. We'll consider us even. Your choice."

"I didn't steal that money because *I* earned it." My lungs feel incapable of taking a full breath. "You pimped me out on the internet for years, selling my image to publicity campaigns I never agreed to participate in. You used me, and I never saw a cent. I didn't want your money, couldn't care less about it when you've scarred me for life. I only used it to get away because I had no other choice. *You* didn't leave me any other choice."

She huffs, turning to my father. "Are you hearing this?" When she looks at me again, I don't see a mother. All I see is a monster. "You privileged, ungrateful *bitch*. We gave you an easy life, influence, privileges. More than a brat like you could've ever strived for, and this is how you thank us?"

My heart can't take any more beatings, so I let that word slide.

But Travis doesn't.

"What did you just call her?" He keeps his voice low, reminding me of the military man he once was even though I never knew him.

"You don't get it. You still don't get it." I turn to my mother before she can answer Travis. Unlike his, my voice has turned meek, quiet, as the fight leaves me for good. "I never asked or wanted to grow up with a camera in my face. And I never..."

I wipe at my tears, deciding that I'm done wasting my time with a mother who won't listen. With a father who never cared. In one last hopeless attempt at clinging to that stupidly idealistic dream of a real family, I turn to Johnny.

"I know you hate me." My voice breaks, and my throat hurts

when I speak, but I push through. Because when it comes to my past, not giving closure to my siblings is the only thing I regret. "I know we've never been close, but I hope one day you'll understand my choices. I hope you will forgive me for the pain I've caused you and Cindy by leaving like that, without giving you an explanation. For never reaching out because I... I couldn't, Johnny. I hope you realize they've used you too. All three of us. You may hate me, but I don't hate you. Despite everything, I don't. I can't. You're victims too. Victims of greed and harmful decisions—"

"*Enough.*" My mother cuts me off, her words bouncing off the walls. "Enough of playing the victim, Allison! Sign the damn NDA."

I'd almost forgotten Travis's presence at my back until he steps in front of me, blocking me from my family's view.

"You have ten seconds to get the fuck out of here before I call the cops."

I hear my father's voice. "You wouldn't—"

"The press would love to know you caused a scene in a bar. That tends to be good for the reputation, I'm sure."

I'm not surprised *that*, a threat to their public image, is what makes my mother sidestep Travis until she's facing me again and say, "Our lawyer will be in touch soon with the NDA, Allison *Smith*. Make a smart choice for once in your life. You have one week."

Nothing feels real for the next few minutes as my family exits The Lair, leaving behind nothing but the broken pieces of my future mixed with the shattered remains of my past.

The ground beneath my feet isn't sturdy anymore.

My vision blurs with tears, dizziness. Both.

My ears ring, but I still hear his voice.

I think it's Travis.

I think he's calling my name.

258

What must be his hands land on my shoulder. My eyesight focuses long enough to see his moving lips, but my hearing hasn't caught up.

It's like there's a flat line inside of me. Like everything my heart had started beating for in the past year is now gone.

Video. NDA. Lawsuit.

The words swirl in my head. Everything turns black again.

I have to get out of here.

I think I say something. I don't know. My mouth is open. I know it because it's so dry, it hurts. I'm not sure if any words come out.

"Allie."

Travis.

"Allie, talk to me."

Everything comes back at once. The sounds, the smells, the feeling of Travis's hands on my shoulders that I shrug off.

My head pounds with embarrassment and regret as I look around and find everyone I've grown to love in the past year staring back at me, shock written all over their faces.

I lied to them. I betrayed their trust, smashed it to pieces. For nothing.

I try to breathe, but my lungs won't fill up. Moisture runs down my cheeks, and sweat clings to the back of my neck.

Travis tries to stop me. Charlie says something, but I can't...

I can't.

I give up.

There's no point in fighting anymore when everything I've tried to build for myself has never been real. And it's all my fault.

"I-I'm sorry."

An apology is the only thing I can offer them. They deserve so much more than the words of a liar.

Using the last of my strength, I exit The Lair for the last time, knowing I can never come back. Not after what I've done.

Chapter Thirty-Two

Age 19

I stared at the Los Angeles skyline from the rearview mirror. When my chest constricted, I took a deep breath through my nose and focused back on the highway, all while trying to convince myself that I was doing the right thing.

Leaving didn't make me a coward—it made me a survivor.

And that video...

It wasn't a mistake. It was my only way out.

Los Angeles took everything from me—my safety, my happiness, my chances at a worthwhile future. I could never come back to a place that never felt like home.

As I sped down the highway, I wondered if I'd ever find a place that did. And I promised myself that if I ever did, I'd never ruin it.

Chapter Thirty-Three

Heavy clouds settle over the Fore River, visible from my hotel room window in Portland. The water matches the muted gray-blue shade on the walls almost to perfection. I would know since I've spent the last four days looking at it.

Four days since I stormed out of The Lair, turned off my phone, packed my things before Travis drove back to his farmhouse, and left.

For good.

I thought I'd hit rock bottom six years ago when I left Los Angeles. I was young, scared, hurt, and lost beyond all sense of direction. Now I look back and wonder how my nineteen-year-old self had the strength to road-trip across the country in survival mode. More than ever before, I wish I could go back in time and give that Allie a bone-crushing hug.

But I wouldn't have the courage to tell her all she went through was for nothing.

My gaze travels from the river-blue walls to my backpack, resting on top of a small desk across the room. I haven't touched my phone in four days. Haven't even turned it on.

Because I'm a coward. I always have been.

An uncomfortable hum sizzles in the center of my chest as my feet meet the plush carpet. The floor grumbles with every step toward my backpack. Slowly, I undo the zipper, and with a lump in my throat, I stare at my phone at the bottom.

Jada must be worried. I should turn it on and tell her what's going on.

But I can't. It doesn't feel right, and I don't know why. Going to Jada with my problems has always been my go-to. So why the hell can't I bring myself to do it when I need her more than ever?

Because a huge part of me is scared of what else I'll find when I turn on my phone. I'm not ready to see a text from Travis, whatever the content may be.

More than that—I'm not ready to *not* see a text from Travis.

It's only now that I'm able to take off the rose-tinted glasses and see that he was never meant to be mine. He doesn't deserve an emotionally unstable liar for an employee, let alone for a life partner. And I certainly don't deserve such an attentive, loving man when I didn't even have the courage to turn in a resignation letter. I simply left.

Coward, coward, coward.

I prove to myself once again what I'm made of when I look away from my phone, making a final decision.

But something catches my eye at the bottom of my backpack.

Tom's business card.

My fingers shake with uncertainty as I pick it up. His name is written in an unassuming font along with the *Production Assistant* tag. The logo of George Eden's production company sits on the left, staring back at me. Daring me.

No. Forget about it.

I should. My parents' threat left no room for doubts. If I ever speak a word about my past, they will demolish whatever scraps of privacy I have left. Plus, talking to George Eden would defeat the purpose of hiding in the first place. I don't want attention. I don't want more chaos.

With a confusion I don't fully understand gripping at me, I put the card back down. I should throw it away altogether and shift my energy into what really matters—what the hell I'm going to do now.

Should I stay in Maine? Try to make it to Canada? Maybe my mistake was always staying in the United States. Maybe—

A sudden wave of anger and sadness washes over me at the sound of my inner voice.

I...

I...

I'm tired of running away.

And I'm angry at myself for treating it like it's always been my only option.

I've convinced myself that I'm only a passenger in my life instead of the goddamn driver. I let fear take over. I've spent the past six years telling myself it wasn't the time to move on yet, that I still needed to be on the lookout, that I wasn't safe despite the distance.

All this time, I've been my own worst enemy.

My eyes prickle with tears at the realization that I'm wasting my life away. A life that doesn't belong to me because, even so many years later, I'm still letting my parents control it.

My promise. I'm breaking it.

How could I have forgotten about it?

That day at the warehouse, as I hid under a car and waited for an imminent death, I promised the sky I would make the world a better place if I survived.

And I did. I survived the worst thing that has ever happened to me and only got stronger as the years passed.

Yet all I've done since is lie, hide, and betray myself.

I grew up in a privileged position. I'm well aware of how many children would kill for a fraction of what I had. And I don't want to sound ungrateful, not even to my own ears, but the truth is, I'd give all of that away for a loving family. Because what I had, no matter how grand, meant nothing if it was obtained through exploitation and abuse.

I hate my parents. Both of them. I hate them with a burning passion that has reignited after their visit six years later.

I hate my father. I hate how he never confronted my mother when she mistreated me, how he never went out of his way to comfort me, how he saw my breakdowns as an inconvenience instead of what they really were—a desperate cry for help.

I hate my mother. I hate how she sacrificed my safety, well-being, and health for money and influence, how she never put her children first, how she's still blind to the pain she's caused me.

I don't hate Johnny and Cindy, but I also can't hold back because of them.

I need to stop this.

I promised.

It's too late for me, but it may not be for others.

My fingers continue to shake as I pick up Tom's card again. They still shake as I grab my laptop and get on the bed.

It feels like the hotel room is spinning when I log into my email account and type in his address, so much so that I have to shut my eyes for a moment and take a deep breath.

Don't do it. Your parents will ruin your life.

A beat passes.

The world shifts and clicks into place.

They already have.

Chapter Thirty-Four

It's funny, I ponder as my driver speeds past a yellow light in downtown Los Angeles, how the more you insist you will never do something, the harder life comes back to bite you in the ass.

Six years ago, I promised myself I wouldn't come back to the city where so much was taken from me. I can only guess the universe is now laughing at the way I'm eating my words.

The navigation system shows we're ten minutes away when the sound of my phone makes me jump.

"Hi." My throat is dry when I speak.

"Hey, Allie." There's a mixture of softness and urgency in Tom's voice. "Are you in the car already? I checked online, and your plane landed fifty minutes ago."

I clear my voice. "Yeah, I'm in the car. We're almost there."

"Good, good." He pauses, and I hear voices and commotion behind him. "How are you feeling?"

I'm surprised he's asking. Hollywood isn't exactly known to care about nobodies, but then again, maybe I'm being unfair. When he emailed me back yesterday, he did it with a contract, a one-way plane ticket, and a promise to make me feel as comfortable as possible through this whole thing. He also wrote that I was really brave for speaking out, and that they appreciated it more than I could ever know. He sounded genuine when I spoke to him on the phone this morning, too, before boarding the flight.

"Nervous," I tell him honestly.

Before my flight, I gave in and checked my phone. I have several missed calls from Jada, as well as texts from her that I couldn't bring myself to open. I need to do this on my own. I can't keep using her as a crutch, even though I love her more than anything. I need to stay in my own bubble right now; a bubble that is fragile enough to be burst by the smallest of doubts. Shutting everything and everyone out is the only way to do this.

I also saw texts from Charlie, Jude, and Sandra. I didn't open them either.

Nothing from Travis.

A sharp, piercing feeling stabs through my chest. *Don't think about him.*

"George will tell you when you get here, but I want to remind you again," Tom starts, pulling me out of my thoughts. "You can speak as much or as little as you want. We won't pressure you. The fact that you'll be speaking out at all is a big deal in itself."

"I appreciate that," I mutter.

"I have to hang up, but we'll talk shortly. Thanks again for agreeing to this, Allie."

The reminder of what I'm about to do bulldozes right through me. Last night, I didn't sleep a wink. I couldn't, not when I knew what would happen today. And so I did something I was sure I'd come regret—I searched my name online.

For years, I'd been terrified of the internet. It's a wild thing, caring about what strangers think of me. I couldn't, and still can't, understand how people I don't know, people who don't know *me*, have such strong opinions about my private life. A private life I never agreed to showcase in the first place.

I'd never felt in control of my own narrative, not as a child and not as an adult. In a way, by looking myself up, I regained scraps of that agency. And even though it was uncomfortable, I pushed through for myself, because it was about damn time I faced my fears.

I saw dozens of differing viewpoints—that I was an attention seeker, that I was a victim, that I should speak out, that I should be allowed to remain silent—and it only proved my long-standing theory that the human brain isn't built to take in so many opinions at once. That we shouldn't have to.

"We're here, ma'am," the driver says, bringing me back to the present.

I let out a shaky breath as I take in the tall building we're parked next to. I can't see much other than the buzz of people coming in and out the main entrance of the TV studio, busy workers with phones pressed to their ears and important places to be.

"Ma'am?"

My cheeks heat up. "Yes, sorry."

I rush out of the car and get my suitcase and backpack. Tom said the production company would pay for my hotel here, but apparently, I don't have time for a stop and a quick shower. All this urgency isn't helping my already-panicked state.

Shortly after I tell the receptionist my name, Tom appears down the hallway wearing a set of headphones and holding a clipboard. His smile is tight-lipped but warm.

"You weren't kidding when you said you were almost here," he says easily. "How was your flight?"

"Good." I don't want to be so awkward, but I'm so nervous I might throw up.

He picks up on it. "Follow me. George is dying to meet you."

The next hour flies by. I'm thankfully allowed to take a quick shower in one of the dressing rooms. Then a man approaches me with a change of clothes—a plain white shirt and dark jeans. Once I'm dressed, someone else ushers me to a makeup chair, where one lady works her magic to make me look less zombie-like, while another straightens my hair. There's a tray with snacks and water there, too, so I eat a granola bar and drink a whole bottle of water before I'm led somewhere else.

Every corner I turn, I spot someone's stressed face. If this is what it's like to work in the entertainment industry, it looks like a nightmare.

Shortly after they tell me I'm ready, Tom somehow finds me again. It feels like he's everywhere at once.

"I apologize for the chaos," he says as if he could read my mind. We start down a well-lit hallway. "I can only imagine how overwhelmed you must be by all this."

"A little." There's no point in hiding it. "Is it always this hectic?"

He throws me a smirk over his shoulder, power walking way faster than me. "You've seen nothing yet."

I gulp, then do it again when we enter a studio, a *real* TV studio, and I spot him—George Eden in the flesh.

I don't know why, but my first thought as he shakes my hand is that he's shorter than he looks on TV. His brown hair looks lighter in person too. My nerves must be making me delirious.

"Allison." His smile is genuine. "I'm George Eden. Thank you so much for coming today. I'm happy to hear you've changed your mind about the interview."

The percentage of people who have never heard of George Eden and his provocative journalism in this country is probably very low, so the fact that he introduced himself calms me down a little. I have no idea why. Maybe it's because I expected to find a demanding, cutthroat man despite Tom's reassurance that he's everything but.

"I..." I start, but my throat closes up. The weight of the last twenty-four hours, paired with what I'm about to do, sinks in.

George and Tom exchange a knowing glance before George says, "Everything's happening so fast, and I understand how you must be feeling. My team and I want to make sure you're as comfortable as possible. We're going to sit down for our interview, just you and me, whenever you're ready. I'll ask some questions, and you can answer however you want. If you feel uncomfortable or overwhelmed at any point, we'll stop."

I nod along, making a superhuman effort to take in what he's saying. My brain is overstimulated in the worst possible way.

"Thank you," I finally say. At least my voice isn't shaking. "This isn't... I mean, this isn't ideal for me, but it isn't because of you. Your team has been great so far, and I..."

Jeez, Allie. Forgot your English?

I shake my head. "I'm sorry. I'm just nervous."

George gives me an understanding smile. "That's all right. Just remember we're here to cater to your every need. Whenever you're ready, we can start."

I've seen George Eden's famous interviews before. They're always engaging, covering controversial and lesser-talked-about topics that soon become relevant conversations people have in the line in coffee shops. He's an industry pioneer, and whatever subject he touches becomes gold, which doesn't ease my nerves.

He's also famous for his interviewing style—casual but intense. I can see it clearly in the sobriety of the set we step in moments later—the same one I've seen on TV. The lights are low, the space empty except for two identical deep green velvet armchairs positioned one in front of the other. To my right, there's a black side table with some water. George has one too.

My pulse accelerates when Tom steps away after putting a microphone on my shirt, leaving me alone with the one man who's about to change my life.

The crew keeps moving around us, positioning cameras and microphones in every corner. Yet despite the crowded set, it feels like it's only George and me.

"Are you ready to start?" he asks me in an easy voice.

I'm only able to nod.

"I tend to be more serious in interviews. Just as a warning," he tells me. "Matches the ambiance."

My lips tilt nervously because yes, he's known for being serious and a little invasive in his interviews. He always gets the answer he's looking for.

Oh god, what have I agreed to?

George signals something I don't understand to the crew before setting his eyes on me. I can pinpoint the exact moment his interviewer mask slips on, and a brief wave of regret hits me —nobody knows I'm here. Not having Jada's reassurance makes me feel momentarily weak before I realize that's exactly why I told no one in the first place.

I'm ready to make my own choices without needing anyone's approval. I can't keep using Jada as a crutch, or even Travis. He makes me feel safer than I've ever known, and I'd give anything to be in his arms right now. I'd give anything to finish the conversation we started in his office. But I can't think about him right now or I'll crumble, so I take a quick gulp of water and focus on the man in front of me.

"Rolling," a masculine voice says somewhere on the set.

George gives me a discreet thumbs-up.

I promised.

Chapter Thirty-Five

"ALLISON BUCCIERI," GEORGE STARTS. HIS VOICE IS relaxed, mirroring the way he's leaning into his armrest. I can tell it's all practiced and measured. "Long time no see."

My hands, resting on my lap, start trembling. My throat hurts when I try to speak, as if I hadn't done it in a long time. "Hi, George."

I feel like a deer caught in headlights, even though I'm here willingly. My fingers are clammy, and I don't think there's enough oxygen in this room. Could they open a window? Are there even windows on TV sets?

"You're anxious," George observes out loud.

My only answer is a short nod.

"You've been hiding for six years," he muses. "Why come out now?"

The set gets blurry, and a buzzing sensation travels to the tips of my fingers. My throat closes, as if protecting me from saying things I will regret.

"Do you need to take a moment?" George asks, dropping his interviewer mask for a moment.

I feel myself shaking my head no.

"All right." He sits back in the armchair, folding one leg over the other. "Whenever you're ready."

I glance around me, at the crew whose attention is all on me, and I wish Travis were among them. If I'd been honest from the start, maybe he'd be. If I'd started living an authentic life after leaving California like I promised myself, maybe I'd have my happy, calm life with him.

George's question echoes in my mind as my eyes find his again, and the fog in my head and my heart clears just enough.

Why come out now?

Because lies are no longer going to write my story.

"I made a promise to myself years ago," I start, my voice quiet. But George doesn't tell me to speak louder, doesn't interrupt me at all. "That I was going to make this world a better place. I don't want to hide behind lies anymore."

George looks at me with intent. "You talk about lies, but what have you lied about, exactly? Other than changing your name to Smith, which isn't a lie. It's a legal process."

"It still feels like a lie," I argue.

"Why?"

"Because I didn't..." I wet my lips. "I didn't tell anyone that Smith wasn't my real name. I never told anyone who my family was. I came up with a fake backstory because telling the truth wasn't an option. And my name... I didn't change it because I wanted to. I changed it along with my looks because I didn't feel safe anymore."

"Because of your family?"

Their threats are still fresh on my mind. I can only imagine what they'll say, what they'll do when they see this, but no part of me feels regretful right now. Whatever the consequences, I'm ready to face them. I'll pay any price if it means I'll finally be free from their shackles—and my own.

My voice is louder, surer. "Yes."

George says nothing for a moment, only looks at me with those intense eyes I swear can see right through me. It's so clear now, the industry shark lying beneath the surface.

"Where have you been, Allison?"

"I left Los Angeles when I was nineteen and moved to Texas. I spent a year there." I remember my time with Jada's sister fondly, but looking back, my soul splits in half just thinking how scared and lost I was. "I wanted to see new places and keep finding myself, so I moved away again. I spent nearly a year in Nashville until someone recognized me."

"You'd dyed your hair by that point, yes?"

I nod. "I'd cut it short, too, brushing my shoulders. A little shorter than it looks right now. I'd always had long hair, so I thought I looked very different."

"But you didn't if someone recognized you," he points out.

"I mean... I flew under the radar for almost two years before someone recognized me. It was bound to happen."

"You say it like it's an obvious thing that you weren't particularly worried about because it was expected. Yet you moved away when someone recognized you. Why?"

"I was in survival mode," I confess out loud for the first time. "I was lost, didn't know what I was doing. I just wanted to be left alone, and moving felt like my only choice to achieve that."

"I'm assuming you had to pay for rent and groceries, which means you had to get a job. Where did you work?"

"I mostly worked at restaurants and bars," I tell him, feeling the nerves leaving my body with each second. Would therapy feel like this too? "As a receptionist at a tattoo parlor, at a bookshop—whatever I could find."

"Those jobs require dealing with customers, though. If your goal was to hide to avoid being recognized, it feels contradictory."

"I graduated high school, but I never went to college," I

explain. "I have some accounting certificates, but they weren't enough to get me the sort of job I would've liked. I had to take risks to keep a roof over my head."

"Mm," he muses before adjusting his position so his legs aren't crossed anymore. "Were you surprised someone recognized you?"

I frown. "I don't understand the question."

"Some may say it's a little... dramatic to change your name and appearance and escape Los Angeles like that. Your parents are well-known, but they aren't Hollywood A-listers."

I realize what he's doing right away. Last night, I saw several comments on forums saying how I'd been too dramatic in my change of identity. That nobody would recognize a social media figure in person, let alone their children all grown up. That I should get over myself.

"My face was on the news for a very long time because of my kidnapping. People knew who I was," I tell George, something uncomfortable rolling in my stomach at the memory of Claudia and that warehouse. "And after it happened, the media still talked about me, and my parents kept posting pictures of my face until I turned nineteen and left. Maybe those people aren't entirely wrong in calling me dramatic. Maybe it is unlikely to be recognized many years later—although it *did* happen—but I was paranoid. I wasn't seeing things clearly and acted on impulse."

"I certainly understand." George nods. "So, Nashville, where you *did* get recognized. Where did you go after that?"

"I moved to a small town in North Carolina. With fewer people, I figured there was a lower risk of getting recognized. I stuck to small towns from then on."

"You stayed there for a year too? That seems to be the pattern so far."

"I wanted to move as far from California as possible." My

275

fingers aren't shaking anymore, but the sweat on my hands remains. "Maine is the farthest state from California. That was always meant to be my final destination, but I wanted to live in other places first. To experience life independently, I guess. To gain self-confidence. I road-tripped my way to Maine over the span of five years, living in different states for about a year each."

"Did you move around so much because, deep down, you didn't feel safe anywhere?"

Dart, meet the bullseye.

"I think... I think I was avoiding reaching Maine too fast, as weird as that sounds. Because when I got there, it meant I'd have to rebuild my life for real. I'd have to settle down and find a stable job, and I was scared of not finding peace there when it'd been my plan all along."

"And did you? Find peace in Maine?"

Travis's face flashes in my head, constricting my lungs. His warm touch, the safety he provided, how validated he made me feel by trusting me with The Lair's accounts, how he opened his heart to me, how right it felt to come home to him every night.

I didn't only find peace in Maine—I found a life worth waking up for.

My throat closes, but I still manage to say, "I found a lot more than that."

I found love. And then I lost it.

He leans on the armrest, his fingers holding his stubbled chin. "I'm fascinated, Allison. How can such a young girl make her way across the United States all by herself, while fearing getting recognized at every stop? That must have been stressful."

His understanding makes me feel better. "It was, but at the time, I didn't think about it. I just kept going, taking it day by day. I was too young to see the real dangers, and I think... I think

I would've given up if I had thought about what I was doing for too long. Why I was forced to do it."

"Given up? What do you mean?"

After I was recognized in Nashville, I briefly wondered why I was bothering to start a new life when my old one would follow me forever. My parents had ruined my past and my future. I was naive to think my story had a happy ending.

I will never forget that night. The moment I thought about how easy it would be to get my hands on some pills and...

Jada called me then to check on me, and the idea disappeared forever. A week later, I signed up for my first online accounting course, finding a purpose again.

My voice comes out raspy. "I don't want to talk about it."

George nods. "Did you have any kind of support during this time? Someone you could call?"

I tell him about Jada, how we got close while I was still in high school, what she and her husband have been doing for me all this time.

And I tell him about Claudia.

"Your kidnapping shocked the entire country," he says, as if I could ever forget. "The news talked about a child trafficking ring."

I swallow thickly. "The police thought that's what it was."

"And what did *you* think?"

The memory of that day is still fresh in my mind, heightened by the near break-in and the car window I now have a strong suspicion my brother was behind.

"I try not to think too much about it," I admit. "It was the most terrifying thing that's ever happened to me. How that woman knew everything about my family without *knowing* them. She was convincing enough to fool a twelve-year-old."

"How did Claudia have access to that information?"

I have an inkling he knows the answer, but he wants me to

say it. He wants me to confirm it and end the speculation once and for all.

I promised.

"My mother shared everything online. Still does." My pulse quickens. It's my first time talking about her in front of someone that isn't Jada. In front of a camera that is recording my words for millions of people to see—*she* will see this. Yet not an ounce of regret fills me as I add, "She shared pictures of me with my school diplomas. In those photos, you could clearly see the name of the school and my grade. That may look harmless to people who don't have bad intentions and may just follow her because they're curious about her life, but evil people exist out there. People like Claudia. And you never know if they're watching."

"It's always fascinated me," George comments casually. "How we share all kinds of stuff on the internet as if it were a private diary. Live locations, pictures of the fronts of our houses, our cars. I feel like we've lost sight of the dangers of social media because we're constantly exposed to it. We don't think what we share could have life-endangering consequences, but it did in your case. Tell me, was your mother warned against sharing so much on social media after the kidnapping?"

"The police told her to share less stuff or do it more vaguely," I recall. Jada told her the same thing. "But she said it was her job, so..."

"So, she didn't care that her negligence got her daughter kidnapped and nearly sold into a trafficking ring, and she kept oversharing on social media," he finishes the thought for me.

My hands start shaking again. "Something like that."

"You've never agreed to being online."

"I mean, she took pictures and videos of me when I was a kid, but I didn't know *what* she was doing with them. I didn't know what social media was or how many people had access to information about me. Eventually, getting so many pictures

278

taken became annoying, and...and when I didn't want to do it anymore, she got really mad. Threatened to send me to bed on an empty stomach and said we'd be homeless if I didn't pose for her pictures because it was her job. I told her to stop as I got older, when I understood what was going on."

"But she never stopped?"

I shake my head.

"What was your father's role in all of this?" he asks next. "His social media presence isn't as big as your mother's, but he does share some things."

"We never got along, my father and I. He wasn't loving, supportive, or understanding. He was never on my side despite knowing that I wanted to be left alone. He said I should listen to my mother because she was right. It was her job, and it paid the bills. That I should stop being a brat and do as they said."

George crosses his legs again. "You know, for a very long time, I also wondered what was up with showing minors on the internet for millions of people to see, criticize, and more. Why do families like yours still do it when it's been proven that the internet isn't as safe as it used to be? When asked, some parents said that by hiding their kids from their audience, they'd create a dangerous curiosity around them. That people would go out of their way to see what their children looked like, and that by showing their faces, they'd take control of the narrative. As one of those children—now an adult—do you have an opinion about this?"

I fidget with my fingers on my lap. It's not something I'd heard before, but I can picture my mother saying it.

"I don't like extremes," I start carefully. "I always try to understand both sides, and in this case... I... I get it. I really do. I understand why some parents think they're doing their kids a favor by showing their faces online. I want to believe most of them do so because their children are a part of their lives, and

they feel proud of them and genuinely don't think it's dangerous. But at the same time, it's so... so *selfish*. So irresponsible.
The internet isn't safe no matter how much we've convinced
ourselves otherwise. We all know this by now. A little girl was
almost abducted not long ago because her mother shared their
address to hundreds of thousands of followers. And then what
happened to me. I just...

"At the start, my mother made it sound like a fun thing.
Taking pictures and videos bonded us, and I liked it until I
didn't. But the thing is, children can't consent to things they
don't understand. And they don't understand how unsafe it is to
have their faces, pictures, and vulnerable moments out there for
anyone to see—nor should they have to, either, at their age.
Adults deal with online hate every day just for being a public
figure, yet they expose their kids to that willingly. *Why* would
anyone do that? It's a sticky situation, I know that. But as
someone who was on the other side, I need parents to understand it can ruin lives. It ruined mine."

"So you're saying it *can* be okay to show children in online
spaces?" George presses.

"I'm not here to tell anyone how to raise their kids. Who
even am I to do that? What I'm saying is that parents should
think twice about what they share. Nothing more." My voice
wavers as I relive the bitter memories. "I don't think it's safe to
post your children's certificates, showing identifiable information. I don't think it's necessary to film your child's temper
tantrums or other vulnerable moments and post them online,
whether you have a million followers or a hundred. I don't think
it's fair to ignore your child when they say they don't want to
take pictures and dismiss them by saying they don't know what
they're talking about. I don't think it should be legal to make
money off your kids and never put that money toward their
education or future."

George frowns. "Your parents never gave you any money when you turned of age?"

I swallow because maybe I shouldn't be confessing this on TV. But...

Fuck it.

"I don't have a Coogan account, if that's what you're asking," I tell him. Tell the world. "I wasn't a child actor or an athlete or a performer or anything like that, so my parents didn't open one. As far as I know, it isn't a legal requirement for children in social media."

"Yet," George says. It sounds like a promise.

"I..." *Deep breath, Allie.* "I took ten thousand dollars in cash from my parents' safe before escaping because I couldn't risk them monitoring my location through my credit card, and I had no other way to get money. It felt like I was stealing, but it was *my* money too. I'd helped earn it by participating in advertising campaigns against my will."

George shakes his head, a hint of sadness tainting his eyes. "You're no thief, Allison. You took what was yours because it was your only chance at survival."

I say nothing. I can't. I'd never told anyone about the money, and I'd been terrified to discover that I was right all along—that I took what wasn't mine.

"You've just mentioned child actors. Do you relate to them in any way?" he asks next. "Minors being exploited and abused in the entertainment industry has been a topic of discussion for years."

"My heart breaks for them. I can understand what they're going through." I hesitate. "But at the same time, I believe our situations aren't quite the same. It's difficult to explain. From my limited understanding, even though there's still a very long way to go, the law protects actors more than it protects us, probably because social media is such a new thing—Coogan accounts are

281

an example. I'm not saying injustices don't happen—they absolutely do—but I think things are different with social media."

"How so?"

"Well… aside from different laws, realistically, how many children and teenagers can be actors? It's a very restrictive industry. There's no room for everyone. Social media is a whole different playing field because *anyone* can become influential overnight. Anyone can post pictures and videos of their kids and go viral. You don't need to pass any audition or background check or be hired by a powerful network. Being an actor is unreachable to most, but anyone can be a social media personality nowadays.

"That's also why I wanted to be here today. We need to protect children in as many ways as we can. The entertainment industry escapes me, but I'm grateful others are fighting for the safety of children in that landscape. Social media is where I, unfortunately, have experience. I don't think we should be censoring these conversations but encouraging more and more people to speak out no matter what their situation is. Only the oppressors benefit from our silence."

An emotion akin to respect shines in George's eyes. Or maybe I'm just desperate for approval, for any sign telling me that this interview won't be in vain. That I'm not about to ruin my life for nothing.

"What you're confessing today is…" he starts after a beat of silence. "Heartbreaking. Honestly, it's heartbreaking. Not only because it happened to you, but because it's happening to other children right now, as we speak, and they're powerless to stop it."

"I really hope that changes," I tell him honestly.

"That's our wish as well," he reassures me. "But inevitably, when these controversial conversations take place—particularly when they point fingers at a public persona for neglect and abuse—skeptics are known to accuse victims of lying. One could argue that you're here because you want attention. That it's your word against your parents', and it wasn't *that* bad. That you're exaggerating."

My chest constricts, knowing where he's going with this.

George sits up straight, both of his feet planted on the ground. "Which is why you've brought irrefutable evidence to the studio."

He turns to look directly into one of the cameras.

"In order to ensure a successful escape from her family home in Los Angeles, Allison Buccieri made a video showcasing her parents' abuse over the years and threatened to release it to the press if they ever contacted her again. Which they did, only days ago. Eden Productions will now show you the video that protected Allison all these years."

Chapter Thirty-Six

Age 19

"Hi, Mom, Dad. I... I don't know how to start this video. I'm shaking a little bit."

For years, I'd watched my mother record countless sit-down videos like this one in her office. She'd show her most recent makeup purchases, new clothes, and answer questions from her audience. She made it look so natural, like it was as easy as talking to us.

But as I sat on my bed with one of her cameras recording on a tripod, my heart raced, and my palms sweated with nerves. Because no, it didn't feel natural at all.

And what I was about to do didn't help.

I forced myself to keep going despite my throat feeling like someone had stuck cotton balls in it.

"I wanted to tell you that I'm leaving Los Angeles, and I'm doing it willingly. Nobody is forcing me, blackmailing me, threatening me, or anything else. This is entirely my choice. I'm not telling you where I'm going. Don't expect any updates from me. I don't want updates from you either. This may be shocking to you, and I understand that. But I've tried talking to you over the years, and you never listened."

I took a deep breath through my mouth and said the same thing I'd said a million times before. Only, this time, I hoped they would listen.

"I've told you countless times that I don't want to be part of this social media circus you've roped me into since I was nine years old. I never wanted to be in your videos or photos. They stopped being fun when both of you forced me to be in them and threatened me if I refused. No parent should treat their child like a slave, but that's exactly what I've been for you for the past ten years. I've been a content-making machine when I never consented to be. Yes, Mom, *consented*. It's a big word, as you mocked not long ago, but I know exactly what it means. Do *you*?"

The red light on the camera stared back at me. The silence in the house became too heavy, and I knew I had to be done with this before my parents came back.

"You've emotionally and physically abused me. You are the reason I got kidnapped and nearly sold into a child trafficking ring. You've put me in danger more times than I can count, more times than I can remember. My teachers and the police have told you to stop, but the fact that I'm filming this video is proof that you haven't. That you put money before your children, and you don't care about the consequences it has for us. I can't protect Johnny and Cindy, but I need to protect myself. And maybe that makes me selfish and a terrible sister, but I can't stay here anymore no matter how much I love them and wish to see them grow up. I don't want to blame you for this because leaving is my choice, but at the same time, I can't deny you're forcing me to do this. I have no other choice.

"I don't want you to contact me again. I don't want you to talk about me online ever again. If you do, you must know I have a copy of this video, and I won't hesitate to show it to the press and expose you for who you truly are. I'm not scared of you."

I was. I really was.

"You might be thinking no one will believe me because I'm a child, and you're influential people, so keep watching and decide for yourself."

My chest deflated with one last shaky breath. I stood from my bed, hovered my finger over the Stop button, and paused.

"You've ruined my life."

I stopped recording.

Before the gravity of what I'd done dawned on me, I quickly transferred the video to my laptop. Then I searched for what I was looking for on my mother's and rushed to take it back to her office.

Over the years, my mother had kept her raw video files on the cloud—including the footage where I complained, cried, and yelled because I didn't want to be on camera. She cut those clips out of the videos she posted, but she never deleted them.

Locked in my bedroom, I spent the next two hours adding those clips to my video—me sobbing uncontrollably when I begged her not to film my red sheets the day I got my first period; our fight in which I snatched her camera when Milo died, including her grabbing me by the back of my hair and pushing me into my room; me complaining when she forced me to be in promotional campaigns I didn't want to participate in; both of my parents calling me a brat and threatening to send me to bed on an empty stomach if I didn't cooperate.

I wished there was proof of every single thing they'd done to me. I wished I had a functional family and didn't need to make this video at all.

I wish, wish, wish.

When I saved the final copy and uploaded it to different accounts on the cloud so it'd never get lost, I shut my laptop and stared off at the garden on the other side of my window.

I couldn't lie to myself—a part of me wished this video was made public so everyone would see the kind of monsters they supported.

More wishes.

Chapter Thirty-Seven

I FIGHT WITH ALL I HAVE TO KEEP MY EYES ON THE SCREEN as George and I watch my video together. When it ends, you could hear a pin drop in the studio.

George has a few more questions after that, but they blur together. Adrenaline pumps through me in powerful waves, making me sick to my stomach. Not because I regret this interview, but because everything suddenly becomes real. My parents are going to see this, and they are going to sue me.

We are done in two hours. Tom and George thank me profusely again, and some members of the crew kindly ask if they can give me a hug. A while later, a car drops me at the hotel George's production company arranged for me. But before I make it to the reception desk, I can't take it anymore and call Jada.

"Allie," she breathes out, the worry in her voice so evident, it makes me feel like the worst human alive. "Is it you?"

"It's me," I whisper, my eyes watering. "I'm sorry, Jada. I'm so sorry. I'm in LA. I talked to George Eden."

She sucks in a breath. "Oh, honey...."

"I'm at a hotel." I rattle off the name. "C-Can you pick me up?"

"Of course, sweetie. Oh, Allie, we were so worried. We'll be there shortly. Please don't move."

I don't. And forty minutes later, I'm sandwiched between Jada and Paul, clinging to their hug as if I'd crumble if they let me go. I'm not convinced that I won't.

We barely speak on our drive to their home. Jada sits with me in the back seat, holding my hand the entire time, while Paul keeps asking me if I'm okay, if I need to stop. I couldn't possibly love them more.

I skip dinner. Jada tries to convince me to eat, but anxiety is knotting my stomach so tightly, I can barely drink water.

One look at Jada's and Paul's faces is enough to know they want to talk about today. Keeping them in the dark makes me feel like crap, but I can't speak tonight. I can't.

They tell me they understand.

I'm so mentally exhausted, I fall asleep the second my head hits the pillow.

The next day, I wake up at noon. Jada leaves me a note in the kitchen, reminding me to eat something and assuring me that she and Paul will rush back home after work. I eat half a banana and go back to bed.

I can't stand being awake.

Hours later, the sound of the front door closing wakes me up. Hushed voices filter under the door of the bedroom I'd once claimed as my own. A bedroom I never thought I'd sleep in again.

I'm rubbing the sleep off my eyes when a soft knock makes my heart do a downright jolt. "Allie? Are you there?"

"Yeah."

"Can I come in?" Jada asks.

"Sure."

Her expression is wary when her eyes meet mine. "Hey, honey. I'm sorry if I woke you up. I sent you a couple of texts, but you didn't reply. I just wanted to make sure you were okay."

With a tired hand, I reach out to my nightstand and grab the glass of water, taking a sip. I clear my throat. "I'm sorry for worrying you. I was sleeping and turned my phone off."

I should just let it die.

"That's okay." Jada hesitates. "Paul and I are going to start making dinner, if you want to join us."

The biggest part of me wants to say no. It wants to fester in bed until fear, anxiety, and guilt eat me alive. It would be so easy to let that part win. *So* easy.

Surrendering to fear isn't scary or even difficult because it's always the safest option. It won't cause your skin to prickle or your heart to stall or your brain to turn to danger mode. It's comfortable.

But then there's a tiny voice inside my head that wants to have this conversation. That needs to. George Eden's interview is airing tomorrow night, and it's okay if I admit to the people I care so much about—and to myself—that I'm not ready for the aftermath.

"Let me take a quick shower first," I find myself saying, swallowing past the lump in my throat.

She gives me what I think is a relieved smile and says, "Take your time," before shutting the door behind her again.

Twenty minutes later, the hardwood floor creaks under my weight as I walk into the kitchen. Paul is whispering something in Jada's ear that makes her chuckle, but all signs of glee vanish as soon as they notice me.

"Hey, there," Paul greets me, trying to sound casual.

I give him a tight-lipped smile. "Hi."

"Was your shower okay?" Jada asks, her demeanor more sober than just a moment ago.

I nod, sitting down at the kitchen table. "I..."

The second I open my mouth, my eyes betray me and start to sting. My lips follow suit and start quivering with the silent words I can't voice because my throat closes up.

"Oh, honey," Jada mutters. A moment later, she's kneeling in front of me, her manicured fingers gripping my hands tightly. "Let it all out, Allie. You're okay."

I shake my head because no, I'm not okay. I've never been, and I only have myself to blame.

"You've been through a lot," Paul says before his heavy hand lands on my shoulder, giving it a reassuring squeeze. "We're really proud of you, Allie. Really proud."

For some reason, that makes me cry harder. It's not that I don't think I'm strong. I *am*, for the most part, and nobody can take that away from me. But what's strength without integrity?

I lied for six years, and it cost me everything. My happiness, my peace, my new life.

It cost me Travis.

Because this is the truth—even if I was brave enough to talk to him again, and even if he was understanding enough to forgive me, I can't forgive myself.

Travis, with a heart so big, it can't possibly fit inside his chest. He's always taken care of me, and he deserves to be with someone who shows the same respect to him. By lying to his face for more than a year, I've betrayed our trust without him even knowing, and I can't move past that.

And so the tears keep falling. Not so much for what's waiting for me once the interview airs tomorrow—as much as it makes me anxious, I don't regret speaking out—but for the life I lost, the one I'll never be able to rebuild.

After what feels like hours of bawling my eyes out in Jada and Paul's kitchen but is probably just minutes, I finally find my voice and tell them everything—how my parents found me in Bannport, how they threatened me to sign an NDA or they'd reveal my new identity, why I talked to George Eden and didn't tell them until now.

"You don't have to explain yourself to us or to anybody," Jada assures me, still holding my trembling hands in her warm ones. "It's *your* life. It happened to *you*. If your parents didn't want the world to know, they shouldn't have done it in the first place."

I let out an uneven breath. "Everything will go to hell tomorrow."

"Then let it happen," says Paul, who's taken a seat next to me. "Nobody in their right mind would question what you did or blame you for your choices, Allie. Not when you showed the video."

"My parents will sue me," I whisper.

"Again, let them. They won't win." Paul sounds so convinced, I want to believe him. More than anything.

"If they do, you won't be alone," Jada says. "We'll be with you every step of the way. We'll help you find an attorney, and anything else you need. You're not alone, Allie. Never."

Travis said the same thing when he showed up after the almost break-in.

I'm here, and you're safe. You're not alone anymore.

I made the mistake of relying on him, of taking too much when I deserved nothing. And now...

"Is there anything else you're worried about?" Jada asks as if she could read my mind. By the way her inquisitive gaze bores into mine, I'm starting to suspect she can.

"There's..." I start but stop when I feel a rush of heat crawling up my neck.

Why does this feel more difficult than talking about my parents on national TV?

Maybe because Jada and I have never talked about love or relationships; my life was too much of a clusterfuck for there to be space for anything else. Plus, it's not like I've had boyfriends in the past. A crush here and there that never went anywhere, sure, but nothing as strong or real as what I feel for Travis.

I have no idea how to tackle this conversation in a way that isn't awkward, so I just blurt it out.

"I hate the way I left things at The Lair. I stormed out of the bar because I was embarrassed after confronting my parents. I hate that I've disappointed my co-workers—who have become my close friends—and I can't bear the thought of them hating me for lying to them. But I regret hurting my boss the most. Travis. He's the man I'd been living with the past few weeks. Because I think I'm in love with him, and I think he feels something for me, too, but I've ruined everything."

Silence is the only response I get until Paul shatters it with the very last thing I ever expected him to say.

"You owe me twenty bucks, Jae."

I blink. "What?"

Jada shakes her head and throws a glance at her husband before her softened eyes land on me again. "It's nothing, honey."

I glance between them. "I want to know."

It's Paul who cracks, a sly smirk on his lips. "When Jae told me you were moving in with your boss, I told her you probably had a thing for him."

"*What*? Why would you even think that?"

He shrugs. "I wasn't wrong, was I? It was just an inkling."

Jada shakes her head, but she can't hide the amusement in the slight tilt of her mouth. "To be fair, honey, I also thought you had a crush on Travis."

My heart somersaults. "And you *bet* on it?"

"That was just Paul being silly." Jada waves it off. "But let's go back to the important stuff, because you're clearly upset about Travis. Did he say anything to you?"

"I left before he could," I admit, seeing—and not for the first time—how childish that was. If I'd stayed behind to explain myself, maybe now I wouldn't be getting nauseous wondering what he must be thinking. For better or for worse, I would know where I stood with the man I was starting to see a future with.

"I called Travis days ago," Jada blurts out, catching me and my poor heart completely off guard.

My tongue feels like sandpaper. "You did?"

The two people in front of me exchange a secretive glance. "You weren't answering your phone. He told me what had happened. That your parents had been there."

I drown out the part of me that tells me it's better if I don't know what went down, exactly, because I refuse to be that Allie anymore. I don't want to be a coward.

"Did he say anything about me?" I ask, my pulse erratic.

"Other than explaining what had happened, no. He sounded..."

"Gruff?" I offer.

"I was going to say pissed off, but yeah."

Pissed off. If I had any doubts after not seeing a single text or a missed call from him, now I know for sure—Travis wants nothing to do with me, and I can't blame him for it. It's all on me.

"How about we take a walk around the neighborhood?" Paul suggests, getting to his feet, probably after seeing the distress all over my face. "Remember the Jenkins? They got the tackiest garden gnomes on their front porch. Jae thinks they're cute, so we need your deciding verdict."

"Fresh air will do you good," Jada encourages.

I glance between the two people who have held my head

above water for more than ten years. Even though all I want is to go back to bed and sulk, they don't deserve to see me crumble. For them, I'll pull myself out of this hole.

"All right."

The garden gnomes end up being tacky after all.

Chapter Thirty-Eight

THE INTERVIEW AIRS ON FRIDAY NIGHT. BY SATURDAY morning, the witch hunt starts.

I don't hide behind Jada and Paul anymore and instead face the music by reading article after article about my parents. About myself.

It starts with the public. The same people who mere hours ago worshipped the ground my parents walked on have now turned against them. They demand a statement explaining the footage they've seen in my video. They demand an apology they won't accept anyway. They demand they take my siblings off their pages immediately, especially Cindy.

On Monday, every company my parents have recently worked with announces they were "parting ways" due to "recent events they deem unacceptable." Those who have included me or my siblings in any publicity campaigns apologize for "the harm we've unknowingly caused" and promise "to do better moving forward."

On Tuesday, I hop on a video call with George, where he explains that, "Your interview is getting far more traction than we had anticipated, and we're working on a law change proposal for Congress. We'd love to have your input, Allison, since you're a direct victim of the very thing we're up against."

I accept. No second-guessing.

On Wednesday, I book my first appointment with a therapist. I owe it to little Allie, who wasn't given a chance to heal. And I owe it to this Allie, who defied her past for a chance at a real future.

On Thursday, my parents speak out.

"Allison was always a difficult child," my dad starts, his voice as robotic as usual. He doesn't talk much throughout the fifty-two-second video they post across all their platforms. I find it funny how he's wearing an old, nonbrand T-shirt he wouldn't be caught dead wearing in public. "We did the best we could with her upbringing. Other parents will understand."

"We are heartbroken by this situation," my mother adds. I don't even bother rolling my eyes at her makeup-free face and old hoodie combination—a clear attempt at looking disheveled to gain sympathy, much like my father. "The clips shown in that video were filmed during a very difficult time in my life when my mental health was at an all-time low."

Mental health professionals didn't take long to react to my mother's words—even if it was true that she was struggling during that time, poor mental health doesn't excuse the fact that she verbally and physically abused her child. That her and my father's carelessness caused a kidnapping.

On Friday, I meet with George and his team to go over my ideas for the law proposal. I haven't left the house all week, and venturing into downtown Los Angeles is the last thing I want, but George, always understanding, agrees to meet over a video call.

The sun is setting by the time I shut my laptop. Rubbing the exhaustion off my face with the heels of my palms, I let my head fall against the back of the couch and close my eyes.

This is my life now. I'm a twenty-five-year-old woman who has just exposed her family on national television and is now helping a production company draft a law proposal in hopes of Congress protecting children from what she endured growing up.

And honestly?

It feels right. Still scary, sure. But for the first time in a very long time, I look at myself in the mirror and don't see an impostor. I don't see a liar or a woman who's living an inauthentic life.

For the first time, I see *myself*. A person who is finally fulfilling her promise.

I place my laptop on the coffee table and head to the kitchen. Jada and Paul won't be joining me for dinner—they asked me if it'd be okay if they met with some friends tonight, if I'd be fine on my own, and I begged them to go. Not because I want to be left alone, but because they deserve to live their life. They've done more than enough for me already.

Since I'm not expecting anyone until well into the night, it takes me far too long to register the sound of a car pulling into the driveway. Thinking Jada and Paul had a change of plans, I peek through the kitchen window and—

That's not their car.

I can't see who's behind the wheel from here, but I don't go near another window in case they see me inside the house.

What if my parents have found me again?

I stop myself.

So what?

I have nothing to hide. I am who I am, and I did what I had to do to end this nightmare and protect other children from a similar hell. I don't regret what I've done, nor do I owe any explanations to people who don't deserve them.

I have no solid plan as I storm out of the kitchen and throw the front door open other than to confront whoever is set on disturbing my newfound peace.

But my steps come to a halt and so does my heart when my eyes land on the person getting out of the car in Jada and Paul's driveway.

I'm still not convinced this isn't a dream as Travis shuts the car door and sets those green eyes on me.

I can't breathe.

Travis is twenty feet away, here, in Los Angeles, and I can't breathe.

Unable to move, I watch as he rounds the car—it's not his truck, so it must be a rental—his tall body coming into full view. He doesn't get close, but he doesn't need to. His eyes don't stray from mine, not once, and that's enough to make everything come back.

The Lair. His confession. The kiss.

My lies. All the reasons he deserves the best, and all the reasons I'm not it.

In the privacy of my mind, I've imagined this moment a thousand, million times. I've allowed myself to daydream about being courageous enough to call Travis. The outcome of that phone call varied depending on my mood that day—when I was feeling hopeful, he asked me to come back and start anew, and when guilt took over, which happened most of the time, he never wanted to see me again.

But now he's here, and I don't know if I'm ready for either to happen.

"Allie."

The baritone rumble of his voice seeps through my skin, coating my undeserving heart.

At my sides, I ball my hands into fists because I don't want him to see how badly I've started trembling. But this is Travis, so he notices.

His face, stoic until this moment, falls. "Sweetheart..."

That word feels like a punch to the gut.

My eyes get glassy, and I can't see him clearly anymore. But I hear his heavy footsteps climbing up to the front porch of Jada and Paul's house. To me.

"What's wrong?" he asks, his voice soft and close and everything that is good in this world. Everything I don't deserve.

I blink the tears away.

"Why are you here?" I breathe out. "Why did you..."

My eyes come into focus, and the sight of him takes my breath away. He looks the same, but his face... his face looks gentle. And no matter how hard I've willed my brain to forget how it feels to have him close, my heart hasn't. Not for one second.

"I'm here for you, Allie."

My chest caves in.

Two conflicting emotions tug at my heart—the blinding need to throw myself into his arms, where everything always feels right, and the overwhelming feeling that I should push him away. For his own good, I should.

Before I know it, I find myself shaking my head.

"No, what?" he asks. His voice has never sounded so patient. When I still say nothing but keep shaking my head, he goes and kills me some more. "You can talk to me. You know that, right?"

Under Travis's confused stare, I ask him again, out of breath, "Why are you here?"

Because I don't understand. Why is he not in Maine? At The Lair? What is he doing in California?

What is he doing *here*?

The man in front of me inhales, his wide chest expanding in size. His face takes on a more somber expression, reminding me of the Travis I met that day I ended up in Bannport by chance.

I'm starting to believe it was a thing of fate.

"I'm here for you," he repeats. "Because we don't belong apart."

I can't breathe normally anymore.

"I lied to you," I whisper, my guilt caving in even deeper.

He sighs. "Allie."

"N-No." My voice shakes along with my head. "I'm a liar, Travis. I lied to you, to *everyone*, for a year."

"I watched you on TV. We all did," he says, making my blood turn cold. *We.* Does he mean everyone at The Lair? "But even before that, Charlie showed me."

"What did he show you?" I ask, not sure I'm ready for the answer.

He swallows, as if it hurt him to say it as much as it hurts me to hear it. "The videos. From your family. The articles about the kidnapping."

My heart stops. "You knew who I was all this time?"

"No," he says. I wouldn't know how to feel if he'd said anything else. "But when your family left, Charlie recognized them and showed me everything. I'm so fucking sorry, Allie."

When I blink, more tears fall. "You don't have to apologize. You've done nothing wrong."

But he shakes his head. "You shouldn't have gone through that shit. A kidnapping, Allie? For fuck's sake. I can only imagine what went through your head the night of the break-in. I should've done more to protect you. Shouldn't have gotten angry at you like I did."

"You had no idea what had happened to me," I point out, my voice small.

"Maybe not, but I could've asked."

"You did. And I lied."

"I knew you were lying," he admits. "I should've insisted. I should've done more to help you."

Is that the sound of my heart shattering?

My brain is telling me that I shouldn't, but my heart doesn't listen as I step closer to him.

"Travis... you couldn't have done anything because I didn't let you. You were just respecting my boundaries. You should be mad at me, not at yourself."

He frowns. "Why would I be mad at you?"

Why would he *not*?

"I lied to you. Omitted so many things about my past," I repeat. "I don't deserve your compassion. I don't deserve you being here right now."

"Allie—"

"No, Travis." My voice sounds firmer, but my tears keep falling. Does he not see it? "You're a good man. The best I know. You deserve better than someone who lies, hides, and doesn't have a healthy relationship with themselves. Someone who doesn't know how to do anything but run away from her problems."

When I swallow, my throat feels as if a bunch of nails were passing through it.

I might have had a couple of therapy sessions this week, and they might have gone great, but I'm far from where I want and should be. My brain is in survival mode, Dr. Rowland said, and it's going to take a long time to learn healthy habits and discard old ones. Until I can get a hold of the version of myself that I know is hiding in there somewhere, I can't...

I can't do this. Not to him.

"You shouldn't be here," I mutter.

"I'm here because I can't fucking stand being in my own house knowing you're not there."

His words leave a sea of goose bumps on my skin.

"I'm not mad at you," he declares, his voice the firmest I've ever heard it. "I understand why you had to lie or omit things. I don't hold it against you. I could never."

"You should," I whisper.

"No, I shouldn't," he argues. "You don't owe anyone your full story, Allie. Not even me. You were going to tell me that day in my office, am I right?" I give him a faint nod. "That's good enough for me. You needed time to trust me, to feel comfortable opening up to someone for the first time. I, of all people, know what that's like."

His words make sense, too much sense, and they're making me feel defensive when I shouldn't. Maybe it's his stubbornness, or perhaps mine, that finally makes me snap.

"You don't know me," I tell him, tired. I'm tired of him ignoring the obvious. He opens his mouth to argue, but I beat him to it. "No, Travis, you don't. I've barely opened up to you because I was scared shitless of getting close to anyone. I couldn't risk people finding out about my past. So don't tell me you don't hold that against me because you *must*. You've let a stranger into your business, into your home, when I've done nothing but hide things from you or lie about them."

"I don't know you?" It sounds like a question, but I know he's not waiting for an answer. "You're gonna look at me with those beautiful eyes and tell me I don't know that you're the strongest fucking person I've ever met, and that I admire you more than I've ever admired anyone? You're gonna tell me I don't know that you love carrot cake beyond reason, that you change into your pajamas as soon as you get home because you can't stand sitting on the couch with your outside clothes on, that you love cooking because it brings you peace, that math gives you a purpose, and that your lips aren't the sweetest fucking thing I've ever tasted? That's what you're gonna do, Allie?"

My eyes fill with more tears as the butterflies in my stomach fly free once again. And even though it pains me to no end, I still tell him, "That's not enough, Travis. You know things about me, but you don't know *me*. I never allowed anyone to get close enough. It's not your fault."

"So allow me to get to know you. And let me show you who I am too. If you've been closed off, so have I."

I'm about to tell him that I know who he is, but I stop myself because he's right. We haven't been fully honest with each other for different reasons—me because I was scared, and him because that's simply how he is.

My voice quivers. "Why are you really here?"

He takes a step in my direction, then another. And when his hand lands on my elbow, cradling it with his gentle warmth, I don't move. Because I may not deserve him, but I want to be selfish right now and take what isn't mine.

"I'm not good with words or feelings," he says in a low voice. Quietly, just for the two of us. "You... you've made me feel things I'd never felt before. It was uncomfortable at first. Until I learned to put a name on it."

I close my eyes, my pulse beating in my throat. "Travis..."

"You don't have to say anything." His voice sounds gravelly. "You may not feel the same, and I'd understand. But I couldn't—"

"I feel the same," I breathe out. "I feel everything. Every single thing, Travis. I have for months."

He lets out an uneven breath. "You mean that?"

I nod. Then I feel rather than see his hand pulling me closer until my body is fully against his. Until both of his arms are around me, and I fall apart.

"I've missed you so much," I croak out.

One of his hands moves to rest at the nape of my neck. "I've missed you more. Trust me on that."

We stay silent for what feels like hours but is probably only a couple of minutes. I allow myself the last moments of selfish-ness in Travis's arms before I force myself to be honest and do what's right. No matter how badly my heart wants something different... my soul calls for this.

"I'm not ready," I admit quietly against his chest. "I don't want to stop talking to you, and I don't want us to become strangers. I want you to get to know me, to *really* know me, and I want to know you better too. I care about you more than I've ever cared about anyone, but I'm not ready for... for more. Not yet, even though I want to. I need to find myself first because you deserve the best version of me, and she doesn't exist yet. I-I'm sorry."

"There's no need to apologize for asking for what you need." He tucks a strand of hair behind my ear so lovingly, it takes everything in me not to bawl my eyes out. *I love him. I love him so much.* "However long it takes you, Allie, I'll be here. You've got me, sweetheart. I'm not going anywhere."

Chapter Thirty-Nine

"ALLIE, HONEY?" JADA CALLS OUT THE FOLLOWING afternoon. "It's for you."

Confused but not anxious—which is a first—I set my pen and journal down onto the mattress and stretch my arms above my head.

The past twenty-four hours have been quite... something.

When Jada and Paul came home and I told them about Travis's visit, Jada admitted that Travis called her after the interview aired, asking if she thought it would be a good idea to come here.

"I hesitated," she confessed last night. "I didn't know if you were ready to see him."

"You did the right thing," I said, not wanting her to feel bad about something I wasn't angry about in the first place. "I needed to see him. I needed the wake-up call."

This morning, during my video call with Dr. Rowland, I told her about what it meant to me that he'd come to California. For me.

"I don't want to run away anymore. Not from myself or my

feelings, and not from him," I told my therapist. "But I'm scared of what comes next."

"In what way?" she asked, tilting her blonde head to the side and pushing her glasses up her nose.

"What if I ruin it? I've been lying for so long, I'm scared it's now part of me, and I can't even see it. What if I find myself lying about small things because that's what my brain thinks will keep me safe?"

During our first video session, she told me I was very self-aware, which would help in my healing process. I'd never been called self-aware before.

"That's a very valid worry to have," she said, her voice always encouraging. "But you aren't lying to me in our sessions. And when you talk to Jada and Paul, you aren't lying about your feelings either. Nor did you lie in the interview.

"Therapy is a long journey. After what you've been through, it's going to take a great deal of effort and patience to overcome these obstacles your family has been throwing in your direction for more than a decade. But you *can* do it. What you need right now is to listen to yourself and respect your wishes. If you want to go out and make friends, do it. If you want to get into a relationship, do it. You're healthy in far more ways than you realize. Yes, you used to lie, but it never came from a bad place. It came from survival. Now that you don't have to just survive anymore, you need to relearn how to trust yourself and take risks. We all have trauma that could ruin our relationships —what counts is that we work on ourselves to prevent that from happening, and you're doing it."

When we hung up, I plugged in my phone, waited until it was charged, and finally faced what I should've never been scared of in the first place.

CHARLIE

> We love you, Allie Cat. We want you to come
> back. You're one of us, and your past isn't
> gonna change that. We'll always be best
> friends.

JUDE

> Not good with technology, but we miss you,
> kid. You did what you had to do. Respect to
> that.

SANDRA

> Oh, sweetie. My heart breaks for you. Please
> come back. The Lair isn't the same without
> your light. Nobody is angry at you. We could
> never be.

LOLA

> Hey, girl. I'm so sorry you had to go through
> that. I can't imagine how you must be feeling
> right now. I'm here if you need to talk. No
> judgment, ever <3

After my conversation with Travis yesterday, the urge to pack my things and catch the next flight to Maine become so strong, I have to force myself to pause.

Yes, I want to be with Travis.

Yes, he feels the same for me.

But no, I'm not ready to take that step yet.

I need to find myself first. Not fully, because I know that's an ongoing process, but just...enough. Enough to give us the chance we deserve.

Now, as I slide my feet into my house slippers and head out of my bedroom, I wonder who could be waiting for me at the door. George, maybe? He hasn't contacted me about Congress again, and I'm not sure he knows where I live, but Travis didn't know either, and he showed up anyway.

God, he showed up.

I don't know what I've done to have such a patient, caring man in my life, but I'm grateful for him every day.

When I round the corner of the hallway, I stop.

Travis gives me a lopsided smile that straight up kills me. "Hey."

Jada sends me a knowing look, her own mouth quivering with the beginning of a smirk. "I'll leave you two to it."

If eyes could smile, his are doing it right now. As his gaze travels from my face to my feet, I don't particularly care that my hair is a mess, that I'm wearing an oversized old T-shirt with a hole in my armpit, or that my house slippers are lobster themed. None of that matters because he's here. Again.

"You said you wanted to get to know me better," he starts in that deep rumble that sounds so soothing, I could fall asleep listening to his voice every night. "And I want to know you better too."

I swallow back my nerves. "I thought you'd already left."

He shakes his head. "I can stay a few days." *Days*. "I'd like to spend them with you, if you want."

Is this real? Is *he* real?

"I know you need time and space. I don't want to be over-bearing. But I'd like to see you every day, just for a couple hours, and do stuff together. Just the two of us. If you want. I can leave for Maine right now if you'd rather—"

"Don't leave," I cut him off, emotion clogging my voice. "Please don't."

Those massive shoulders visibly relax. "I won't. Not unless you ask me to."

"I won't ever ask you to leave."

His smirk is devastating. So, so devastating, it makes me weak in the knees.

"Give me ten minutes to get ready," I tell him, forcing myself to act like a normal person. "Or did you not want to hang out today?"

The corner of his mouth tilts a little higher, and I swear this is the happiest I've ever seen him. "I want to, if you're free."

I waste no time nodding.

"I'll wait in the car outside," he tells me, suddenly sounding a little shy. "Take as much time as you need. I'm in no rush."

As he shuts the front door behind him and I head back to my room, my heart pounding, I wonder if this would count as our first date.

* * *

January in Los Angeles isn't exactly cold, especially compared to the East Coast, but the light breeze makes me hug my jacket tighter against my front all the same. Maybe it's just nerves.

Travis is waiting for me in the car as he said he would. Right as I'm closing the front door behind me, he steps out into the driveway to open the passenger door for me—which melts my insides but also isn't helping my first date suspicions. Is that what this is? Or does he just want to spend time with me as a friend?

I could always ask, but I enjoy torturing myself.

"Thank you," I tell him shyly, pretty sure my cheeks are bright red.

If they weren't before, they sure are now that he's smiling down at me in that handsome way.

"Where are we going?" I ask him once he's behind the wheel again.

He starts the car and checks the rearview mirror before pulling out of Jada and Paul's driveway. "First, to get food."

I smirk. "That doesn't sound vague at all."

"This is about getting to know each other, isn't it?" He starts down the residential road, my eyes falling on his hands as he drives. God, I'd forgotten how attractive he makes everything look. "Tell you what, I like surprises."

My eyebrows shoot up at that. "You do?"

"You sound shocked."

"I just thought..." *Honesty, Allie. Speak your mind. He won't be offended.* "I've always thought you were kind of a control freak, and they don't usually like surprises."

"You're not wrong. I like to keep things under control," he concedes as he takes a turn. "What I meant is that I like surprising people. Those I care about anyway."

"What's the biggest surprise you've given Uncle Neil?"

"Other than that one time I went home with my hair cut in odd places, like he told you?" I nod, the reminder of our conversation making me laugh. I'd give anything to see a picture of that. "I got him a car a few years ago. Told him it was mine, sat him behind the wheel so he could try it out, and then gave him the keys and told him it was for him. He almost cried. He will deny it if asked, but those eyes were glassy."

And I thought this man couldn't get more attractive. "That's the sweetest thing ever, Travis. How about getting surprises yourself?"

He shrugs those massive shoulders. "Only if I trust the person who's giving me a surprise."

"Makes sense. So, food. I don't know what you had planned, but I want us to eat your favorite food tonight."

He sneaks a quick glance at me. "My favorite food?"

I hum.

"What if you don't like it? Today is for you as much as it is for me," he says with a hint of worry.

"I'll like it," I tell him with conviction. "And if I don't— which I doubt because I'm not a picky eater—then I'll never eat

311

it again. Simple. But I want to know this about you. Pretty please?"

He shakes his head, the corner of his lips tilting upward. "Can't say no to you."

We end up getting Chinese takeout. I haven't had it in years, and I don't remember if I liked it or not, but the car is filled with the most heavenly smell as Travis drives us somewhere else—another surprise.

Twenty minutes later, he stops the car at a place I haven't been to before. Perched on a hill, the imposing cupola of the observatory offers a clear view of the Los Angeles skyline. Paired with the sun that's starting to disappear on the horizon, giving the sky an orange-pink glow, it takes my breath away.

Travis grabs the takeout bags and something else from the trunk, but I'm barely paying attention. My eyes stay glued to the horizon, and before I know it, my throat clogs up.

Los Angeles has never felt like home to me. Home to the worst years of my life, sure. Home to fond memories, happy times, and freedom? No. Not at all. I couldn't wait to get out of here when I was younger, and I swore I'd never come back.

So why is my heart constricting now—and not in an uncomfortable way—as I look at the skyline of the place that has taken so much from me?

"Everything okay?" Travis's heat seeps into my skin as he places a hand on the small of my back.

I lean into his touch. "It's stunning, isn't it?"

If I'd been looking at him, I would've noticed his eyes on me as he says, "Beautiful."

My throat is so dry, I have to swallow. "Why don't I hate it anymore?"

"The city?"

I nod, finding that speaking about this is easier than I'd ever expected. "I told myself I'd never come back, but here I am. I don't want to stay here for the rest of my life, but I also don't... I don't want to run away like I used to."

He pulls me closer until my forehead is pressed against his chest and I'm wrapped in the familiar scent of him. "I'm so fucking proud of you," he mutters against the top of my hair. "I'm proud of you for feeling that way. You know what it means?"

I'm starting to, but I want his perspective. "What?"

"Growth." One simple word. One simple truth. "You're not letting them take your joy away anymore."

I'm grateful he sees it that way because I do too.

His stomach chooses that moment to rumble, and I pull away, chuckling. "Someone's hungry."

Is that a blush on his cheeks?

With a half-amused, half-embarrassed shake of his head, he intertwines his fingers with mine. "Come on. Let's find a spot."

With my heart frantically beating inside my rib cage because *Travis and I are holding hands*, I don't notice the picnic blanket in his other hand until we stop on the manicured lawns in front of the observatory.

He only lets go of my hand to lay the picnic blanket on the grass, and then he takes it again to help me sit down. As we get out all the takeout containers and arrange them on the blanket, I get a comforting sense of privacy despite us not being alone in the gardens. No, not privacy—intimacy.

"I can't believe you're taking me on a picnic," I tell him with a smile once we start opening the delicious-smelling containers.

"Maybe I should've asked first," he muses out loud.

"Hey." I cover his hand with mine, stopping that train of thought. "I've never been on a picnic before, so this is perfect. I trust you, Travis. And you have great taste, you know? This place is amazing."

He visibly relaxes, turning our hands around so he's holding mine. It's that subtle act of dominance that makes my lower area tingle, a foreign sensation that's not unwelcome.

"I do have great taste. I hired you after all, didn't I?" he teases.

We let go of each other's hands so I can open a container with spring rolls, my mouth salivating. "You know, I've always wondered why you hired me in the first place. I thought you hated me."

He grunts. "I had a gut feeling."

"A gut feeling, huh?" I tease him right back as I take a bite. It takes everything in me not to moan. "This is delicious, by the way."

"Glad you like it." His smile is small but genuine before he dives into one himself. "I don't know what else to call it. I didn't like you that much at first."

I gape at him. "Excuse me?"

His low chuckle makes it impossible for me to even stay fake mad at him. "Wasn't personal. I don't like anyone at first."

"So what did that gut feeling tell you about me?"

He takes his time to chew and swallow before speaking again. "I don't exactly know. I'm not great at identifying my feelings. Takes me a while. I suspected you'd be a good worker, and I was right."

I plop a sweet-and-sour shrimp into my mouth. "You keep saying that you're not good with feelings."

"Because I'm not. My therapist says it's a childhood thing."

"I like that you're going to therapy," I tell him honestly. "I mean, not many men do. Or women, I suppose. It took me years to book an appointment because I was scared of them judging me for my past, but my therapist is amazing. Best decision I've ever made."

He grabs another spring roll. "It took me years to take that step too. I started with group therapy."

"For veterans?"

He nods. "It helped me understand that getting professional help didn't make me weak. I've been with my current therapist for five years. She's helping me with the whole feelings thing, but it's a slow process."

"Well, if it's any consolation, I think you're doing great. I'm not that good with feelings, either, so I get it."

"Why not?"

The sky is clear, turning darker as the minutes go by. "Same thing, I suppose—my childhood. My parents would dismiss my feelings, call me dramatic and such."

A muscle in his jaw ticks. "I hope you don't believe that anymore."

He sounds angry, but I know it's not at me.

"I'm learning to let it go. Jada and Paul have always helped me a lot with that. With everything, really."

"You're close with them," he observes, sounding calmer.

"Jada knew what I was going through at home and stepped in, even after I graduated from her class. Her husband too. They've always had my back."

"I could tell she really loves you from a phone call alone."

He passes me the kung pao chicken, and I smirk. "Right. I keep forgetting you've become buddies behind my back."

"She seems like a sensible woman. I like her. Haven't met her husband, but if he's good to you, I'll like him too."

Conversation is easy throughout dinner. As the night descends upon the city, he tells me about his time in the Navy— he sticks to the more lighthearted stories—and I tell him about my good memories with Jada and Paul. He tells me what it was like to grow up with Uncle Neil, and I tell him what it was like to live in different parts of the country.

When we're done cleaning up, Travis gets up and holds out a hand in my direction. "Next surprise?"

I have a feeling I already know what it'll be. But I only smile at him and accept that the butterflies in my stomach will keep growing the more time I spend around him, and that's fine by me.

Because Travis feels like the home I never expected to find.

After we throw our empty containers in the trash and take the picnic blanket back to the car, we head for the observatory. Every corner is fascinating, and as we make our way through the different exhibits, I can't help but ask Travis, whose hand hasn't left the small of my back since we walked in, "Not that I'm complaining because I'm having fun, but why did you bring me here?"

As we both look up at the giant models of the planets hanging from the ceiling, he tells me, "I'm not sure my uncle even remembers this, and I haven't told anyone else, but I'm a huge space nerd."

"That's the cutest thing I've ever heard."

Heat climbs up his cheeks. "Not sure anyone's ever called me cute before."

"Well, you are." I get on my tiptoes and press my lips to his bearded cheek because it feels right. "Thank you for bringing me here. For the picnic, and everything else you're doing for me."

His hand moves until he's holding my waist. The intensity of his gaze makes my breathing stop. "I'd do anything for you, Allie."

My eyes drop to his mouth, and I debate how idiotic it'd be to kiss him right now when we both agreed to take it slow.

"Excuse me?" a shy, feminine voice asks behind us.

Turning, I come face-to-face with two women around my age. "Hi," I greet them a little nervously.

The two women exchange a quick look before one of them

316

says, "We're really sorry to bother you. We just wanted to know if you're Allie Buccieri? From that TV interview?"

I expect my stomach to turn, my mouth to get dry, my hands to start shaking. Everything around me disappears for a moment, even Travis, and I hear it—my heart telling me that I'm safe. That whatever these women want to tell me, I'll be fine.

Because my past no longer holds the power to destroy my future.

"I am," I say. I feel Travis's eyes on me, but he stays quiet.

"We just wanted to tell you that you were very brave," the other woman says. "We had no idea you'd gone through all of that. It must have been horrible."

"It really opened our eyes to what we should post online," her friend says. "Like, *really*. It was so admirable."

"Thank you," I tell them honestly.

I don't know what else to say because I've never been in this situation before, but luckily, they speak again before it has the chance to turn awkward.

"No, thank *you*," the same woman says before sliding her gaze up to Travis. "We just wanted to tell you that. I hope we didn't ruin your date."

My heart jumps at that word. "It's fine. I really appreciate you being so kind to me."

"It's nothing," her friend says. "Hope you guys enjoy your night."

"You too," Travis tells them, squeezing my waist. When they're gone, he lowers his mouth to my ear and whispers, "Did I tell you I'm fucking proud of you?"

I turn my head until his lips graze my cheek. "And did I tell you I'm glad you're here?"

He nuzzles his nose behind my ear, a whole sky of goose bumps erupting on my skin. *I love him. I love him so much.*

Nobody else comes up to us as we finish looking at the

exhibit, and I find myself not paying attention to my surroundings. It's weird, I realize, how I'm not in survival mode anymore despite my face being all over TV and social media these days. I don't feel in danger, and I know it's partly because I feel strong and capable having Travis by my side and partly because my worst fear came to life and I'm still standing.

I survived, and I'll do it again as many times as I have to.

Chapter Forty

"If I squint my eyes, I think I can see a star," I mutter, my neck craned up toward the sky sometime later that night.

We're probably not in the best spot for stargazing, with the city skyline right in front of us, but that doesn't stop me from trying.

"This is why I don't do big cities," Travis says next to me, eyes lost on the horizon. "Too much noise, too much pollution. Too much of everything."

"Is that a Navy thing?" I can't help but ask. "I mean, do you prefer quiet after the Navy?"

"I've always liked small-town life. Offers me everything I need." I stop looking at the sky to glance at him, only to find that his eyes are already on me. "Do you miss living in a big city?"

"Not really. I'd always lived in a big city, so I didn't know how much I'd grow to appreciate the quiet until I moved to a small town. Now I can't imagine myself living in this chaos again."

I can't imagine living anywhere else but in Bannport. With you.

"I never asked you," I start, my voice quiet. "You're playing hooky."

"I'm the boss, sweetheart. I call the shots."

Why did that sound so hot?

"Who's in charge of The Lair, then?"

"Jude is taking over until I come back."

A shiver travels down my spine. The wind has picked up—not enough to freeze me, but it's chilly. The fact that I'm leaning against a cold, metallic handrail doesn't help.

He notices.

Travis moves behind me until his front is covering the span of my back, shielding me from the wind. He rests his hands on the handrail, his fingers grazing mine. His long-sleeved shirt rides up, and I notice for the first time the beaded bracelet still wrapped around his wrist.

Touching my fingers to it, I mutter, "You're wearing it."

"I never took it off."

Neither did I. I couldn't.

I lean back against the comfortable hardness of his body, resting my head over his heartbeat. It's rhythmic, fast, and my favorite sound.

"Allie."

When I turn to glance at him, I find those green eyes looking down at me with a longing expression I can see clearly even in the dark.

"I've missed you so much," he rasps before one of his hands cups the side of my neck. "I felt like I couldn't breathe in my own house because you weren't there. It felt empty, soulless. I hated every second you weren't with me because I knew I should've fought harder for you. Should've gone after you and made you stay.

"We weren't mad at you, Allie. I could never be. But I also wanted to give you space, even if it killed me to think of you all sad and alone and anxious. I've hated everything about the past couple weeks. Every fucking thing."

It takes me a few tries to find my voice. For someone who isn't good with feelings, he's just said one of the most heart-breaking and beautiful things I've ever heard.

I rest my hand on his bearded cheek, caressing his skin with my thumb, hoping this one touch is enough for him to know how much he means to me. But just in case it isn't, I tell him.

"I've hated everything about the past two weeks too," I confess in a whisper. "But I needed to go through it alone. I needed to find my strength and take the reins of my life without depending on you or Jada or anyone else."

When I lick my lips, his gaze drops to my mouth.

"I can never thank you enough for giving me space, Travis. It was what I needed, even if it wasn't what I wanted."

"What do you want?"

Distant voices drift over to us, reminding me that we aren't alone even though we've come to a secluded area in the observatory gardens. But as quickly as I've heard them, they fall away when Travis tilts my chin up.

"I want you," I whisper into our bubble. "When I'm ready, I want everything with you."

His throat bobs with a swallow. "Everything?"

"I want to go back home with you. And I don't want to sleep in the guest bedroom anymore," I tell him over the sound of my heartbeat. "I want to work at The Lair again, as a waitress and as an accountant because I love both. I want to explore Bannport with you, do all the fun things you like and all the fun things I enjoy. I want to host dinners with Uncle Neil, Barbara, and our friends. I want to travel, try new things, do all the things I used to be scared of before. I want to have the rest of my firsts with you. And one day... one day, I don't want that bedroom in your house to be empty anymore."

He shuts his eyes and rests his forehead against mine. "I want that too, sweetheart. All of it. Whenever you're ready, it's yours. Every single fucking thing you ask me for."

Our noses graze in a featherlight touch, and I wonder if it would be a mistake to kiss him. If it would ruin things. But then I remember how I'd wasted so much time before—lying, hiding, ignoring my desires and needs. I remember how I was about to tell Travis about my past that day my parents showed up. I remember all the missed opportunities, the regret.

No more.

The slim distance between our lips disappears. This isn't our first kiss, but it feels new in many ways.

I sigh, melting against the cocoon that is his body. His lips move against mine, gently, carefully, as if he was savoring every second. I know I am.

He makes a growling sound at the back of his throat as my hands thread through his hair. It feels like my body melts into his when both of his hands land on my hips, bringing me closer to his warmth and the hardened bulge now pressing against my stomach.

Without warning, Travis pulls at my lower lip with his teeth, lighting up something dangerous in me. I feel his kiss through my whole body. My skin heats with his every touch, my lips tingle against his, and my legs are suddenly not strong enough to hold me up.

I know there's no coming back from this kiss, from this *claiming*.

I didn't have doubts before, and I sure have none now— Travis is it for me. My constant. My anchor. My home. And I want to be all that for him too.

He's gentle as he pecks my lips once, twice, three times before he pulls away. Dropping his forehead against mine, he whispers thickly, "You're the best thing that's ever happened to me, Allie. I don't know how I ever managed to live without you."

Emotion clogs my throat, and I hug him as tightly as I can. "You're the best thing that's ever happened to me," I whisper against his ear, not bothering to hide the tears that are starting to pool in my eyes. "You're my best friend, Travis, and I lo...I..."

"I know, sweetheart. I know." He cradles the back of my head, tangling his fingers in my hair. "You don't have to say the words now. I feel them too. I'll wait until you're ready."

Travis loves me.

He loves me enough to wait to hear it. And I love him enough to tell him when the time is right.

Chapter Forty-One

Travis and I go on a date every day for the next five days.

I sleep late in the mornings, join my daily video session with Dr. Rowland, go grocery shopping or clean the house or meet with Jada during her lunch break at her school, and then, in the afternoons, Travis picks me up.

Since he chose the observatory for our first date, I decide the spot for our second. We spend hours exploring the Santa Monica Pier while I tell him all about the memories I have from when I came here with my family, just once, ten years ago.

In Fisherman's Village, on our third date, Travis confessed that he flinched during the fireworks show at the New Year's party because of his PTSD from the Navy. That it never fully goes away, and he's made peace with that. I tell him about my kidnapping—how I escaped, the promise I made to the sky, and the nightmares that still make themselves at home in my mind some nights.

While we stroll through Palos Verdes on our fourth date, I tell him about my time in Dallas, Nashville, and all the small towns I'd lived in before reaching Maine. He laughs at the fact that I only ended up in Bannport thanks to a car malfunction, and it's the most beautiful sound I hear all day.

In Little Tokyo, on our fifth date, I tell him that I'm a natural blonde—he must know since he saw the interview, but I want him to know because *I* told him—and he asks if changing my last name was a tough choice.

"By that point, it wasn't," I admit. "I've never felt connected to my parents, so becoming a Smith didn't feel like a big deal. I don't know. Last names mean nothing to me. Buccieri doesn't anyway."

And after our sixth date, as he stops the car in Jada and Paul's driveway when we come back from a drive-in theater, this fantasyland we've been living in for the past week comes to an end.

"I have to fly back home tomorrow," Travis says into the night, his eyes on me, while we're still inside the car.

"Okay," I say slowly. I knew this moment would come. He's the boss, but he can't stay away forever. So why do I feel nauseous?

"Sorry it's so last-minute." His voice has an edge to it, almost as if he was mad at himself. "I didn't want to ruin tonight by telling you before the movie."

"It's okay." My throat works a swallow. "Thank you for coming here. You didn't have to."

His expression softens. "I'd do it a million times over."

I resist the urge to throw myself into his arms. How am I supposed to control myself around him when he says things like that?

"Before I go, I..." He pauses, and I can almost see the gears turning in his head. "I need you to know that I don't expect anything from you. Me coming to Los Angeles wasn't meant to guilt-trip you. I just wanted to see you and talk to you."

"I know," I reassure him.

"I want you to spend as much time as you need here with your loved ones," he says, his voice serious. "And when you're ready, if you ever are, The Lair will always be your home. *I* will always be your home. Okay?"

My chest falters when I try to take a deep breath. "I don't... I don't want us to become strangers."

"We won't." He reaches out his hand until he's holding mine over the console. "Whenever you're ready, Allie. I'll be there. I mean it."

We haven't kissed since the observatory. I'm aware that he's giving me space, but not knowing when the next time I'll see him will be is making me want to kiss him again.

"Slow," he rasps out, as if it pains him to say the word. As if he could read my thoughts. "We'll take it slow."

He doesn't want to kiss me.

No.

He wants to make sure I'm in the right headspace for things between us to happen.

The cutthroat way in which my own head interrupts my obsessive thinking takes me aback. I'm not used to it, but it's not an unwelcome change.

Plus, my non-catastrophic inner voice is right. I know what Travis feels for me, and what I feel for him. But the time to act on those feelings isn't here yet, and I don't know when it will be.

* * *

For the next five weeks, I stick to a firm routine—runs in the mornings, daily video chat with my therapist, meal prep, and quality time with Jada and Paul.

For the next five weeks, I only do things that I enjoy. I fight against the guilt of what I did to my parents, the regret of not having lived for myself before, and the nightmares that have gone nowhere.

For the next five weeks, I relearn how to live.

And I listen. Not to my self-deprecating thoughts, not to online forums, not even to Jada and Paul.

I listen to myself.

There's something to be said about selfishness. Why is it considered self-centered to have boundaries? Why would it make me a bad person to say no or to refuse certain things and accept others? Why is loving oneself and *showing it* so frowned upon sometimes?

So, for the next five weeks, I become selfish—if that's what it means to start living for myself. Personally, I'd call it authenticity.

And it's that authenticity, that refusal to waste any more time, that desire to follow my heart, which leads me to the living room five weeks after Travis left for Bannport.

Jada and Paul are watching a romcom hours after dinner when I walk in.

Paul pauses the TV. "Everything all right?"

"I thought you'd be asleep," Jada says.

"I'm leaving," I announce.

Silence.

"I want to go back to Maine."

More silence.

I want my life back.

No.

I want to build a new life from the ground up. A life that feels authentic this time.

I know I haven't healed in five weeks. I doubt I'll heal in five *years*—and I'm okay with that. I've also learned to be patient with myself, and I'm ready to take on the challenge of self-growth.

"I'm tired of waiting around for everything to be perfect and under control to start living the life I deserve. So, I... I'm leaving tomorrow. To Bannport. Because that's where I want to be," I tell them.

Jada swallows. "Are you sure?"

"I love you both. So much. You're my family, and nothing and no one will keep me away from you anymore—not even myself. I'll come back to visit you. But I want to leave. I want to go back to Travis and my friends. I'm never hiding again."

Because this is *my* life. And as cheesy as it sounds, I only have this one, and I'm done wasting it obsessing over how unfair my past was or how little control I have over my future.

I deserve to move on, and I'm tired of waiting to *be* ready. I *feel* ready, and that's enough. It doesn't mean I'll stop going to therapy or that I won't have bad days. But I was abused, and I told my story because I had every right to. Society needs to have a conversation about online safety for children, and I'll never understand why I was among those who had to initiate it, but I'm done wondering.

I deserved to speak out. Everything I said was my truth, and I don't regret a single word.

"You have helped me grow into the confident woman who has been hiding inside me all along," I continue. "I could never thank you enough for protecting and loving me. So yes, Jada, I'm sure. I'm very sure. I'm ready to start again."

She's the first one to get up from the couch and hug me tight, tighter than she ever has before. Paul follows her, holding us both, and a thought crosses my mind.

My parents didn't ruin my life.

Yes, what I went through was horrible. Yes, the abuse I was put through should've never happened. And yes, not every bad situation needs to have a meaning or lesson behind it.

But I choose to see it this way.

Without my parents' questionable choices, I would've never gotten Jada and Paul.

I would've never gone to Maine or met Charlie, Sandra, or Jude, and I wouldn't have worked at The Lair.

I wouldn't have fallen in love with Travis.

And most importantly, I wouldn't have found my voice. My authentic voice.

Good luck, world, trying to silence me again.

Chapter Forty-Two

CLOUDS COAT THE BANNPORT SKY, THREATENING RAIN, AS I shut the cab door behind me.

The streets are quiet. Nobody knows I'm here, standing in front of The Lair. Not even Travis, because I wanted this to be a surprise. A part of me was and still is afraid of his reaction when he sees me. He did say he'd always be there for me, but what if—

No.

I'm here because I *want* to be. I can't control how he's going to react to me. What Charlie, Sandra, Jude, and everyone else in this town will say when they see Allison Buccieri.

I spoke my truth. This is who I am. This is what happened to me. If people have an opinion on it, it has nothing to do with me. And honestly? Even attempting to control the narrative sounds exhausting.

Life is uncertain, but I've learned to find the beauty in the unplanned. To appreciate the puzzle pieces falling into place at their own rhythm without having to force them to fit.

With that thought in mind, I push the door open and instantly revel in the familiar voices that filter through it.

"I'm telling you, boss. This is my best idea yet."

Charlie's words are followed by an unmistakable grunt. "I've heard this before."

"A pool tournament will bring us new customers," Charlie argues. "People my age too. You know, a new kind of crowd."

"We don't need new customers," Travis argues back.

They're standing near the kitchen at the back. Neither has noticed me.

"I know we don't *need* them, but it'd still be good for business. I'll organize everything. You won't have to lift a finger."

"Sounds good to me," Jude says. Is Sandra in there somewhere too?

Their shift has already ended, so the bar is empty when I walk in. Holding my breath—not that I can breathe that well in the first place—my voice doesn't shake when I say, "Hey, guys."

Everything stops as the three men in front of me turn their heads.

Jude gapes.

Charlie blinks.

And Travis...

Travis smiles. A devastating, beautiful smile I want to see every day for the rest of my life.

"Holy fucking shit," Charlie breathes out.

Before I know it, he's wrapping his arms around me in a sealing hug. Not even a second later, my feet leave the sticky floor as he spins me around.

"You're really here. Holy fucking fuck," he says as he sets me back down, only to stare at me with a mixture of amazement and breathlessness.

"I am here," I confirm, my smile still in place because *this* is where I want to be. Where my heart has begged me to come back to.

"Sandra!" Jude bellows before he takes a step forward, then

another, and another—that's when I notice his glassy eyes. "Come here, girl."

It's not a request he needs to repeat.

Jude hugs me tightly, as if attempting to glue all my broken pieces back together. "We're so proud of you," he mutters into my hair. "So, so proud. We had no idea what you'd gone through. God..."

A gasp makes me lift my head from the comfort of Jude's shoulder. I barely have time to react before Sandra is hugging me too.

"Oh, sweetie," she says. "You should've told us. We would've never blamed you for it. *Never*, Allie. You're a survivor."

"I'm sorry." I choke up, their collective hug finally managing to break me. "I'm so sorry I lied to you. You didn't deserve it."

"Shush," Sandra says. "None of that. We aren't mad at you. We all wanted you to come back."

"Especially that big guy over there," Jude whispers playfully in my ear as they both let me go.

My eyes land on Travis then, as tall and imposing as I remember.

During those five weeks I remained in Los Angeles, we spoke on the phone some nights, texted a little bit throughout the day too... and learned that neither of us are big on calls or texts. We didn't force ourselves to contact each other daily, and it was fine. Because I knew he'd be waiting for me when I was ready. I knew he'd keep his promise to me, just like I'd kept mine to the sky.

"Hi," I say shyly.

His smirk kills me. "Hey, sweetheart."

"I think this is our cue, people," Charlie chimes in, throwing me a wink. "Allie, please tell us everything later, okay? You two, don't do anything I wouldn't do."

332

I roll my eyes at him at the same time as Sandra grabs my arm and asks me in that motherly voice I've missed so much, "You're staying for good, aren't you?"

There are no doubts in my mind when I say, "Yes. For good."

For good. Nothing has never sounded more right.

"Then that's worth a welcome back party," Jude suggests.

Charlie gasps dramatically. "Jude? Suggesting we throw a party? Quick, someone check if pigs are flying outside."

"Respect your elders, boy," Jude chastises him, but he's smiling.

"Yes, sir. Wouldn't dream of ever offending you, sir."

Sandra chuckles. "Let's get out of Travis's and Allie's hair, yeah? See you lovebirds tomorrow."

A blush creeps up my cheeks at her words, but weirdly enough, I don't feel self-conscious. Travis and I... make sense. Despite our age difference and our opposing personalities, he complements me in every way. I'd like to think I complement him too.

Being with him is easy, familiar, and *right*. And so, when the door closes behind our co-workers and friends, I don't waste another second.

He catches me with ease as I throw myself into his arms, breathing him in. Standing on my tiptoes with my arms around his neck, I pull him closer until there's no space between us.

The way I want him, the way I need him, is beyond anything else I've ever experienced before. And it's time I let him know.

I've already wasted too much time hiding who I really am and what I truly want. I refuse to waste any more.

"I love you," I breathe out. "I love you so much, Travis. I'm ready for this. For *us*. I'll have bad days, and I can't promise I'll be happy and cheery all the time, but I'm done waiting. I want to spend the rest of my life with you, and only you."

He wipes away a tear I hadn't noticed. The love shining in his eyes fills my heart, my soul, every fiber of my being.

"I love you too, sweetheart. More than I've ever loved anyone else. I'll always be here for you, Allie. On your good and bad days. You're it for me. Until the day I take my last goddamn breath."

I let out a throaty chuckle, smiling through the tears that have started to fall. "Oh, no way. You're stuck with me forever. That includes the afterlife."

He brushes his nose against mine. "Is our next life included too?"

"Absolutely."

"Good."

The world turns quiet for the next two seconds. And on the third, his lips find mine as if we'd kissed a thousand times before.

His hands rove over my back as his mouth moves in sync with mine, devouring me in the sweetest yet most possessive way. And when he tears his lips from mine, he starts kissing his way down my neck in a slow way that has my knees buckling.

Travis can say whatever he wants—that he has trouble identifying his feelings, that he struggles with voicing them—and I believe him, of course I do. But I don't need flowery love confessions to know what he feels for me is raw and true. I don't need grand gestures or pretty words when life has taught me that actions are all that matter.

And Travis? He shows me every day that I matter. That I deserve to take up space. That I'm lovable. For me, that's enough.

"I'm so fucking in love with you," he mutters against my skin as he kisses his way back up to my mouth—and all right, it feels incredible to hear it too.

Chapter Forty-Three

TRAVIS SHUTS THE FRONT DOOR OF HIS HOUSE BEHIND US A while later. The sound echoes through the hallway as I scan every corner of this place I don't ever want to be away from again. Why does it feel like I've been gone for years? Cooper and Buddy sure feel that way, seeing how they ambushed me as soon as my feet touched the driveway moments ago.

Travis notices me watching them through the window. "They missed you too."

"Don't say that unless you want me to burst into tears." I'm only half-joking.

"Would never want that. Come here, beautiful."

Travis holds out his hand for me. After he pulls me into his chest, he presses a soft kiss to my inner wrist, desire glinting in his eyes.

We don't speak. The passion in his gaze, the tenderness of his touch, the trust we've built together—they tell me everything I need to know.

This man who grunted at me the first time we met, who installed an extra lock on my apartment door without me having to ask, who made friendship bracelets with me, who opened up about his past, who offered me a safe haven when I needed it the most—he was always meant to be mine. And I, his. Irrevocably.

My mouth meets his. Gentle at first, and then hungry at once. His big hands cover nearly the entire span of my lower back when he pulls me closer, and that one detail sends my body into overdrive.

Some people might think I'm weird if they read my mind right now, but the fact that Travis is so huge all over makes me short of breath. I don't know what it is exactly—that he's so intimidatingly large, nobody would look at me the wrong way if he's near, that he's so strong, he could protect me from anything, that it's just... him. All of those combined.

Now, as he kisses me in the middle of the hallway, I wonder if he'd be big in other places too.

And if I should tell him I'm freaking out about it.

"Travis," I mutter as I pull away. Suddenly my shortness of breath doesn't have to do with how good he makes me feel.

"Mm..." He brushes his nose against mine before pecking my lips once softly.

I hesitate. What if he thinks I'm lame?

He pulls away a little further, a notch forming between his brows. "Did I do something?"

"It's not that. It's not you at all."

"What's wrong, then?"

I'm being dumb. I know that. But the words get stuck in my throat until Travis, this patient man who has chosen me despite everything, squeezes my waist. And then he says in a gentle voice, "We're a team now. Whatever is worrying you concerns me too."

Despite feeling like my cheeks are on fire, I confess, "It's just that I've never done this before. I don't mean kissing, obviously, but what comes after that."

Why can't I say the word *sex*? Very mature of me.

Travis tilts his head in a way that shouldn't look so adorable. "Sex?"

There it is.

"Yeah." My face is officially flaming hot. "I've never done it."

"All right," he says calmly. "That's something you're worried about?"

"I'm just nervous. I mean, I kind of thought for a second there that you'd find it lame, but that was just me self-sabotaging."

My therapist says I tend to do that a lot, so it doesn't surprise me that the tendency makes an appearance during an intimate moment.

"Allie, you're the furthest thing from lame." His voice turns serious. "Your life wasn't exactly normal. But even if it had been, being a virgin isn't something to be ashamed of. You hear me?"

My throat is dry. "I hear you."

He rests his forehead against mine, one of his hands traveling the length of my spine until it settles around my neck in a loose grip. "We don't have to do anything, today or ever."

I find myself shaking my head, breathless. "I need you, Travis. I want to do this now."

His nose grazes mine, his grip on my neck tightening in a way that doesn't feel restrictive but deliciously possessive. And when he presses his front against mine and I feel his rock-hard bulge against my stomach, my head becomes void of all thoughts but the blind need to have him.

His voice is raspy when he says, "You're killing me, sweetheart."

"I'm not doing anything," I whisper.

"You standing there, looking at me, fucking *breathing*, is enough to drive me insane."

My head spins. Travis is so huge, so imposing, so capable of being tender and rough, a part of me wonders if I should feel at least a little intimidated right now. And I do feel somewhat nervous, but Travis... There's simply not a world where I feel incapable, uncomfortable, or insecure if he's with me.

My mouth finds his again, and I let go of the what-ifs, of the nerves swirling in my stomach, and focus on how good his hands on my body feel as he effortlessly hoists me up.

Before I know it, we're moving. I don't stop kissing him to see where we're going because there's no place I wouldn't want to be if he's there.

My fingers tangle in his short hair, and I hear him opening a door. My mouth descends on his neck, earning me a shiver, and I hear him shutting the door behind us. When I open my eyes, moonlight filters through the curtains of the one bedroom in this house I'd never been in until tonight—his.

Travis sits on the edge of his mattress with me straddling him as I shamelessly look around. A king-sized bed, one night-stand, the same wooden wardrobe I have in my bedroom, and an ajar door, which I'm assuming is the bathroom.

"Like what you see?" His voice is teasing, but his gestures are tender as he places a loose strand of hair behind my ear.

"You're not a fan of pictures on the walls, are you?" I tease him back, eyeing the empty space.

"I didn't have anything worth putting up on my bedroom walls before," he says, his voice low. His hand moves from my ear to cradle the nape of my neck. "Now I do."

"You're going to plaster my face all over your walls?"

"Sure, but I'd rather have the real you sleeping in my bed every night."

"Deal. I'd need my own nightstand, though. I need a place to keep my bedside water bottle and e-reader."

"I'll build you one with my bare hands if you want me to."

I chuckle, hugging him around his neck. He hugs me back, pulling me closer. "No need to build it with your own hands, although that would be sexy."

"Sexy, huh?"

"It's just..." I take advantage of the fact that my face is buried in his neck, and he can't see how furiously I'm blushing. "Your hands."

"My hands," he repeats. I can *hear* his smirk.

"Yeah."

"What about them?"

"They're hot," I admit.

He chuckles, and I can't help but think being this happy and playful suits him. So much.

"You think my hands are hot, sweetheart?"

"Very," I whisper.

"Mm..." The heathen moves them so they're resting on my hips. And then he squeezes. "You think it's hot if I do that?"

The muscles in my lower area squeeze too. How can I be all hot and bothered already?

"Yes," I breathe out. "I love how big and strong they are."

"Let me tell you a secret," he whispers in my ear. His voice no longer sounds playful but charged with heat. "These hands can make you feel good too. Want me to show you?"

As soon as I say a perhaps-too-desperate yes, they travel from my waist to my sides. Up, up, up, and then he stops.

"Can I?" he asks.

I nod, my throat too dry to speak.

"Are you sure?" he insists.

I don't answer. Instead, I cover his hands with mine and move them slowly, tentatively, until they're holding my breasts. Travis's breath hitches as he stares at my chest, and a sudden burst of confidence boosts through me. It's *me* causing *him* to have this reaction.

"Fuck, baby," he grunts. The bulge in his pants becomes all the more evident when he shifts under me. "You can't do this to me."

I move again, watching how his hands swallow me up. Gently, as if he wants to revel in every touch.

"Travis," I breathe out when I can't take it any longer. "Take it off."

His eyes collide with mine. "You sure?"

"Yes. I want to feel you against my skin."

He curses under his breath.

My fingers move with urgency as I help him take off my sweater, then the T-shirt I'm wearing underneath until I'm only in my bra. Travis curses under his breath again before his mouth descends to the valley between my breasts. His open-mouthed kisses on my bare skin leave me panting, begging.

In the midst of my wanting, I still manage to taunt him by pulling the straps of my bra down my shoulders at a torturous pace, then a little further until only my nipples are covered. He grunts, a borderline animalistic sound I can't help but chuckle at, only for my laugh to get cut off when he pulls my bra down completely and sucks one of my nipples into his mouth.

I gasp at the sensation. It feels strange at first but *so good* soon after. His groans mix with my whimpers as he switches from one nipple to the other, showing both the same hungry attention.

My hands claw at the hem of his shirt, desperate to take it off and feel his skin against mine. He obeys, pulling back enough to get himself naked from the waist up, before he kisses my skin again.

Shamelessly, I run my hands over his impressive upper body, the warm and rough planes of his chest I'd never seen until now. "I feel like I'm going insane. I need you so badly."

341

He grunts, burying his face in my neck. "Are you wet for me already?"

My heart hammers. Nobody has ever spoken to me like that, and I never expected such words to light me on fire.

"Yes," I whisper.

"Can I feel it?"

I nod.

"Use your words, sweetheart."

"Yes." My voice is charged with heat. "Touch me, Travis. Please."

A pleased groan leaves the back of his throat. "That's my girl."

In one swift move, he places me on his mattress. Travis hovers over my half-naked body, his bare chest so imposing, I can't help but run my hands down it. My fingers are met with hard, hairy skin, and it's the hottest sight I've ever laid my eyes on. *He* is.

Wordlessly, he grabs the hem of my leggings and pulls them down. He keeps his eyes on me, watching for any clue that he should stop. And I love him for it, but stopping is the very last thing on my mind.

Cursing under his breath when he sees my half-naked body lying before him, he leans down and plants a kiss on my stomach. Then another, lower.

"Have you ever been touched before?" he asks in a husky voice. When I shake my head, he mutters, "Fucking hell."

Nerves swirl in my stomach. "Is that a problem for you?"

"Far from a problem," he rasps. "I'm trying not to come in my pants like a fucking teenager, just from thinking I'll be the first and the last man to touch you."

I arch my back at his words, craving his touch, as a heavy breath falls from my lips. As always, Travis gives me what I need.

Even if I wanted to, I couldn't suppress the moan that escapes when his finger caresses my covered center. It's a faint touch, barely there, but enough to set me off.

He grunts, applying more pressure. I don't hold back as my sounds of pleasure echo through the empty house. He runs circles with his middle finger on my most sensitive spot, still covered by my underwear, chasing my whimpers. I've never felt freer, or happier to be out of control.

"I need to touch you." There's a desperate edge to his voice. "I need to sink my fingers inside that tight little pussy, then my cock, or I'll go fucking insane."

God.

My back arches again, and I nod rapidly, *begging* him to do those things. And do them *now*.

Despite his urgency, he's gentle as he moves my underwear aside, baring me to him completely. Yet I don't feel one bit self-conscious about it because this is Travis. This is the love of my life.

When his middle finger breaks through my folds, I lose all sense of reality for an instant. Instead of pain, I'm met with an overwhelming sense of relief and desire I've never experienced before. And when he starts pumping his finger in and out, slowly, his curses mixing with my moans, something inside of me *snaps*.

"More," I beg him, my back arched and breaths uneven.

"You want another finger?"

I shake my head. "I need *you*."

He throws his head back, grunting, "Allie."

My hands reach for his belt buckle, and he eases his finger out of me so he can undo it himself. He gets out of bed and drags his pants and underwear down his strong legs as I watch with nervous excitement.

The sight of Travis fully naked stops my breathing altogether. If I thought he would be big, it's nothing compared to the real thing. His generous inches stand proudly against his stomach, and I gulp. I need him badly, but I'm not so sure I can take him.

Travis reads my mind.

"I'll be gentle," he promises, and I know he means it, but...

"That's..." *Too big. Huge.* I gulp again. "I hope you don't take this the wrong way, but what the hell, Travis?"

His low chuckle sends a thrill through me. "Way to boost my ego."

"I'm just telling the truth."

He climbs over the bed again and presses a soft kiss on my lips. "We'll go at your pace. Do you trust me?"

My nerves ease at that. "Always."

He kisses me again slowly, helping me relax. And it works. Because within seconds, I'm writhing under him, his stiff member between us, and I can't wait any longer.

"I'm ready," I whisper against his lips.

"You sure?"

"I trust you, Travis. And I want you to make me feel good."

He grunts. "Condom."

Right. We probably should use one, but I find myself shaking my head instead. "Can we go without it?"

Another grunt, this time buried in my neck. His hips buck against my middle. "Allie."

"We can use one if you want to," I'm quick to say. "I just wanted...I want..."

He nips at the sensitive skin behind my ear. "Tell me."

"I want to feel you without any barriers between us. Is that okay? I tested negative."

"Me too. Are you on the pill?" When I nod, his hips meet my center again, as if he couldn't help himself. "All right. I'll pull out just in case."

He pecks my lips softly, easing the nervous rhythm of my heart.

Time stops when I feel his thick head penetrating my entrance. Wet sounds fill the silence, followed by our heavy breathing. He pushes inside of me a little further, gently and slowly, as he promised, and I lose all sense of reason.

"Deep breaths, sweetheart," he instructs, sounding like he's struggling to breathe too. "Let me fill you up."

I do as he says, finding that it hurts a little before the pain transforms into pleasure.

"That's it. Keep taking deep breaths for me," he praises. "You're taking my cock so well."

By the time he buries himself inside of me to the hilt, I'm a mess. I've never known a deeper or a more intense pleasure. Not like this. I feel full in ways I didn't know were possible. And when he starts moving inside me, my wetness coating his every inch, a flame lights up inside my chest.

Moaning, I beg him to go faster. Harder. He's hesitant at first, saying he doesn't want to hurt me, so I start using his shaft as I please, moving up and down on it to prove a point.

That throws him over the edge. He grabs one of his pillows and places it under my lower back, angling my body in a higher position. He grabs my hips, pounding in and out of me at a punishing rhythm. Soon, the only sounds filling the room are our moans and the slapping of our bodies coming together.

I can't stop staring at him. His lips are parted, frowning, as he watches himself ease in and out of me. He looks so powerful right now, so raw and manly and *primal*, a powerful wave crashes through my body, and I know I'm close.

"Come for me, sweetheart," he demands as his finger starts rubbing circles on my center. "Soak my cock."

A physical reaction I don't fully understand takes over me, and suddenly I feel like I'm falling. My mouth opens, but no sounds come out. My back arches, taking him deeper, and I'm hit by such a strong wave of pleasure that I lose my breath.

Travis pulls out in time to come all over my stomach with a heavy grunt. He fists his length, pumping it until he empties out on my skin. It's the hottest thing I've ever seen.

"*Holy fuck,*" he grunts when he's done. "*Fuck.* I went too hard. I'm sorry. Did I hurt you?"

I shake my head. "You were perfect, Travis. It was perfect."

He leans down to kiss me on the lips. "I love you, Allie. So much. You're my life."

His words squeeze my heart. "And you're mine."

I sleep in his bed for the first time that night, with one of his arms protectively wrapped around me. The first of forever.

Chapter Forty-Four

One year later...

"Allie, I'm serious. This idea tops every other one I've ever had."

"You say that a lot," I point out. Jude jokes it's become his catchphrase at this point, and he's not wrong. "Also, your last one is hard to beat."

Two months ago, Charlie suggested The Lair sponsor a local elementary school T-ball team, which brought us a ton of new clients, including from out of town.

"Okay, yeah. That was pretty cool," he admits. "But how about this—home delivery on game nights. I can't believe I didn't think of this sooner."

I purse my lips, unsure. "I'm not sure Travis will be on board. You know how he gets."

Game nights are stressful already. I can't imagine adding a delivery service to the mix, especially since Travis likes to keep things simple to avoid burnout.

Charlie's groan is nothing short of dramatic. "Work your magic on your big, scary boyfriend for me. Pretty please, Allie Cat? He never says no to you."

I stick out my tongue at him. "Ask him yourself, you coward."

"Damn right I am."

Amused, I shake my head. "Char, he hired you as our marketing manager after you left for Boston. Don't you think that means he trusts you?"

Shortly after I came back to Bannport for good, Charlie found a job at a renowned marketing firm in the city. He comes back to visit as often as he can since his family also lives here, but we still miss him a lot—even Travis, as much as he tries to hide it.

"I guess he *does* trust me a little," he concedes. "I mean, we go way back if you really think about it. I gave him his favorite mug, and I caught you hooking up by the pool table that one time and never told anyone. Fond memories all around."

"You're incorrigible," I tell him as heat climbs up my neck.

No matter how much time passes, I still get flustered every time someone talks about me and Travis as a couple. It doesn't help that people love to tease us about our relationship too.

Uncle Neil is as much of a menace as Charlie or worse, and he's unapologetic about it. He's been asking for grandkids since we broke the news one year ago.

Jude and Sandra are happy for us, and they join in on the teasing whenever they can. Sandra is a lot more benign, but Jude lives for giving Travis shit about how smitten he is with me. He says his tough-guy facade is slipping, only for Travis to scowl at him and prove him wrong.

Charlie, Lola, Barbara, and everyone else are equally as happy for us. I was scared Jada and Paul would frown upon our age difference or the fact that he's my boss, but after seeing how he treats me and how happy he makes me, they're fully on board with our relationship. Their support wouldn't have been a deal-breaker, because I'm finally living for myself, and being with

Travis is what I want, but it means more to me than they could imagine.

Charlie, perched on one of the stools, smirks as he watches me tidy up behind the bar. "I may be incorrigible, but I'm also a psychic. I totally called you and Travis being in love before you even knew it yourselves."

That's not a total lie.

"Stop bothering my girl, Charlie."

Something else I won't get used to anytime soon is the sound of his deep, soothing rumble calling me his. To the way the weight of his hands feels when he hugs me from behind, just like he's doing now. To the way he's so openly affectionate with me no matter who's watching.

"I didn't think you'd be into PDA," I teased him shortly after we started dating, one night when he kissed me in front of Jude and Sandra. And not exactly in a discreet way.

"I want to kiss you all the time. I'm not holding back just because people want to watch."

Now, Travis rests his hands on my waist and drops his chin on top of my head as Charlie says, "Me? Bothering Allie Cat? Never. I actually wanted to talk to you."

"About?"

Something that hasn't changed in the past year is Travis's no-wasting-saliva policy. He and I can have hours-long conversations about anything and everything, but when it comes to other people, he likes to keep it short and not sweet.

"Some new marketing ideas," Charlie says. "I have this one that..."

I don't hear the rest of his sentence.

I can focus on nothing but the two people who have just walked into The Lair. On the tall, brown-haired boy and the younger blonde girl.

I know Travis has seen them, too, when his powerful body stiffens behind me.

Johnny and Cindy.

My siblings are here.

"What's wrong?" Charlie asks, noticing how both of us have stopped paying attention to him.

My eyes lock with Johnny's, and I don't answer. I give Travis's forearm a squeeze. "Stay here."

"Allie—"

Swirling around, I get on my tiptoes and peck his lips. "I've got this."

In his eyes, I see a mixture of worry—Travis is the biggest mother hen I know—and the softness he can't hide every time I kiss him. "All right. I'm here if you need me."

I give him a small smile. "I know. I love you."

"I love you too."

Charlie turns around in his stool, and I don't think I'm imagining him muttering, "Shit."

The last time I saw Johnny, he came to the bar with our parents a year ago. His disgust for me was evident then, and a part of me is scared he's back to tell me what he didn't get the chance to last time—that he hates my guts, that he wishes we weren't related, that I've ruined our family for good.

My chest constricts when I look at my little sister. I haven't seen her in seven years. It shouldn't surprise me that she isn't a baby anymore, yet I can't stop staring at her, wondering if she's real. She's fifteen now, a full teenager, and I...

I missed all of it.

Will she even recognize me?

When I stop in front of them by the front door, I don't know what to say. I must look different to them too—I've let my hair grow a little longer, and I'm slowly getting rid of my bangs. I think the brown dye will stay because I'm fond of it, but I no longer feel the need to look like a different person. To hide in plain sight.

"Hi," Johnny starts. Did his voice sound so gravelly the last time we saw each other?

My throat feels too dry. "Hi."

He not-so-discreetly squeezes Cindy's arm, who quickly lets out a meek, "Hi."

I have to blink several times to avoid crying. I'd completely forgotten my own sister's voice.

"Can we talk?" Johnny asks.

We're nearing closing time, but a few tables are still occupied, so I usher them to the nearest booth, far from everyone else's ears. My siblings sit together in front of me, and then... nothing.

For what feels like hours, we don't speak. My gaze shifts between them. Johnny alternates between looking around and at me. Cindy keeps her eyes glued to her lap, her long hair partially hiding her expression. I don't know why they're here, but I can't imagine they've come all the way to a small town in Maine to see me and say nothing. So, I let them take their time until my brother finally speaks up.

And says the last thing I expected him to.

"I'm sorry, Allie."

Is that my heart stopping?

"Why?" I ask, my voice abnormally calm. A part of me is happy to see them, but another part—a bigger one—doesn't trust Johnny. Not after what he did and said.

He glances at Cindy for a brief moment, then back at me. "Because you were right about everything, and I didn't listen."

I'm starting to think my brain is playing tricks on me. There's no way *this*, this moment I've dreamed of for longer than I'd like to admit, is happening right now.

"Johnny..." I start, unsure of what to say to that.

"I'm not finished," he chimes in, but his voice is soft. Not demanding, not aggressive.

He takes a deep breath before continuing, "Allie, you are..."

He hesitates, and my breathing becomes labored while waiting for whatever he has to say. Despite having worked with my therapist for a year on my family issues, the truth is that the boy-man in front of me still wields the power to hurt me.

"We watched your interview a year ago," Cindy blurts out.

I don't know what to say. It makes sense that they watched it, but I'm still struggling to believe the interview happened in the first place. The fact that they're aware of it shouldn't feel weird, but it does.

Johnny speaks next. He sounds serious, somber, and I don't know what to make of it. "At first, we were... I was angry, but then they showed that video."

Even if I wanted to, I don't think I could speak right now.

"I had no idea all of that had happened," Johnny continues. "I was too young when the kidnapping happened. I'd heard things, but I thought they were rumors. It was stupid of me, I know, but Mom and Dad never talked about it. The people around us either. It was a taboo thing, and I thought I'd imagined the little I'd heard. I didn't know about Mom and Dad's punishments if you didn't want to film either. They never said anything."

At this point, it doesn't surprise me that our parents kept so many things away from Johnny. He was their golden child, the one who was always up for taking pictures and cooperating in *family activities*.

"I didn't know either," Cindy says, her voice soft. "I was a baby when it happened, and growing up, nobody talked about it. We weren't allowed to go online without supervision, either, so..."

"After the interview aired..." Johnny starts, only to pause a moment later, as if he was struggling to find the right words. "It's been difficult, Allie. Very."

I don't need to ask to know what he means.

The plan was to do a little more therapy before I fully ventured online. Dr. Rowland said I needed to be emotionally ready for all the conflicting information I'd find, and I agreed. Much like my relationship with Travis, I didn't want to rush my relationship with the internet either.

I was doing okay. Healing day by day, taking it slow, allowing myself to break down when I needed to and live guilt free.

But then my parents sued me for defamation.

After I got the email from their lawyer, Travis had to spend nearly an hour holding my hair back as I threw up in the toilet. Fortunately, George Eden was quick to reach out to me and offer to pay for my legal expenses.

"We got you into this mess, didn't we?" he argued.

I told him that no, I'd come forward because *I* wanted to, because I'd promised myself, but he wouldn't have it. And after a quick trial, the judge ruled in my favor.

But that was months ago, and I have no idea what's been going on since then.

"I saw what our parents had done to us for what it really was—abuse," Johnny keeps going. "They put us in danger and disguised it as a fun thing. They... They lost custody of Cindy after your trial. Social services got involved."

Guilt like I've never felt before punches me right in my gut. "What?"

"It's okay," my brother rushes out, probably noticing my freak-out. "Well, it's not *okay*, but I was able to get her guardianship. I'm her legal guardian now. Right, Cici?"

"Yeah." She clears her throat. "We manage."

"Where are they now?" I ask before I can stop myself.

"Lying low somewhere in Colorado," he tells me. "We haven't heard from them in months."

I let out a long sigh. "That's a lot to take in."

Cindy snuggles to his side, and he puts an arm around her as he tells me, "We wanted to tell you."

"You did?"

"I'm sorry, Allie. For treating you like an asshole when you were nothing but a victim," he says. "You said Cindy and I were victims, too, when I came over with our parents last year. I couldn't stop thinking about that. You said you could never hate us, so I thought we would come here and... I don't know. I don't even know if you want us in your life anymore. Maybe this family is broken beyond repair."

I can tell his words are genuine. For some reason, I can.

I lean over the table, keeping my voice quiet. "I meant what I said a year ago, and I still mean it now. I don't hate you. Neither of you. I never did."

A beat of silence passes. Johnny hesitates. "My friends nearly broke into your apartment," he confesses, turning my blood cold. I've suspected he was involved for a long time, but hearing him admit it is an entirely different thing. "I wasn't with them, but I still regret it every day. Our parents asked me to do it, but I could've said no. I was blinded by my hatred for you—unfounded, unfair hatred—and I'm so sorry."

I've always hated when people say, "You have to be the bigger person." Because what if I want to be the smallest person in the room? What if I don't feel like suppressing my feelings for the sake of someone else's comfort?

But then I started therapy, and Dr. Rowland explained that it's not always about the other person. Would forgiving bring *me* peace? Or would it make *me* feel like crap? There's nothing wrong with putting ourselves first. If we don't, who will?

"Thank you for being honest with me," I start, thinking my

words through. "When your friends almost broke into my apartment... it took me back to the kidnapping. It scarred me for a while."

"I'm so sorry," Johnny repeats.

"I had an inkling you were involved, but I still couldn't... can't hate you. Maybe I should."

"I'd understand if you did."

"Well, I don't."

"Allie—"

"Maybe this makes me extremely dumb," I continue, ignoring him. "Maybe Travis won't understand, or my friends, but this is *my* life, *my* choices, and I choose to give our relationship a second chance. I want to take it slow, just like I'm doing with everything else now, but I don't want us to be strangers. We went through something horrific together, felt forced to do things we then hated ourselves for, and I don't know about you, Johnny, but I'm tired."

His shoulders sag with relief. "I'm tired too."

"Me too," Cindy mutters.

I slide my gaze toward her and give her a genuine smile. "What do you say we start over, Cindy? Would you like that?"

With her eyes holding mine, she nods. "I'd like that."

"We're still living in California," Johnny tells me. "Not in Los Angeles, but in Santa Barbara. We're leaving tomorrow, but we'd like to see you if you ever come back to California."

A gigantic weight lifts off my shoulders at his words. "I will stop by Santa Barbara to see you," I promise them. "And if you ever need anything at all, you can call Jada. I'll give you her number. Remember her, from my school?"

"Yeah. Are you sure she wouldn't mind?"

"She was there for me when I couldn't rely on any other adults. She'll be there for you just the same," I tell him, knowing it's the truth. Jada is an angel, and she would never leave my siblings stranded. To her, they're victims of my parents' neglect as much as I am.

"If you change your mind about this—" Johnny starts again, but I don't let him finish.

"Circumstances forced you to break into my apartment to get a copy of the video. I was forced to lie to the people I loved. It's not quite the same, I know, but Johnny, we both became people we aren't proud of because our parents forced us to, in a way. And I'm willing to give us a second chance if you promise to take it seriously. No more shenanigans."

"No more shenanigans," he echoes. "I promise, Allie. I want to start anew. Cindy deserves as much."

She hugs him a little tighter, and I'd be lying if I said their bond doesn't spark a hint of jealousy in me. Of longing. *I could've had that too.*

Slowly. We'll get there.

"Everything okay?" a new voice asks to my left. A voice I know too well.

I'm not imagining Johnny's wince as he glances up at Travis, who's towering over all of us. And I know he remembers him from last year, if only because a man as imposing as my boyfriend is nearly impossible to forget.

"Everything's fine," I tell him, breaking the tension. "Travis, this is my brother, Johnny, and my sister, Cindy. And this is my boyfriend and boss, Travis."

Travis glares at Johnny for a beat too long until he slides his gaze to Cindy. The shift in his eyes from hard to soft is so drastic, I could laugh.

"Hey, there," he starts, addressing my sister in an easy voice. "Do you need anything? A glass of water?"

She nods timidly. "Thanks."

He smiles. "I'll be right back."

But before he does, one of his big hands lands on my shoul-

356

der. A silent question. I glance up at him with nothing but adoration in my eyes. "Hurry up, you grump. We're thirsty."

He throws me a wink before disappearing behind the bar.

Johnny wastes no time asking, "You're dating him?"

I get a little defensive. "Yes. What about it?"

"Nothing," he hurries to say. "He's just... scary. And huge. Like a bear."

I can't help my smile. That sounds about right.

* * *

I'm sitting by the edge of the lake, a blanket wrapped around my shoulders as the sun disappears behind the clouds, casting a lavender sky, when I hear his footsteps behind me. I know it's him because Cooper and Buddy are whimpering instead of barking as if their lives depended on it.

Turning in my chair, I spot Travis only a few feet away. My chest constricts with how much I've missed him even though it's only been a few hours.

"Hey, handsome," I tell him when he reaches my side. "How are your uncle and Barbara? Still denying they're a couple?"

Some things don't change in a year.

He smirks. "Aside from that, they missed you today. I told them we'd visit together this weekend. I also brought back some of Barbara's carrot cake."

After the unexpected visit from my siblings, I went to yoga with Lola while Travis went up to Uncle Neil's to fix a faulty cabinet.

Leaning down, he pecks my lips. "I've missed you today."

"I've missed you too. Sit with me?"

He helps me up so he can take the chair, then gently lowers me to his lap and shields me from the cold with his arms. I bury my face in his neck, wrapping myself in his familiar scent. His presence calms me down so much, I would fall asleep in a heartbeat if it weren't so freezing outside.

"How are you feeling?" he asks quietly, not needing to add anything else for me to know what he means.

A tired sigh escapes me. "I'm... not sure." Travis plants a soft kiss on my forehead, encouraging me to keep going. "I wasn't expecting them to contact me ever again. A part of me hoped they would so we could talk things out, but..."

"You're unsure about reconnecting with them?"

I fidget with my fingers above the blanket. "We've never truly connected. It's like starting from scratch, only the scratch is more of an open, bleeding wound."

"Be patient with yourself, sweetheart." His voice is low, soothing something inside of me. "Don't put any pressure on yourself to make it work. There's no use in worrying about the what-ifs. They're infinite."

I sigh again, melting against him. "You're right. I'll talk to my therapist tomorrow."

His beard tickles my forehead as he kisses me again. "I'm so fucking proud of you, you know?"

"Stop saying things like that. It makes me want to climb you like a tree."

My body shakes with his chuckle. "And that's a bad thing?"

"For our immune systems, probably. This isn't exactly outdoor-activities weather."

"So what you're saying is that you'll let me do all sorts of things to you outside when spring comes?"

"Don't sound so pleased with yourself. You know that's exactly what I'm saying."

Another chuckle, followed by him lacing his fingers through mine. "Only you, Allie. Only you."

It was a pleasant surprise learning that Travis is in fact one big, cuddly bear. He can't be in the same room as me without touching me now—not that I'd ever complain about it.

"Allie?"

"Yes?"

"I've been thinking about something."

It's the way he says it that makes me lift my head to look at him. His voice doesn't give away any nerves, but it also doesn't sound... normal. There's a weird edge to it I can't read like I usually do.

"What is it?" I ask.

A tiny part of me is scared of what he'll say. In the year we've been together, we've had rough days—during the trial against my parents, when his nightmares struck, when my anxiety took over. Despite it all, there's nothing we haven't been able to get through together. So I tell myself this time will be no different.

"I've been thinking about something you said in Los Angeles."

Even a year later, the fact that Travis traveled all the way to California for me still feels like a dream.

"I asked you how you'd felt about changing your last name. Remember?"

I nod. He starts caressing the skin on my hand with his calloused thumb as I ask him, "Why have you been thinking about that?"

"Because I know last names mean nothing to you, but I still wanted to ask you if you'd take mine."

Everything in me stops.

My heartbeat. My breathing. My train of thought.

Travis reaches into the pocket of his jacket and takes out a tiny black box.

"You're the best thing that's ever happened to me." He opens it, revealing the most stunning diamond ring I've ever seen. "I know we agreed to take things slow, and we still can do that, but I can't imagine my future without you. I don't want to. I love you so damn much, Allie. If I ask to be yours forever, will you say yes?"

My hand starts trembling between his. I blink, my vision clearing as the tears fall. When my lips curve into a smile, his shoulders visibly relax.

"Oh, Travis. Do you even have to ask?"

He slips the ring on my finger easily, as if it was always meant to be there.

"Come here, sweetheart."

And when my lips meet his under the moonlight, I realize that luck has always been on my side after all.

Epilogue

Three years later...

THE PAST WEEK HAS BEEN INCREDIBLY BUSY AT THE BAR, SO it's no surprise that I get home past dinnertime. Travis warned me I'd be stuck in the finance booth, as he likes to call it—because I always use the same one—for longer than usual today, and he wasn't wrong.

By the time I pull into our driveway, I'm positively exhausted. The back of my neck is throbbing, and my butt hurts from sitting for hours on end. Glancing at the time in my car, my soreness gets put on the back burner as I realize how late it truly is.

Even if I still love accounting with all my heart, at times like this, I can't help but feel guilty about getting home this late. But Travis insists that he has everything under control, that he's the other half of this team, and that he will "damn sure act like it." He proves it every day.

There's light coming from the living room window. Cooper and Buddy are probably inside the barn since I don't see them outside. Just as I'm about to get out of the car, my phone pings with a notification. A text from Johnny, confirming they will be able to make it. I can't help but smile as I text him back.

If someone had told me ten years ago that my brother and sister would be celebrating my thirtieth birthday with me, I would've asked them if they had hit their head. But Johnny has kept his promise to stay in touch all these years, and Cindy has slowly opened up to me, and now I can say we are... okay.

We aren't super close—and that's fine—but we have visited one another a handful of times in the past three years, and we get along. They even gave George Eden their input for his law proposal and celebrated with me when it passed through with Congress last year.

To me, that's enough for now.

The chilly night air hits my cheeks as I start for the front door. There's not a single cloud in the sky, and I crane my neck up to watch the stars twinkle above my head. It's magical, but the beauty of the infinite universe doesn't hold a candle to what I'll find inside our home.

Travis is finishing up two burgers in the kitchen when I walk in. His hair is all over the place, his beard needs a little trimming, and he has a vomit stain on his shoulder. He's never looked hotter.

"Hi," I greet him quietly, careful not to make much noise.

"Hey, sweetheart." The baritone of his voice turns my insides into goo as if it were my first time hearing it. I've already accepted he'll always make me feel this giddy. "How was your afternoon?"

"All's taken care of."

I get on my tiptoes to kiss his cheek, but he moves his head at the last second and captures my lips with his. I chuckle into the kiss, then squeal when Travis abandons his burgers and grabs me by the waist, pulling me onto an empty space on the counter. It's instinctual, the way my legs wrap around his middle.

Our kiss turns urgent, and I pull away before we get too

carried away. We both know what happened the last time he took me on the kitchen counter.

"Did you manage okay?" I ask, giving him another peck before he steps back to finish up dinner.

"They're angels, just like their mama."

Great, now I want to throw myself at him and finish what we started a moment ago. I'd wonder if I'm still hormonal or if something's up with me, but this is Travis. He always has that effect on me.

"I'm going to check on them," I tell him, but before I can move, his hands are back on my waist, helping me off the counter.

"I'll join you in a minute. Let me make sure I won't burn down the kitchen first."

"Please don't. Your reputation as the burger master of the family is at stake here."

No matter how much he teases me about it, I've got to give it to him—his burgers are better than mine.

"Wouldn't want to ruin it."

I'm quiet as I make my way toward the bedroom across from ours. And just like always, my heart fills with unmeasurable love as I push the door open and spot the two small figures snoring peacefully in the room that was never meant to be empty. Our favorite room in the house.

Thanks to the dim light coming from the hallway, I can easily see the two little faces I love the most. Our twin girls, sleeping without a care in the world.

Travis comes up behind me a moment later, hugging me from behind like he knows I love, and kisses my neck. "Dinner's ready."

I lean back against him, not taking my eyes off our daughters. "I could stand here and watch them forever."

He squeezes my middle. "Let's do it, then."

That earns him a quiet chuckle. "Don't indulge me. One of us is supposed to be the stricter parent."

"You three have me wrapped around your fingers. It's not gonna be me."

"Travis, we talked about this. We need to keep the spoiling to a healthy amount."

He hums. "I don't remember that conversation."

I glance up at him, amused. "I'm sure you don't."

Those powerful shoulders move up and down with a shrug. "I'm a girl dad now to two little princesses, and I'm the husband of a fucking amazing wife. You can't expect me not to spoil you."

My heart soars, but I keep teasing him. "Poor you. Must be so hard."

"It is," he whispers before pecking my lips again.

After we got married—an intimate ceremony by the lake with our loved ones during the spring—I thought I knew everything about Travis and that I couldn't possibly love him more. I've always cherished every virtue and flaw because they make him the incredible man I want to spend my life with. But then...

Then we had our daughters, and I fell in love with a Travis I'd never met before—the one who spoke to my pregnant belly every night, who cried when he held our daughters for the first time, who shows us every day that we're his entire life.

Remembering where we started and seeing where we are now always makes me smile. Tonight is no exception.

"Can I make a confession?" I ask him, my voice quiet.

There's an amused glint in his eyes. "Am I about to regret saying yes?"

"Probably." He squeezes my waist. "I used to call you 'bear-man' in my head all the time when I started working for you. I may or may not still do it sometimes."

"Bear-man," he deadpans, but he can't hide the smile in his voice.

"Because of your beard," I explain. "Also, your height. You're enormous. Grouchy, too, which is kind of like a bear— one look is enough to know that getting close to them may not be the best idea."

"And yet here you are. Right in the bear's lair."

I smile. "I wouldn't want to be anywhere else."

THE END

A Note from Lisina Coney

Deciding to publish *The Lair* wasn't easy for a number of reasons I'm sure you'll understand.

Have you ever read a sexually explicit book about a woman who grows up in an influencer family, gets kidnapped because of her parents' questionable behavior, and runs away to escape the exposure? Me neither. That's reason number one. It's an... interesting concept for a romance novel, and the market doesn't always love out-of-the-ordinary stories. Yes, I write for myself, but I also have bills to pay. Considering what might sell isn't a bad thing, even if I always end up doing what feels right to me.

Reason number two is that the subject of child stars and child influencers is being very heavily discussed right now, which I feel wasn't so much the case when I started working on this book in 2022 (Allie isn't a child star, but I've been told her situation is similar in some aspects). I have the utmost respect for everyone who's bravely speaking out about their experiences. My intention with *The Lair* is and always has been to shine another light into the dangers children could face while in the public eye, specifically on social media. I believe in freedom of speech as long as it doesn't interfere with someone else's wellbeing. I'd like to think I've been respectful and mindful in the way I've handled this theme. If I haven't, I'm always open to learning from my mistakes.

The last reason is fear. *The Lair* is my shooting star. It represents aiming for something new, uncertain, and hopeful. *Shrek* has an outstanding soundtrack, and I love every minute of it, but sometimes shooting stars *don't* break the mold—sometimes they fizzle out and die. As I'm writing this, I don't know if this book will end up being a shooting star that fizzles out before I get a chance to wish upon it.

It took me two years and endless therapy sessions to understand that I have the right to write and publish freely (and that's a wonderful thing). That I have the right to use my voice, and use it to remind us to protect children and teenagers on all fronts as our world evolves.

In the end, I decided to publish *The Lair* because if we keep important conversations in the shadows to avoid confrontation, we're only abandoning those who suffer in silence. And, sometimes, that includes ourselves.

This book is entirely fictional but not unrealistic. Allie came to me when I asked myself, "What would happen if exposing children on social media took one of the worst possible turns?" She isn't based on any real person, living or dead, because I would find that extremely violating. *The Lair* is inspired by a general behavior I've noticed over the years that I don't agree with, and Allie's journey is a reflection of what I could see myself doing if I were in her unfortunate position.

Allie's family isn't based on any real family, living or dead, either. I didn't bother giving her parents first names because they're only an archetype. They represent my idea of narcissistic people who failed to protect their daughter from the dangers of social media. I hope people like them don't exist in real life.

My heart goes out to anyone who sees themselves in Allie, for one reason or another. You deserve peace and safety, and I'll always cheer you on.

If nothing else, I hope her story has urged you to protect the children in your life from online threats more than you already do.

Thank you for reading this far.

With love and gratitude,

Lisina Coney

Acknowledgments

You wouldn't be reading this book if it weren't for Alexis, who helped me through so many emotional breakdowns, it's a little concerning. I'm so lucky to have found a best friend and a life partner in you. You're the most patient man ever, which also helps. I love you endlessly.

Additionally, you wouldn't be holding this book in your hands—or any other of my published stories—if I hadn't worked my ass off in therapy. If you've been asking for a sign to seek help, this is it. Much like Allie, you also deserve a happy, calm life.

To my readers. I bet you weren't expecting this kind of book after The Brightest Light series (or maybe you totally were). Hopefully you enjoyed it anyway. Even if you didn't, thank you for being here and giving it a chance.

To Tía. Thank you for encouraging me to stay true to my creative impulses when my self-doubt took over. You are the voice of reason amidst my chaos. I love you.

To Alejandri. No, you can't read this one either (yet). But I hope you know you're the kindest, funniest, sweetest cousin I could ever ask for, that I love you more than anything, and that I'll always be in your corner.

To my parents. I'm thankful every day that I can't base my evil characters on you. Love ya!

To my friend and talented author, Zarin Madiyha. I live for your reaction videos crying in the car. (Also, sorry for making you cry with this book.) (No, I'm not, and we both know it.)

Thank you for being such an amazing cheerleader and for formatting this baby. Love you!

To Savannah Greenwell. Thank you for being a superstar agent and fighting for Allie and Travis. At the end, their home was always meant to be with me.

To Melissa Doughty. Talk about a stunning cover! Thank you for being so wonderful to work with.

To Keeley Catarineau for being the best, most supportive editor in this entire world (we're totally work besties now), Kim Deister for her valuable insights on combat-related PTSD, and the rest of the team at Hot Tree Editing. Thank you for elevating my stories every time.

To booksellers, librarians, reviewers, and everyone who supports my books in one way or another. I wouldn't be here today without you. Thank you for everything.

Para Tata y Abue, siempre.

Also by Lisina Coney

An emotional romance between a tattoo artist who takes care of his baby sister and his sister's ballet teacher, who's healing from her past.

A slow burn romance between an injured ballerina and her grumpy physical therapist, who thinks he's too broken to deserve her.

A forbidden romance between a Master's student and her internship supervisor, who's also a family friend.

About the Author

Lisina Coney is a Spanish international bestselling romance author in her twenties.

She's a lover of slow-burn stories with happy endings and main characters who help readers feel less alone in their journeys.

When she's not reading or writing, Lisina can be found fighting people over the last French fry, spending too much time on social media (Gen Z habits die hard), and pestering her two very patient cats.

Made in United States
Orlando, FL
30 March 2025

59993197R00225